ELEMENTS
BASIC
7
BASIC

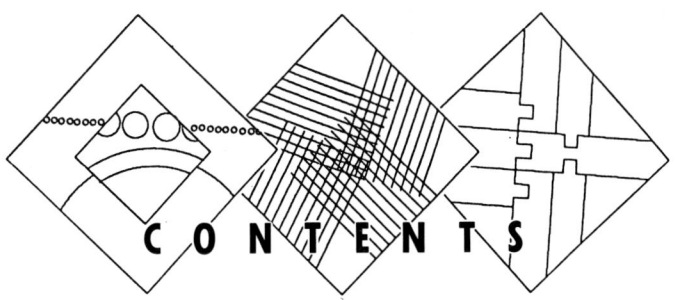

CONTENTS 1 | ELEMENTS 7
BASIC
BASIC

PRODUCED BY
AIM CREATIVE PRODUCTS CO, LTD
JEUNESSE PLANNING CORPORATION

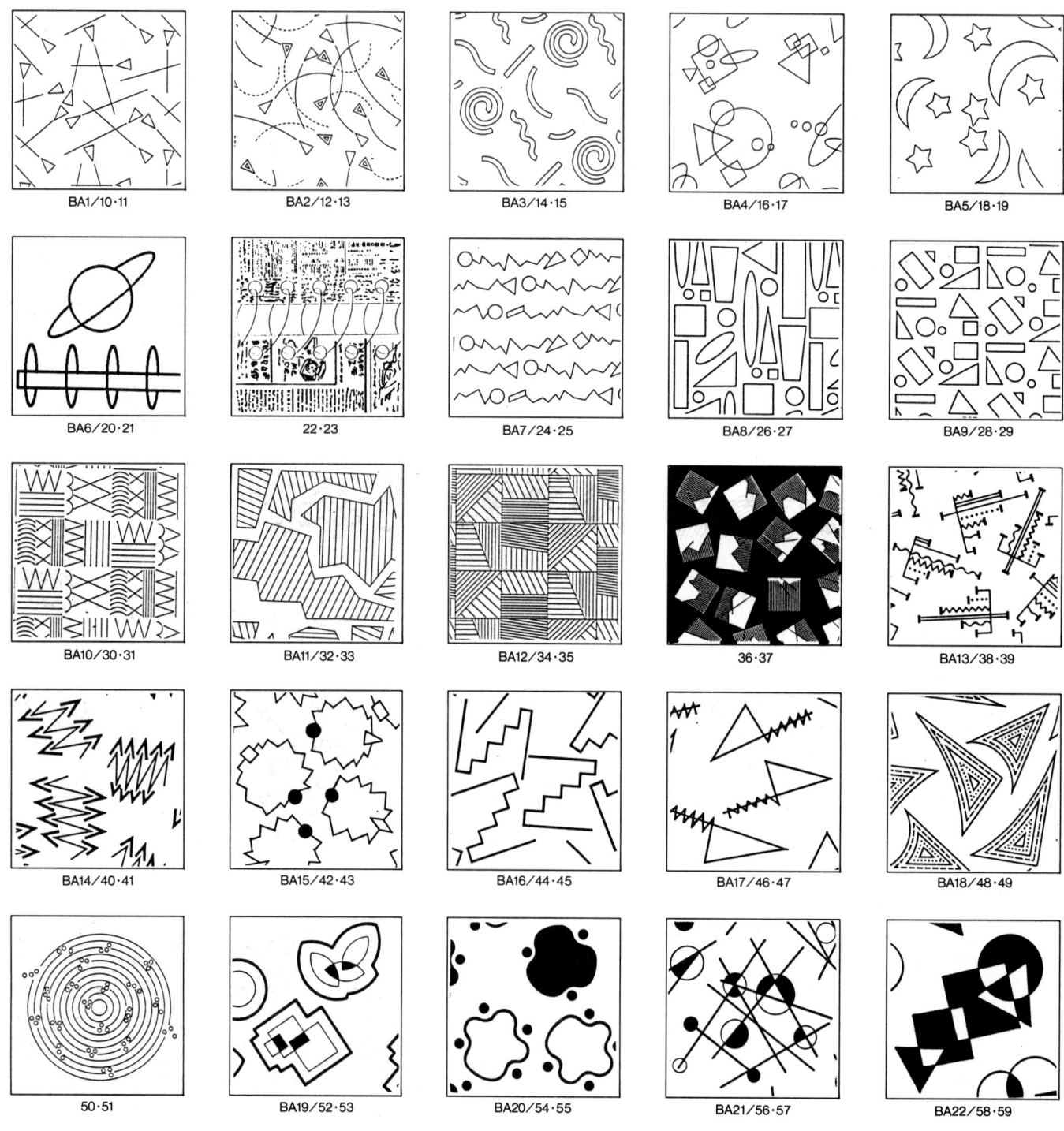

CONTENTS 2 | ELEMENTS 7
BASIC
BASIC

PRODUCED BY
AIM CREATIVE PRODUCTS, CO, LTD
JEUNESSE PLANNING CORPORATION

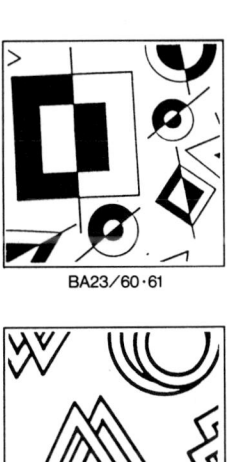
BA23/60·61

BA24/62·63

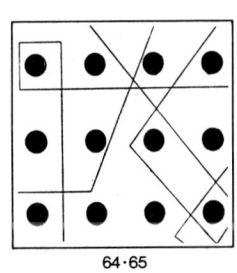
64·65

BA25/66·67

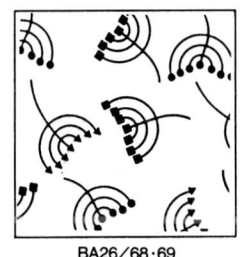
BA26/68·69

BA27/70·71

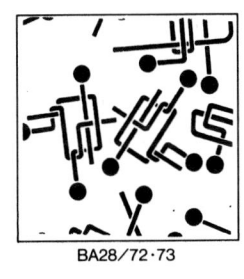
BA28/72·73

BA29/74·75

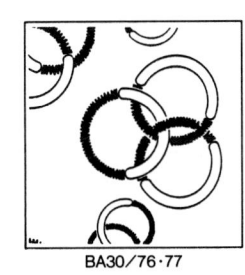
BA30/76·77

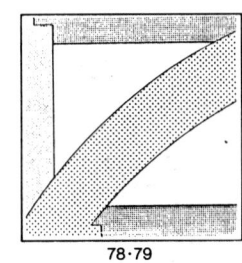
78·79

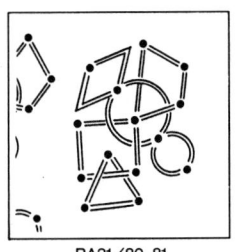
BA31/80·81

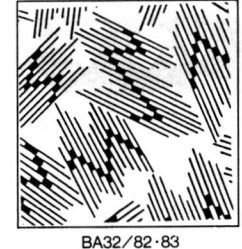
BA32/82·83

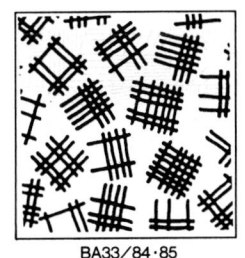
BA33/84·85

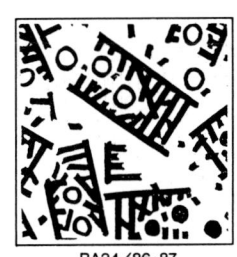
BA34/86·87

BA35/88·89

BA36/90·91

92·93

BA37/94·95

BA38/96·97

BA39/98·99

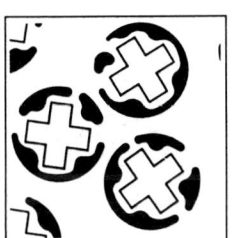
BA40/100·101

BA41/102·103

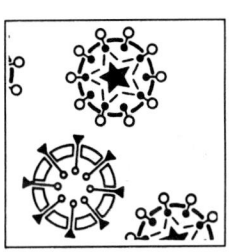
BA42/104·105

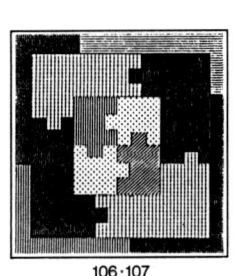
106·107

BA43/108·109

CONTENTS 3 | ELEMENTS 7
BASIC
BASIC
PRODUCED BY
AIM CREATIVE PRODUCTS CO, LTD
JEUNESSE PLANNING CORPORATION

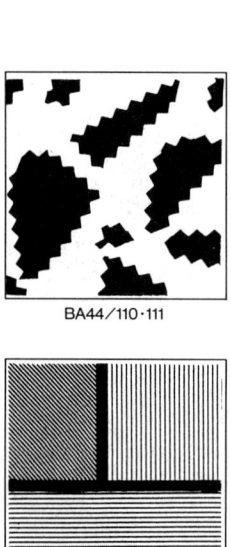
BA44/110·111

BA45/112·113

BA46/114·115

BA47/116·117

BA48/118·119

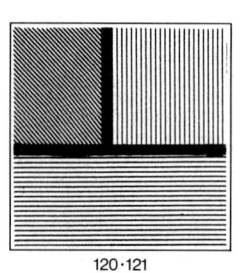
120·121

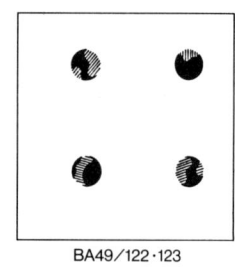
BA49/122·123

BA50/124·125

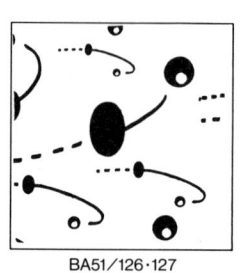
BA51/126·127

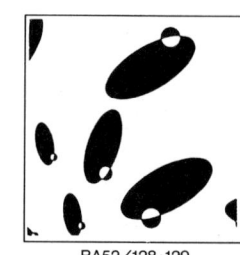
BA52/128·129

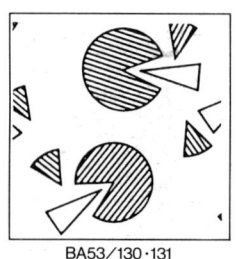
BA53/130·131

BA54/132·133

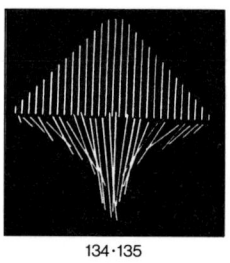
134·135

BA55/136·137

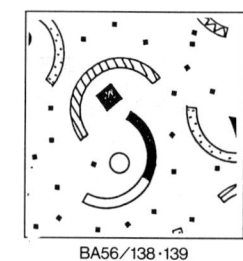
BA56/138·139

BA57/140·141

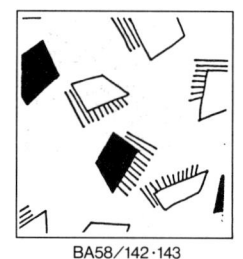
BA58/142·143

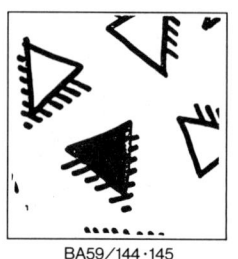
BA59/144·145

BA60/146·147

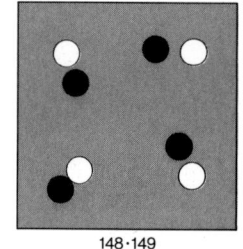
148·149

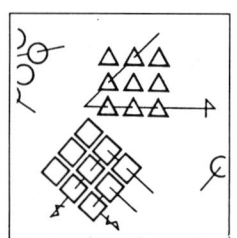
BA61/150·151

BA62/152·153

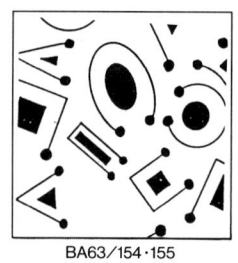
BA63/154·155

BA64/156·157

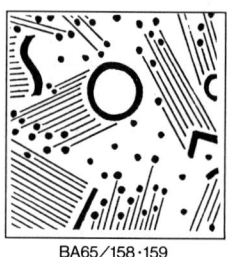
BA65/158·159

CONTENTS 4 | ELEMENTS 7
BASIC
BASIC

PRODUCED BY
AIM CREATIVE PRODUCTS CO, LTD
JEUNESSE PLANNING CORPORATION

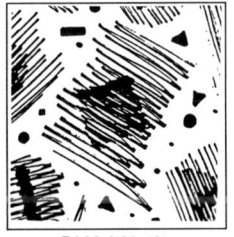
BA66/160·161

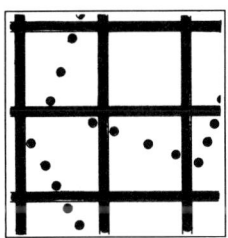
162·163

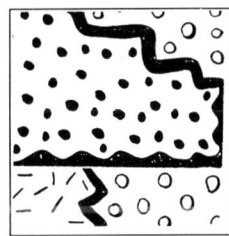
BA67/164·165

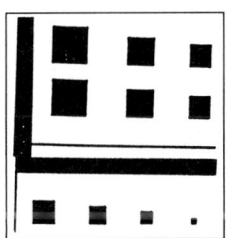
BA68/166·167

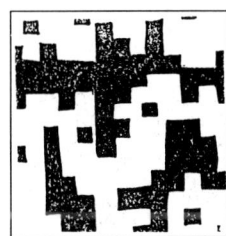
BA69/168·169

BA70/170·171

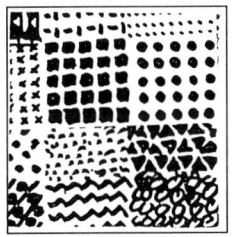
BA71/172·173

BA72/174·175

176·177

BA73/178·179

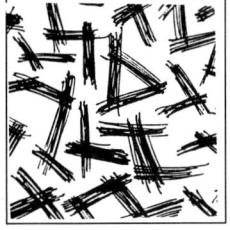
BA74/180·181

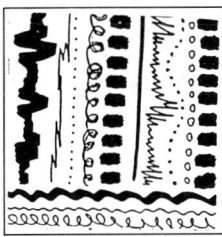
BA75/182·183

BA76/184·185

BA77/186·187

BA78/188·189

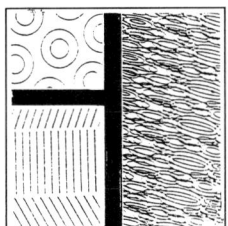
190·191

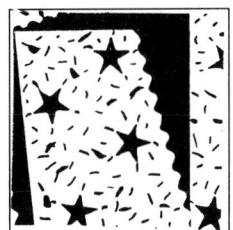
BA79/192·193

BA80/194·195

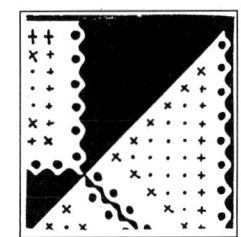
BA81/196·197

BA82/198·199

BA83/200·201

BA84/202·203

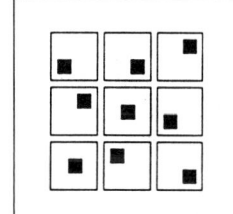

ELEMENTS
パターン清刷集・エレメンツ

BASIC
7
ベーシック
BASIC

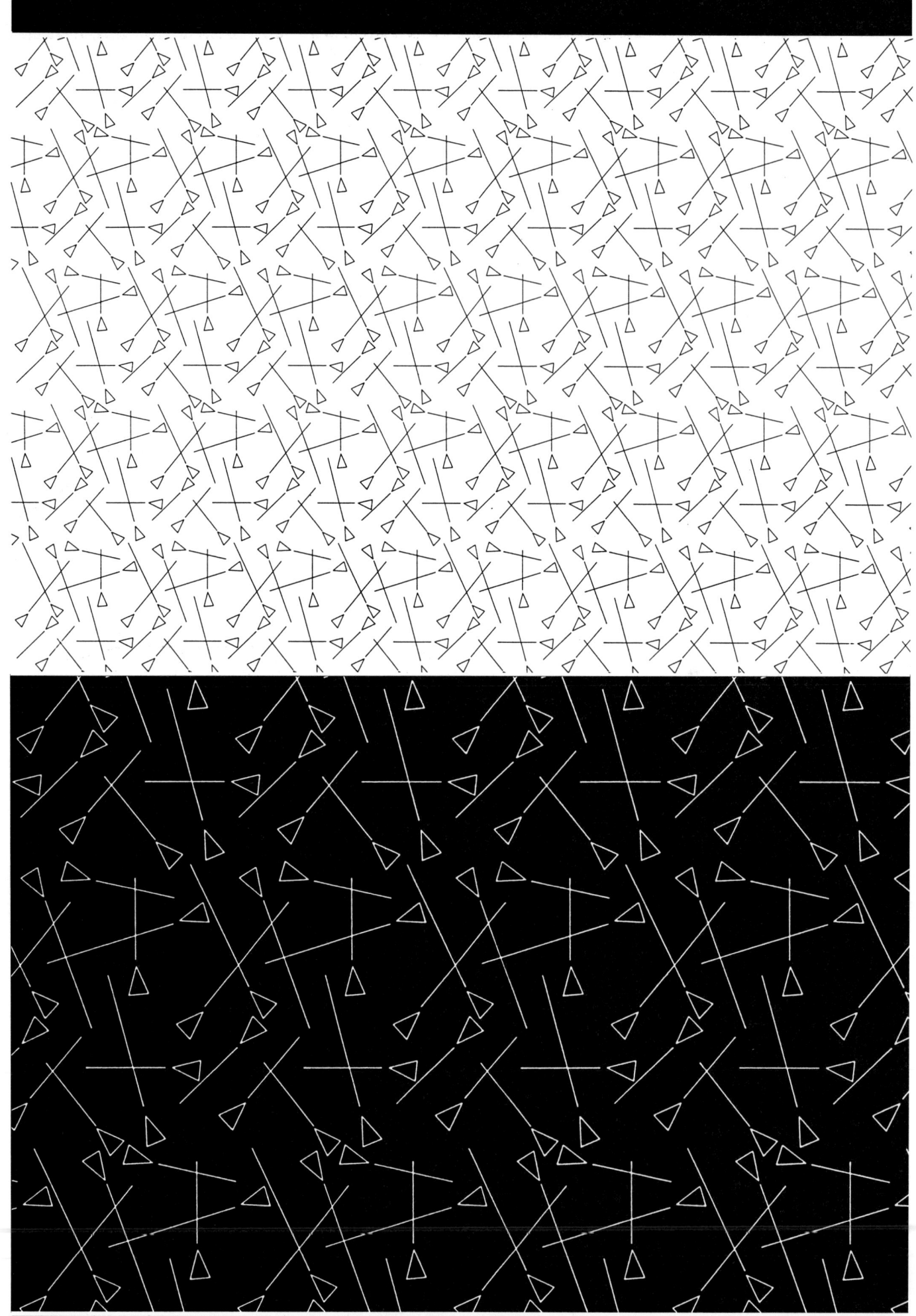

BASIC ELEMENTS

BA1

BASIC ELEMENTS BA2

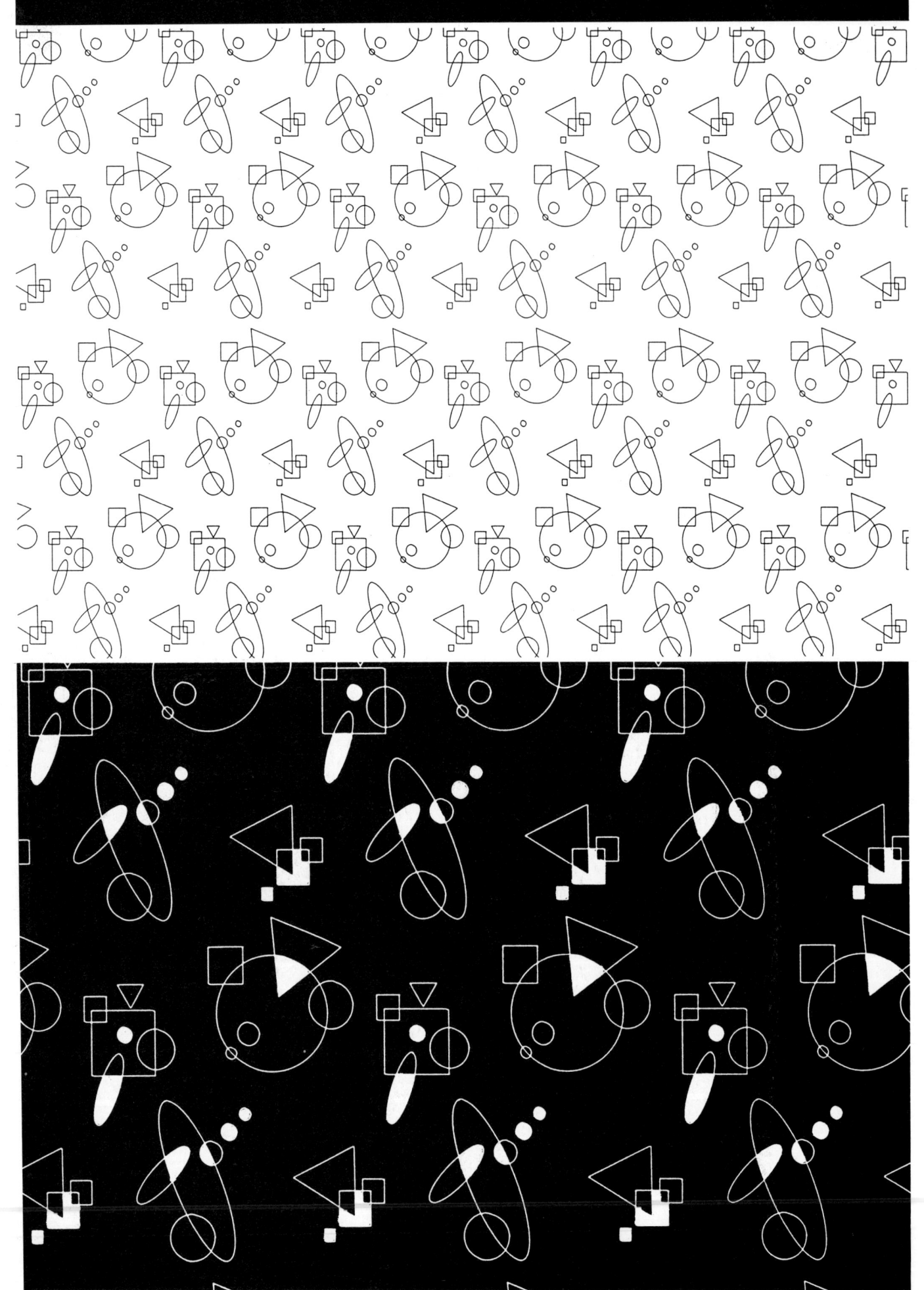

BASIC ELEMENTS BA4

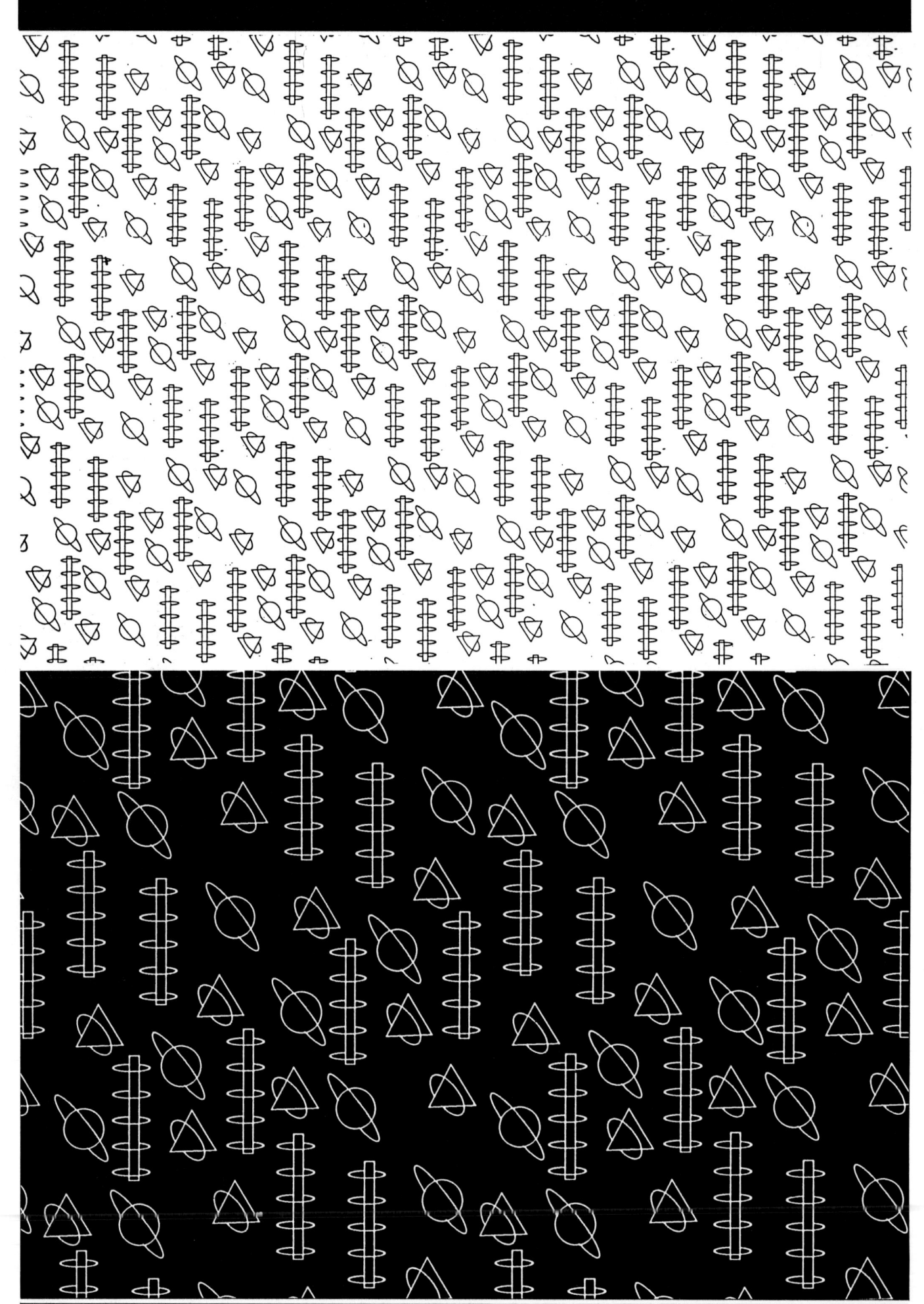

BASIC ELEMENTS BA6

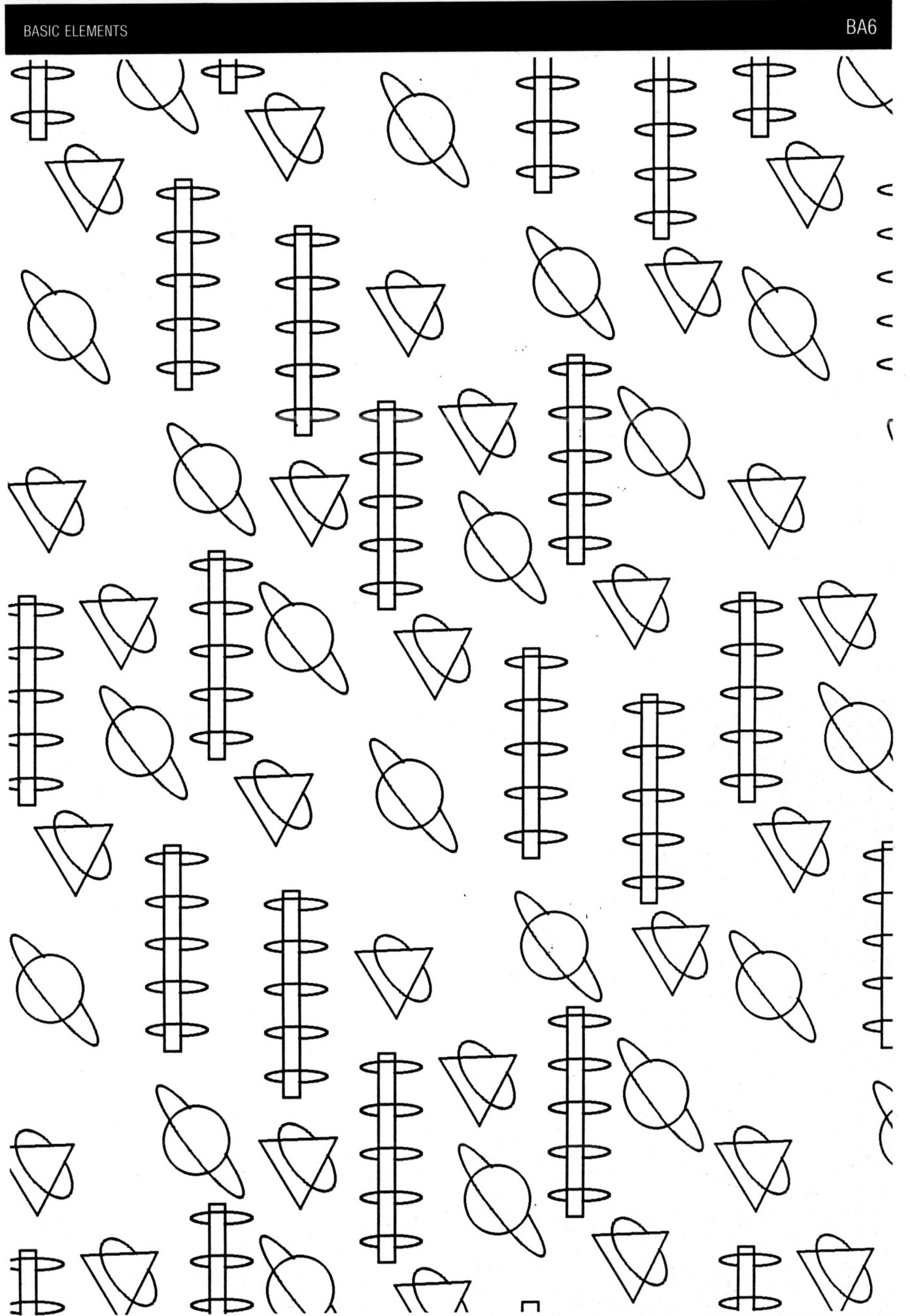

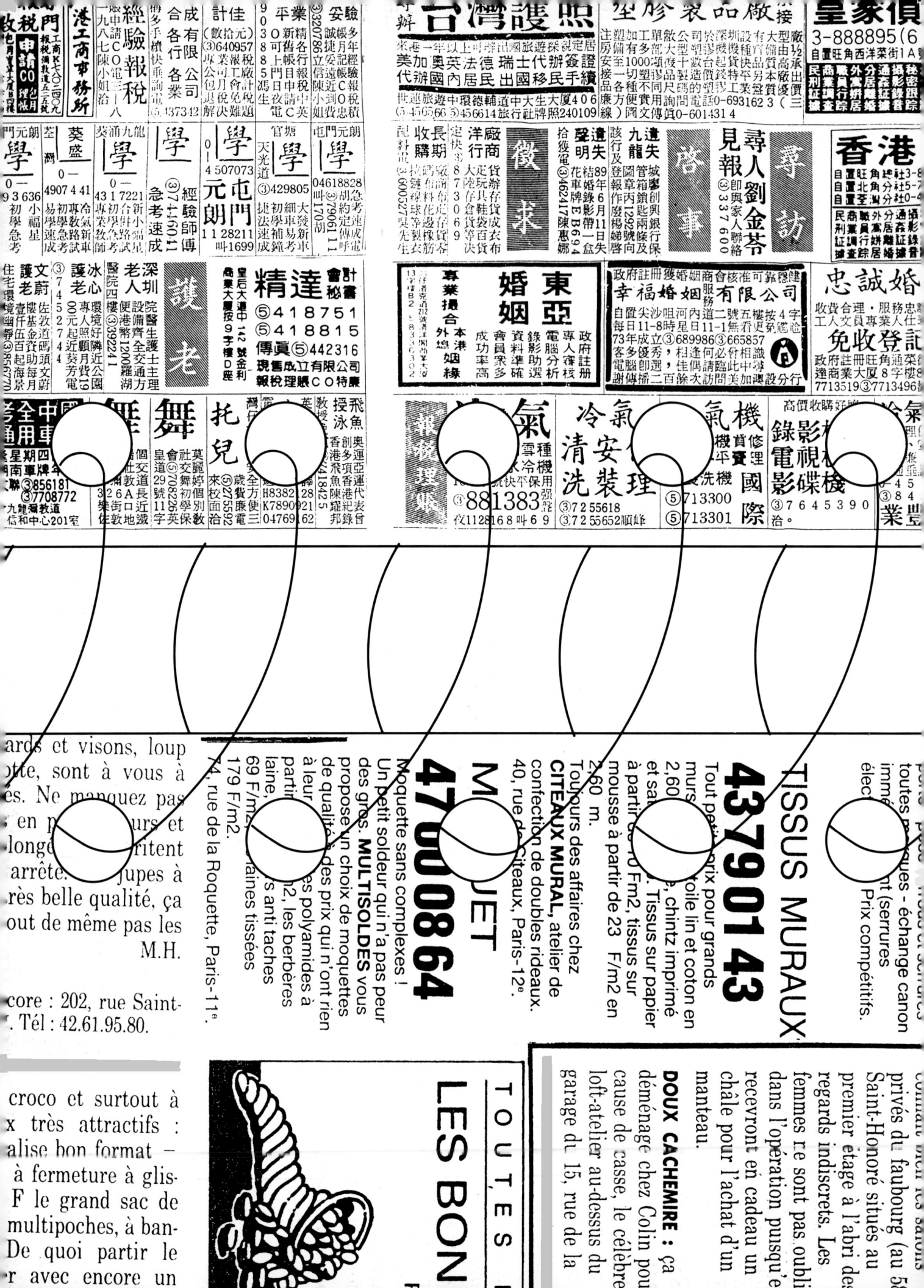

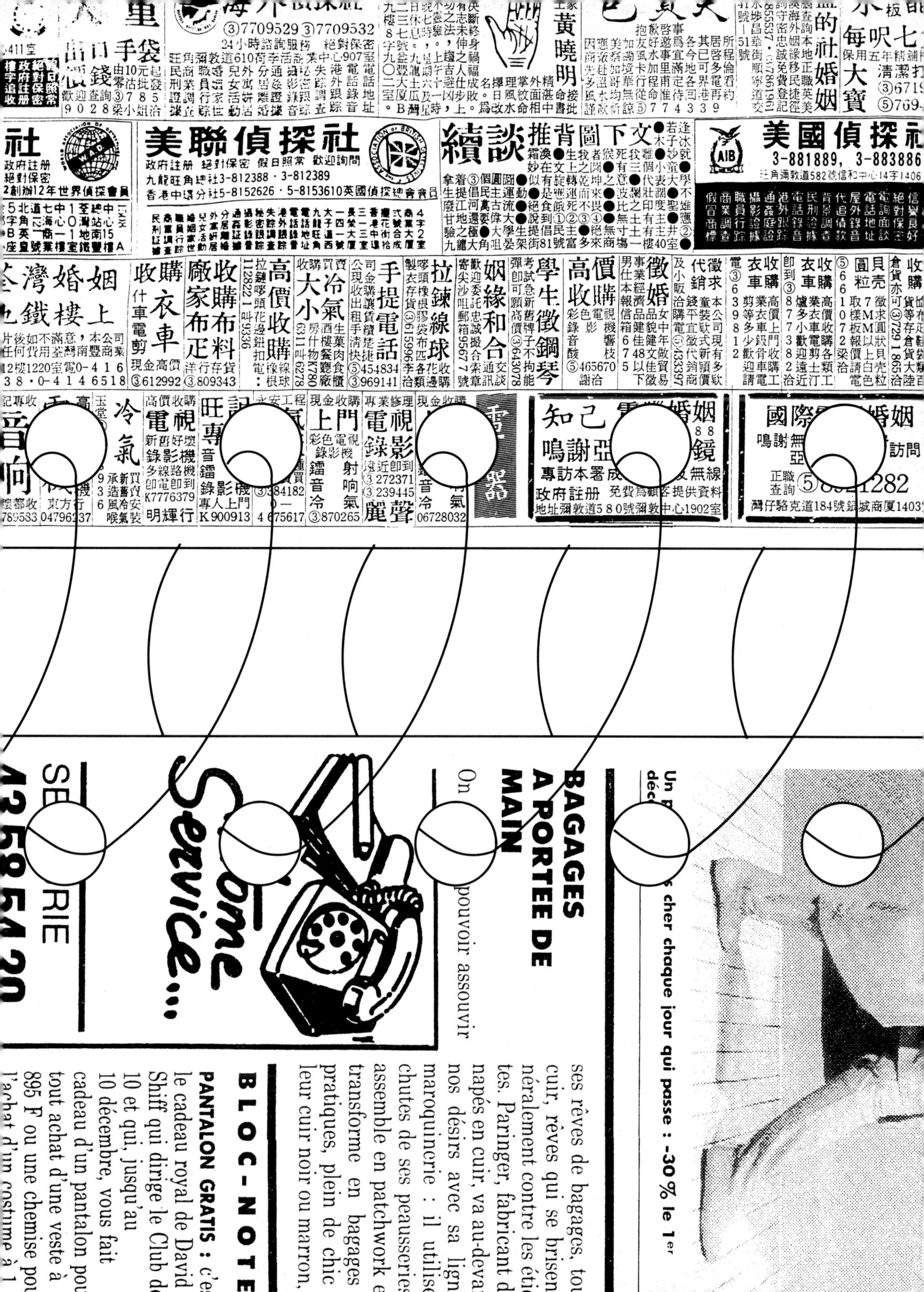

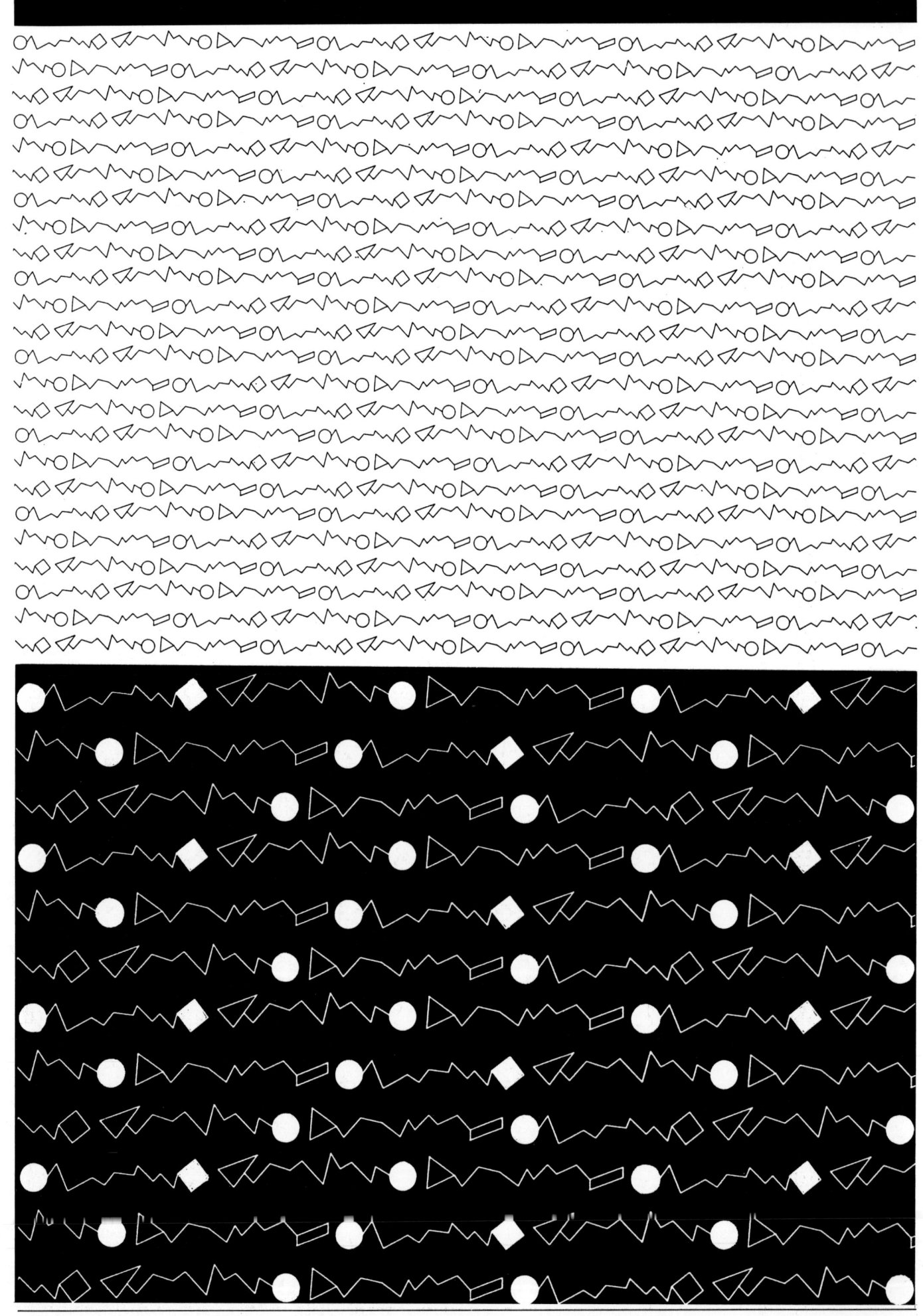

BASIC ELEMENTS

BA7

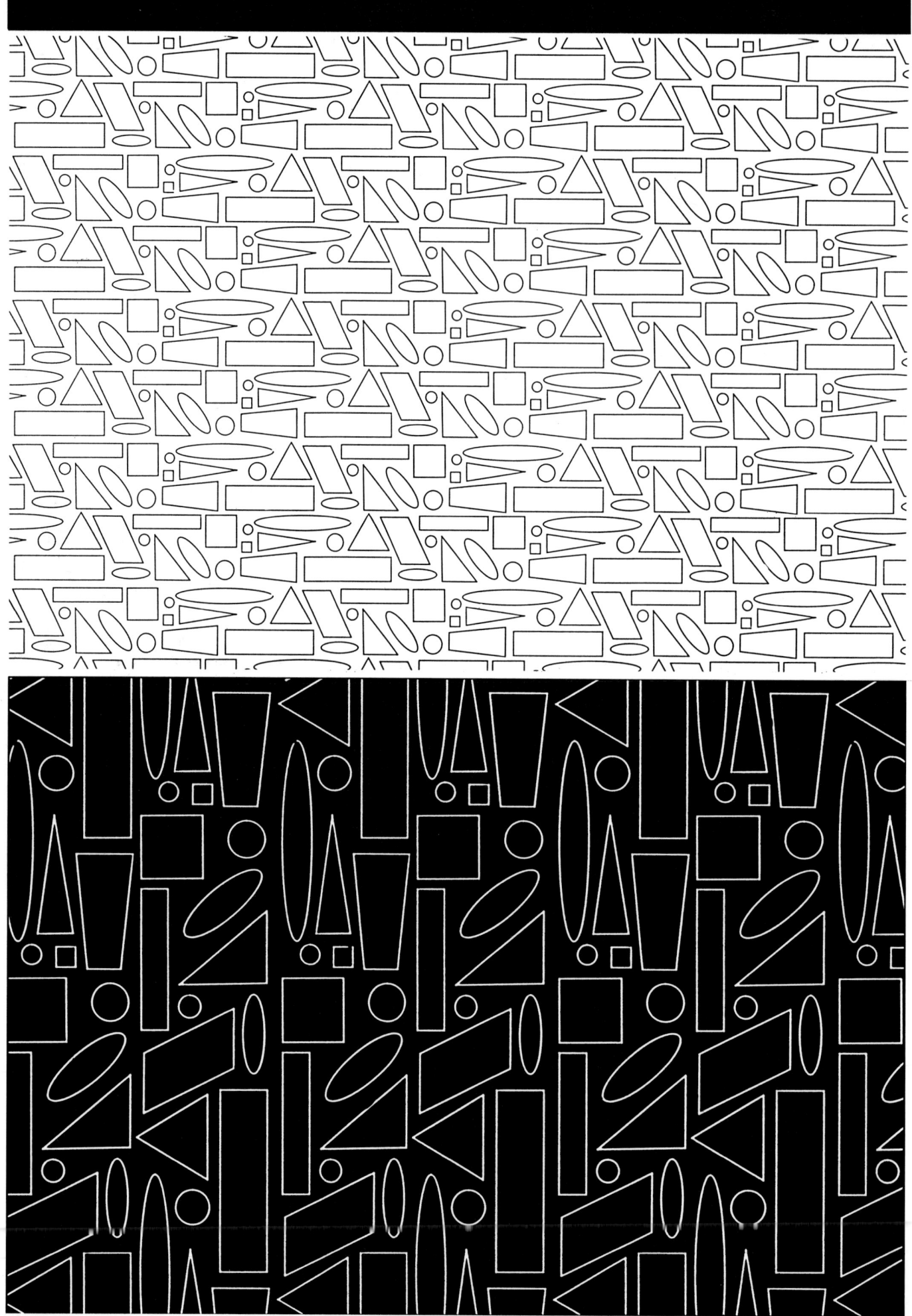

BASIC ELEMENTS BA9

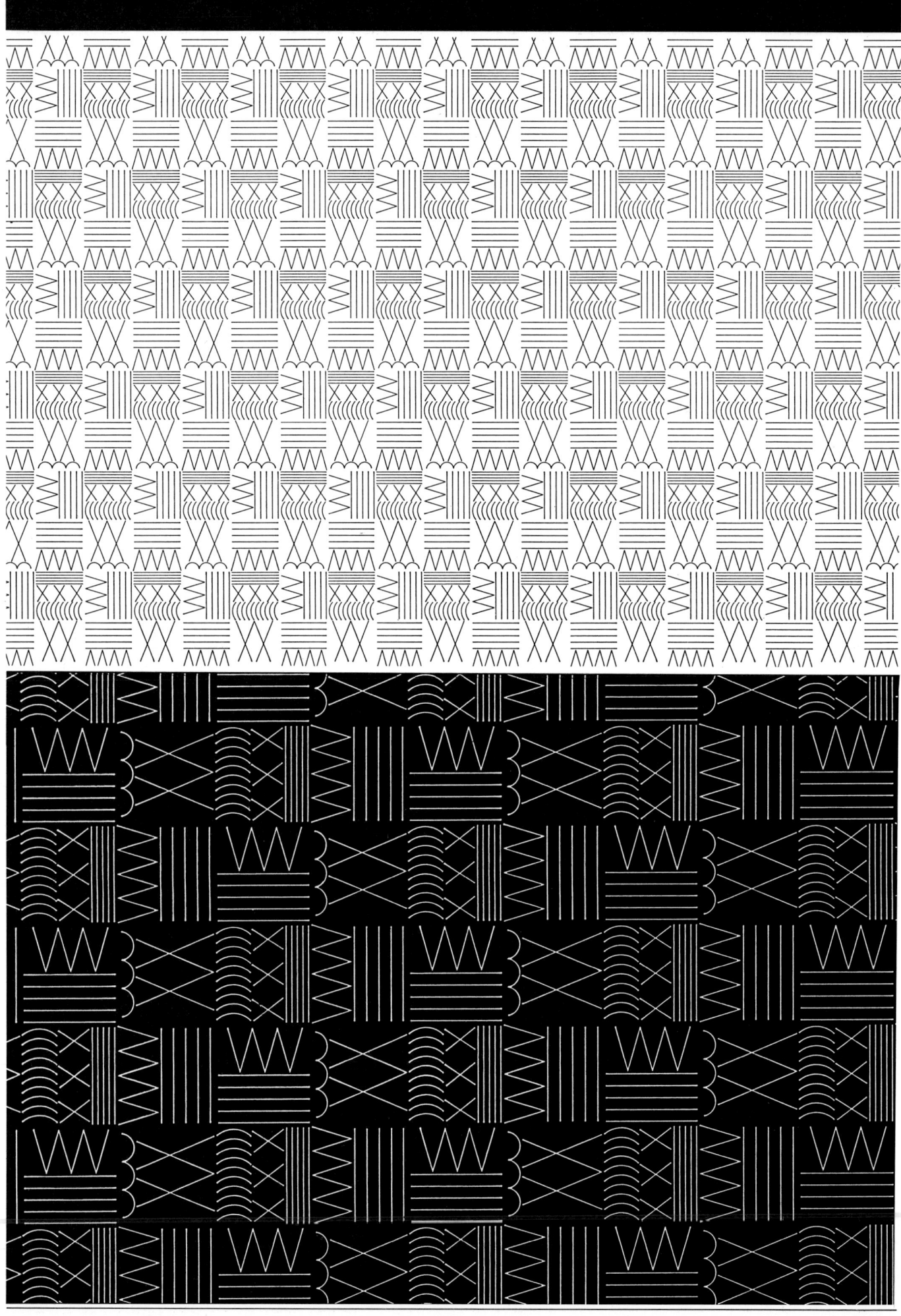

BASIC ELEMENTS BA10

BASIC ELEMENTS

BA11

BASIC ELEMENTS   BA12

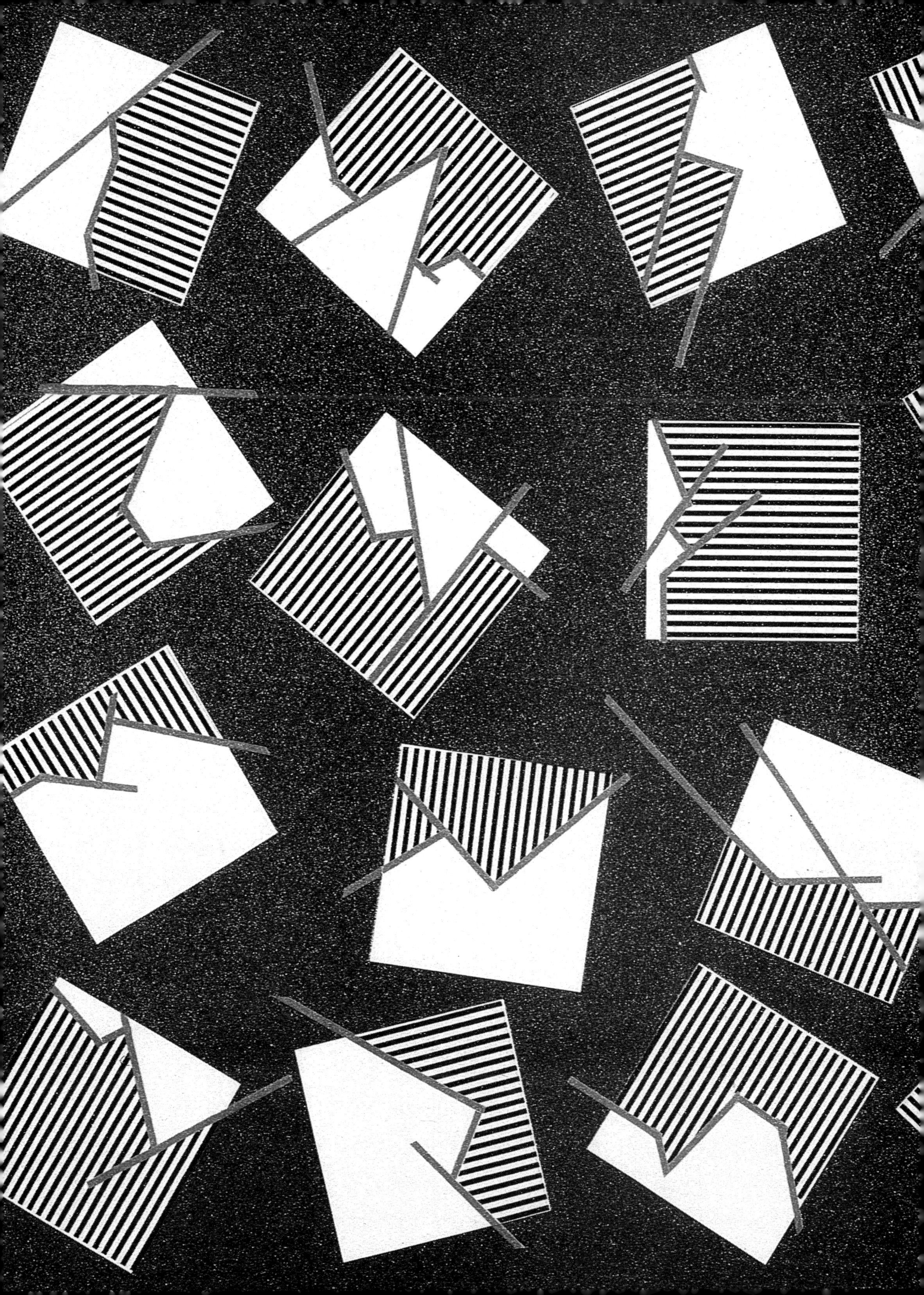

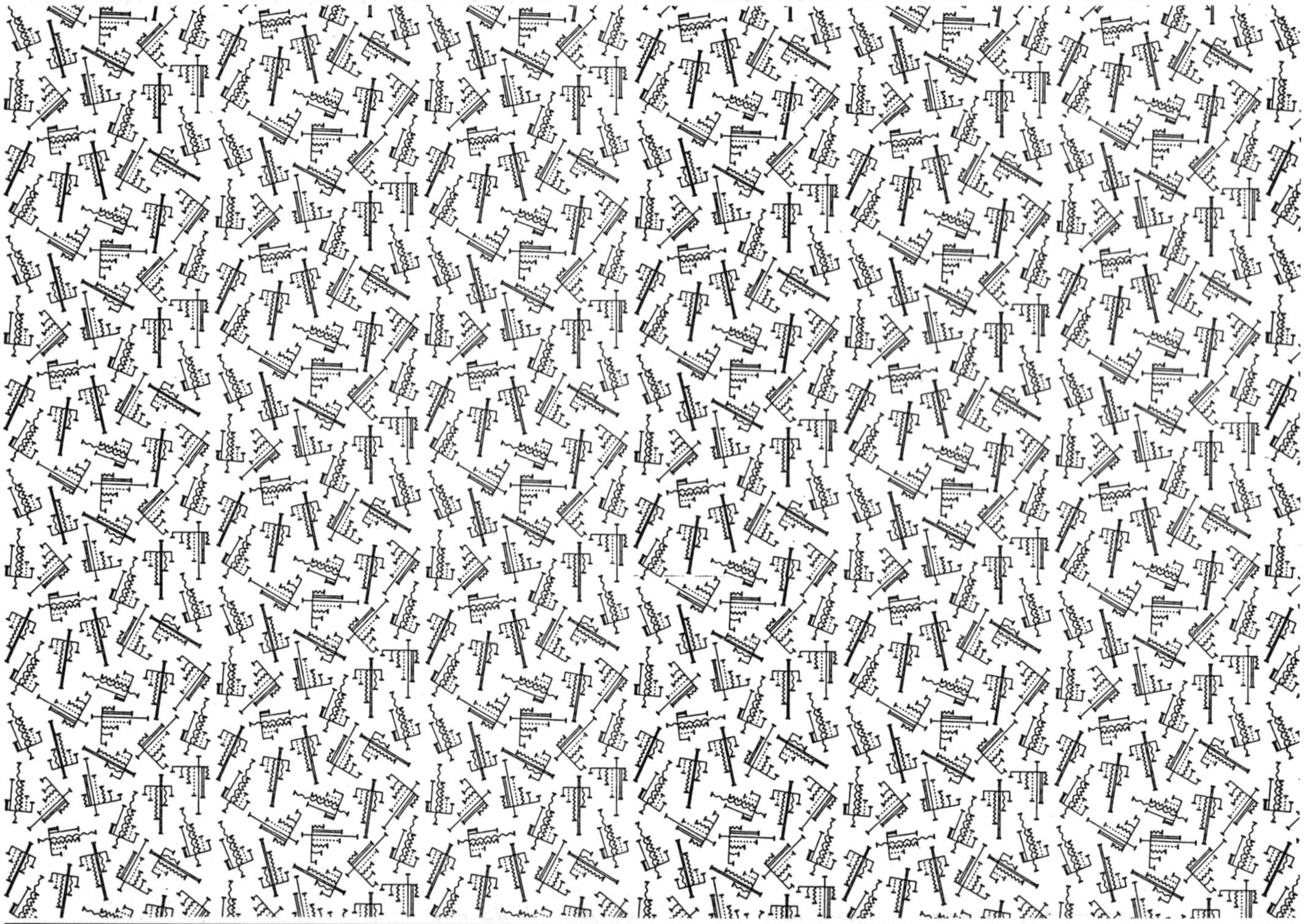

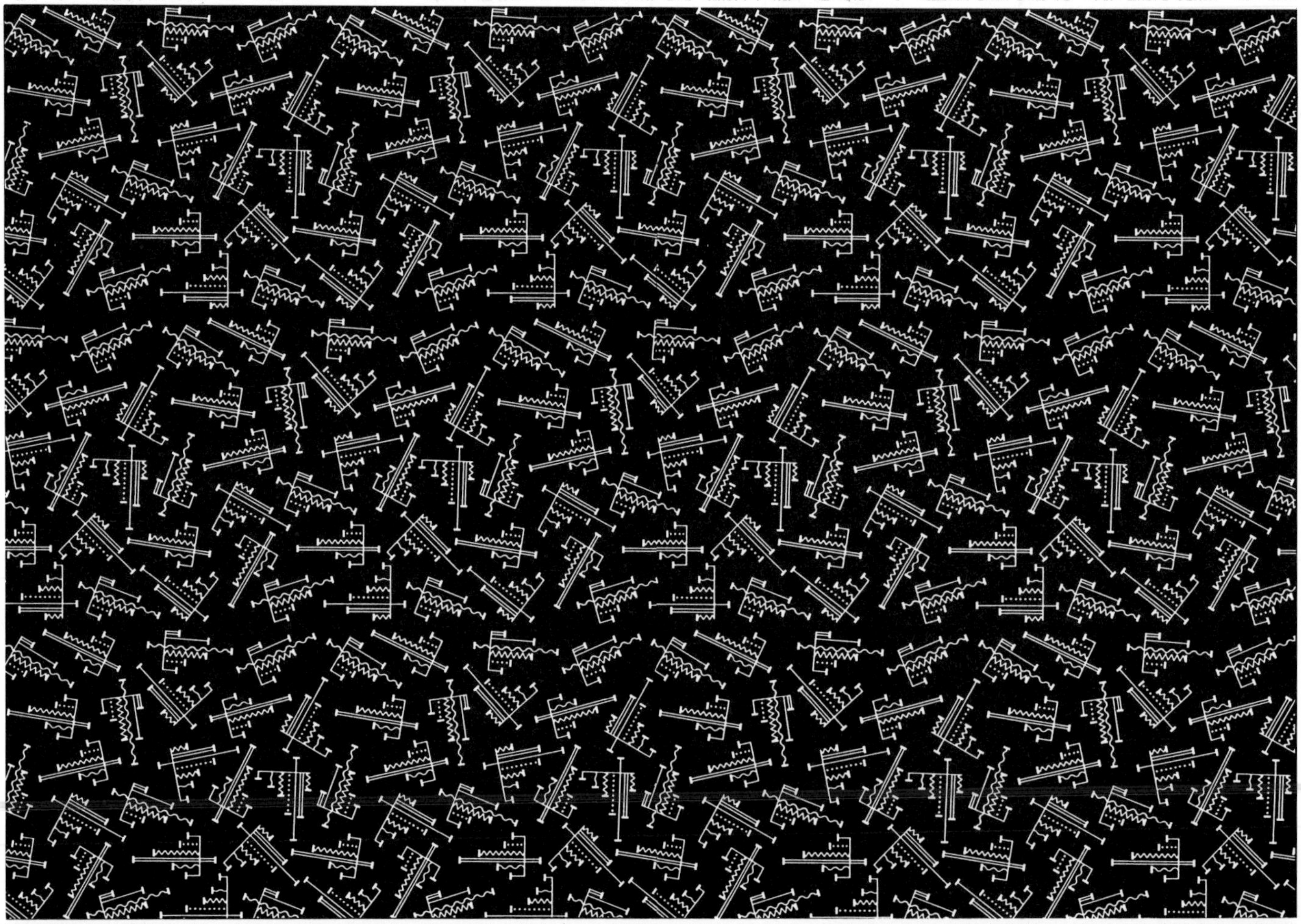

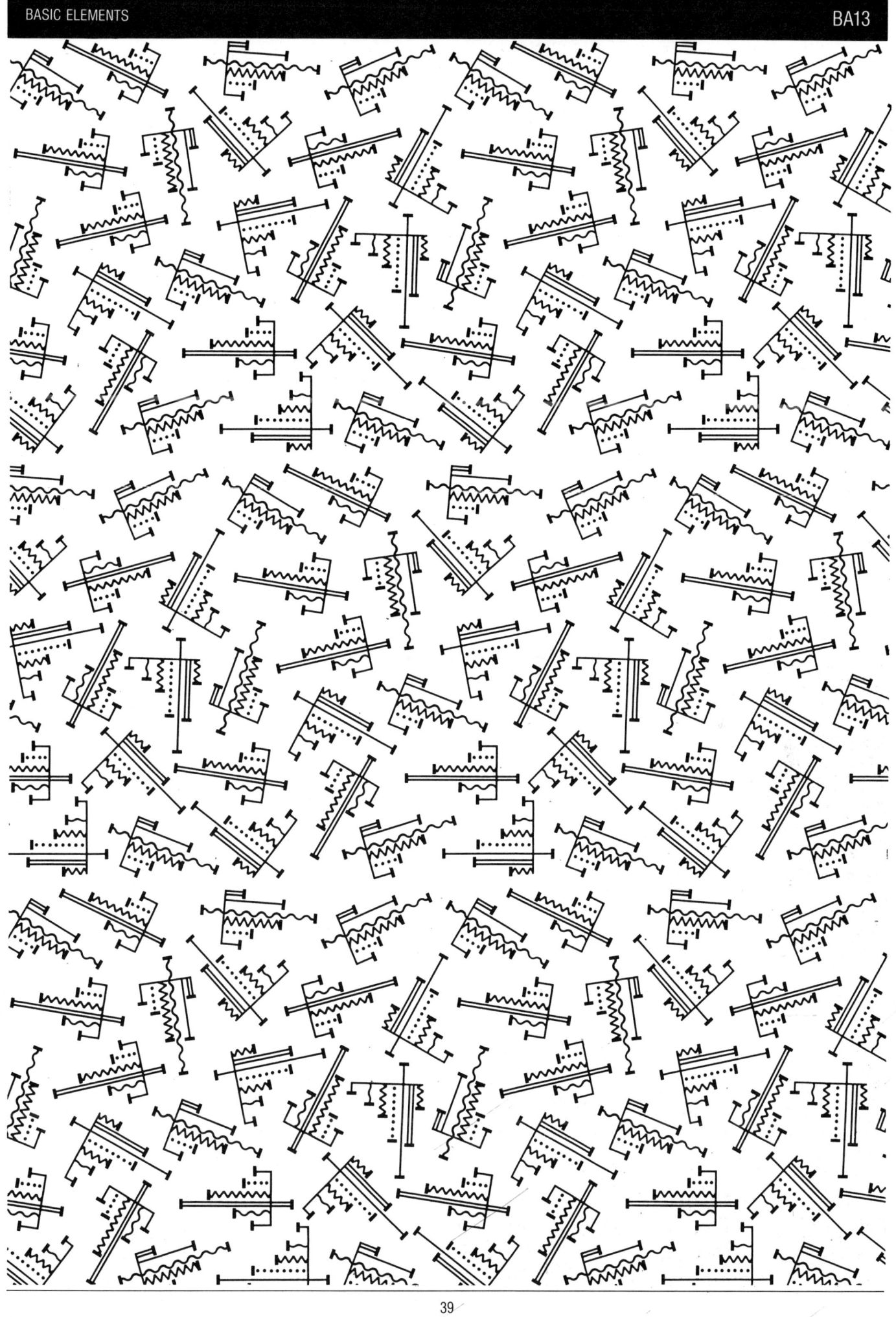

BASIC ELEMENTS

BA13

40

BASIC ELEMENTS

BA14

42

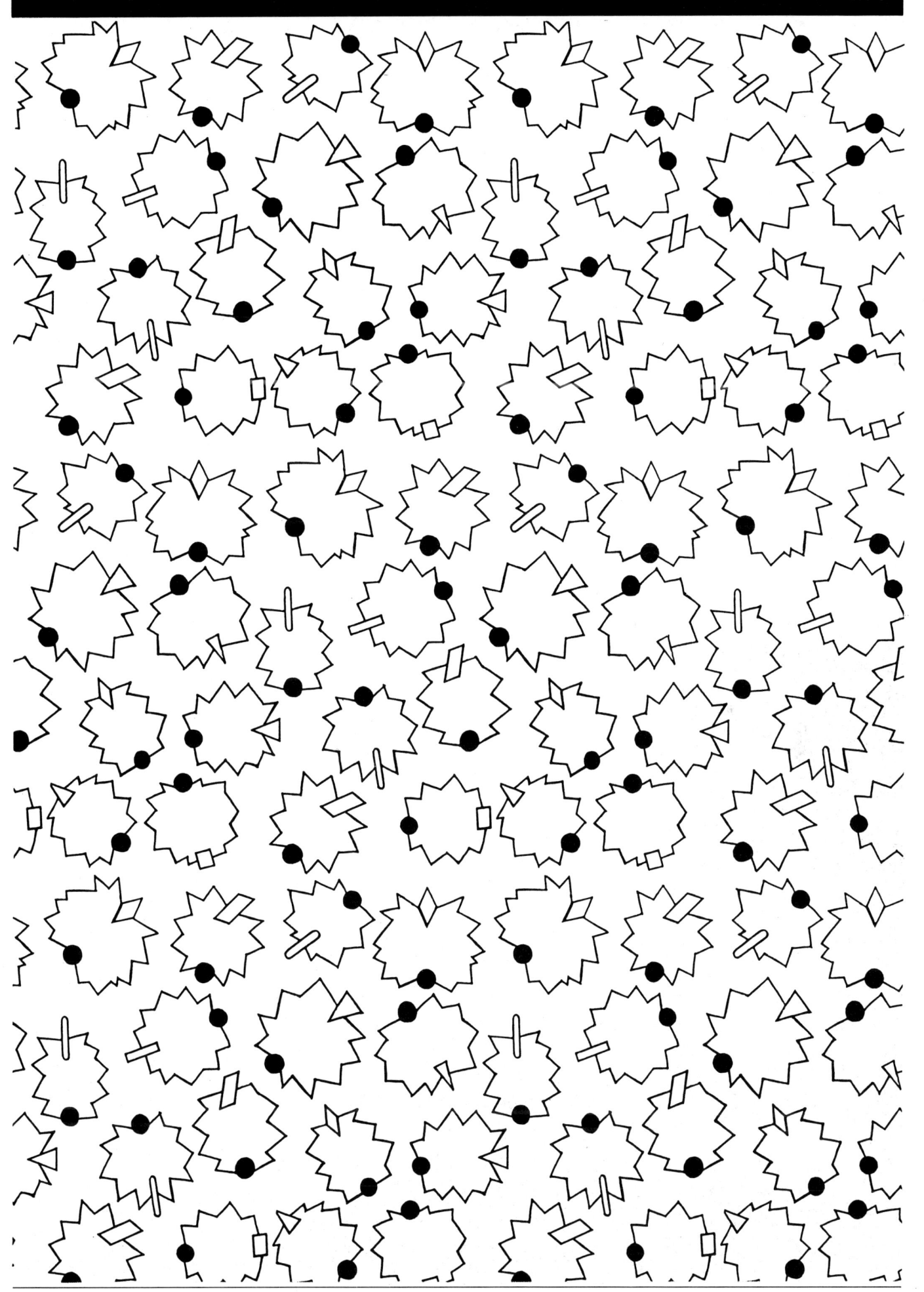

BASIC ELEMENTS BA15

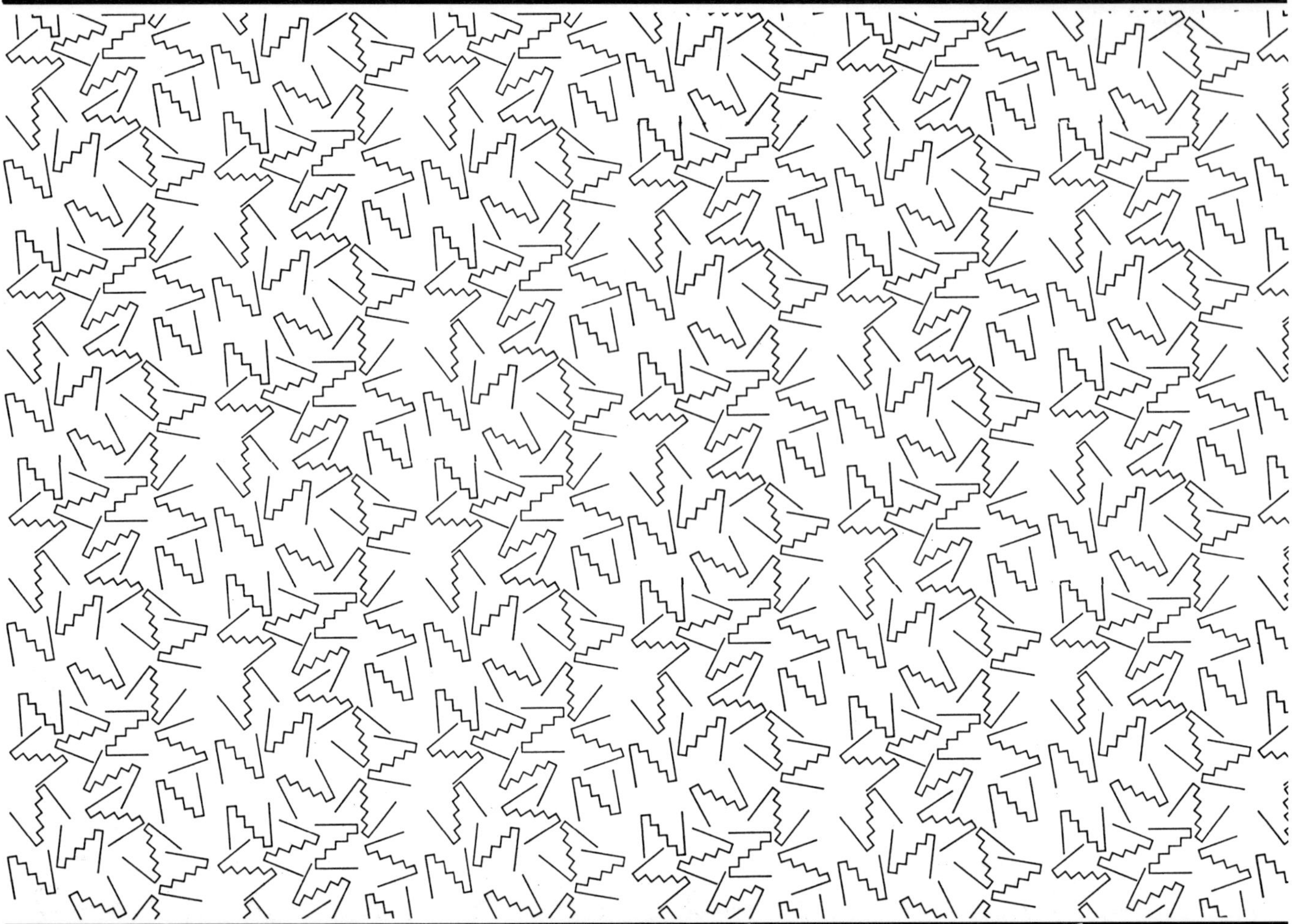

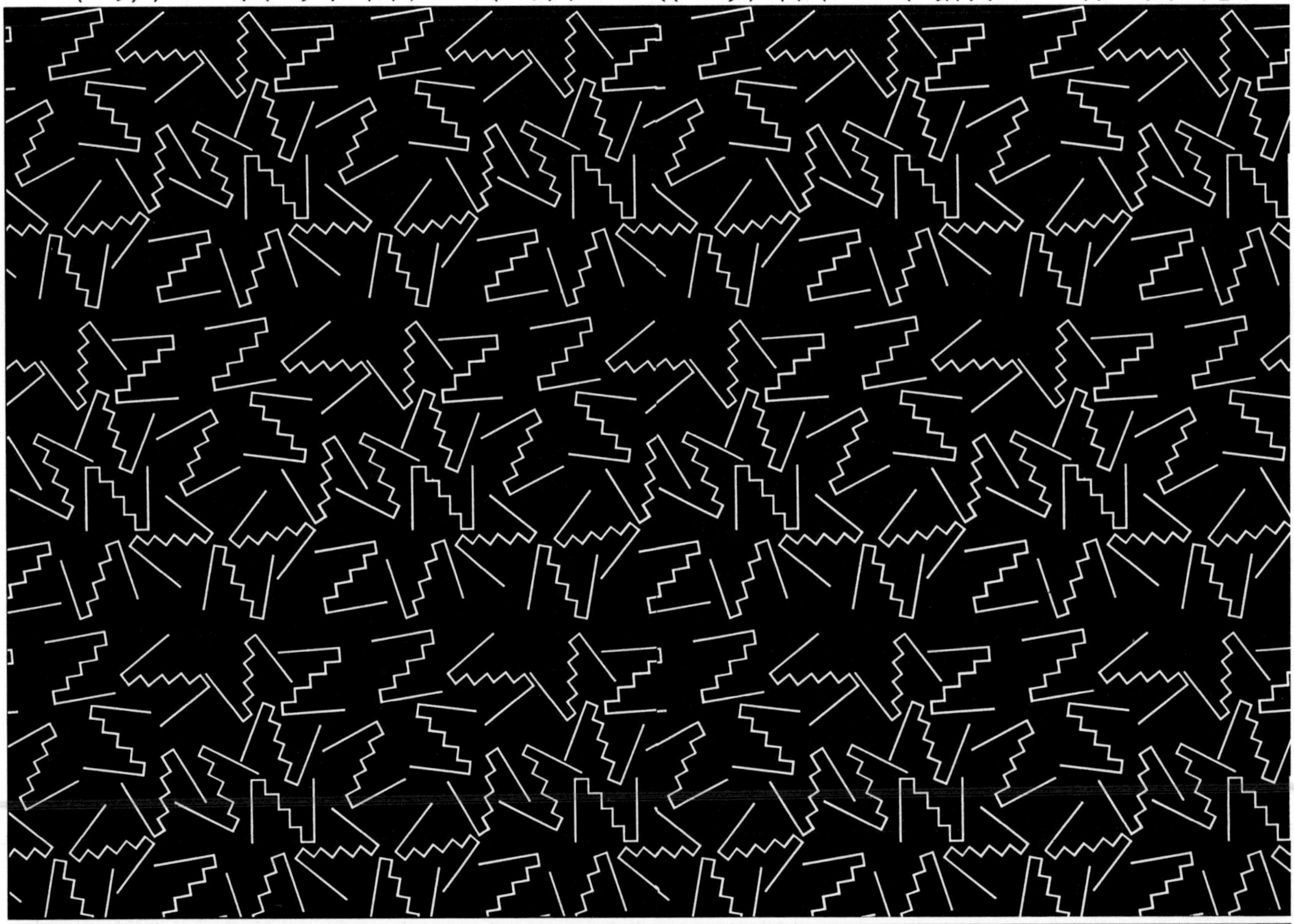

BASIC ELEMENTS BA16

46

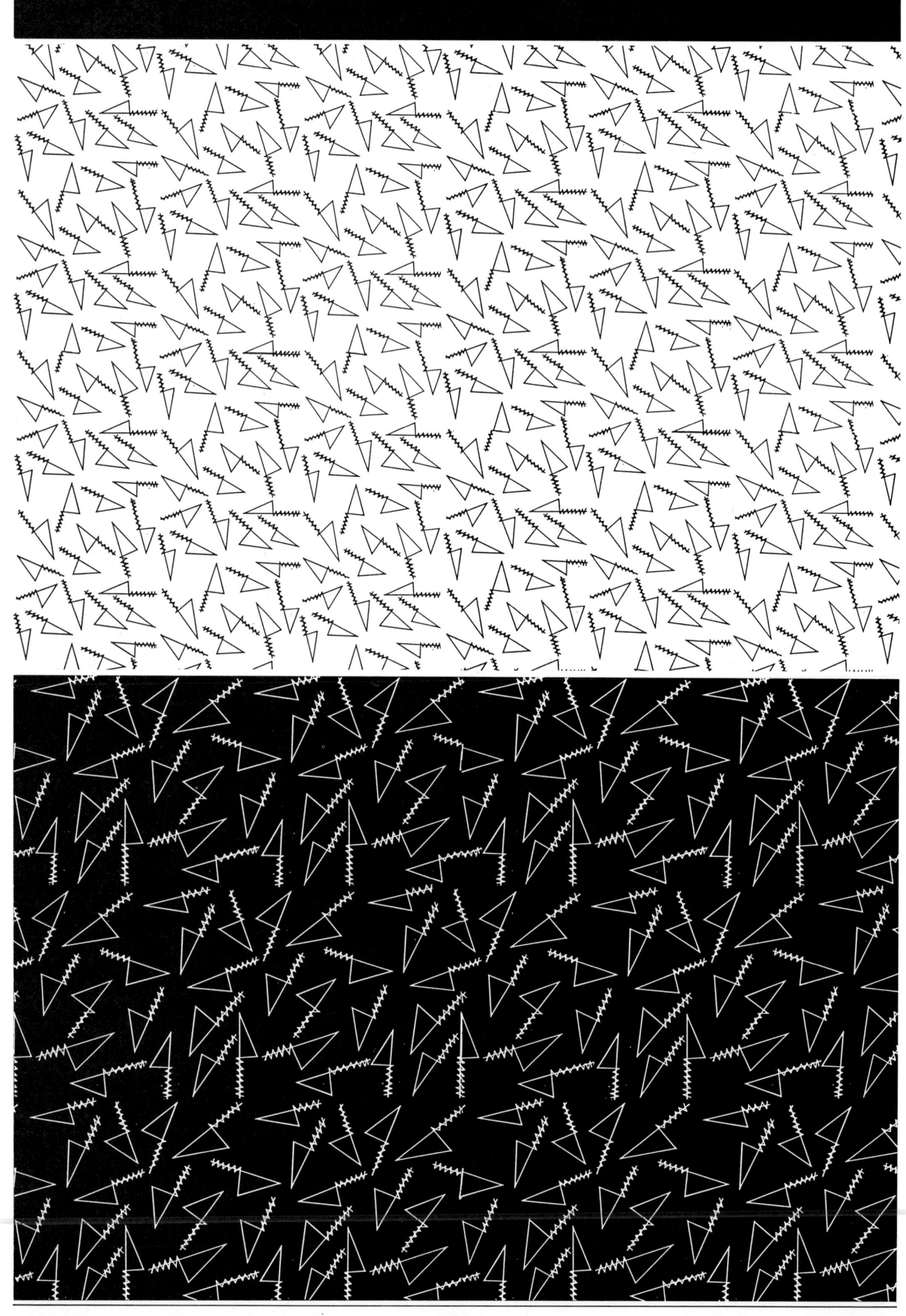

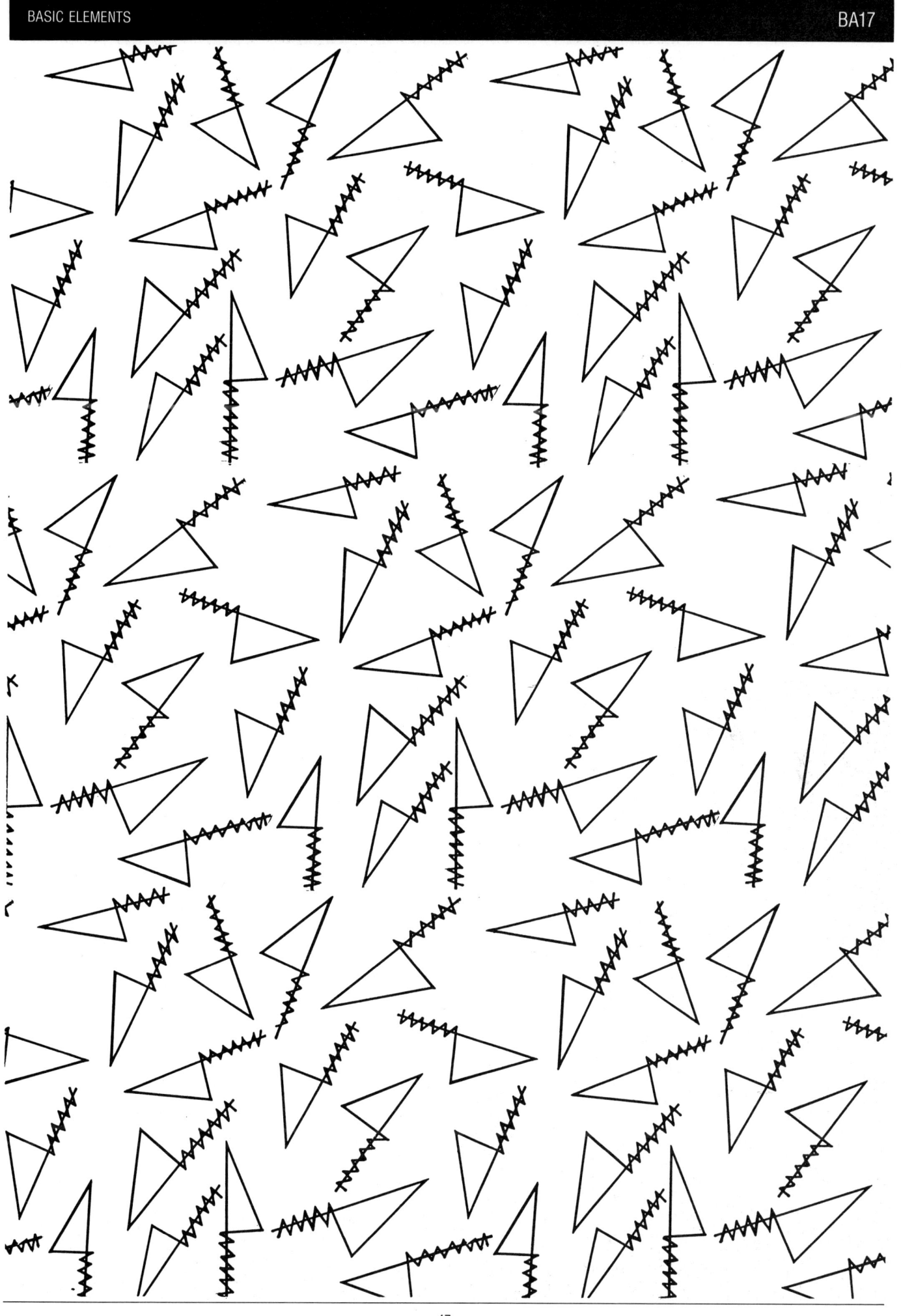

BASIC ELEMENTS BA17

48

BASIC ELEMENTS BA18

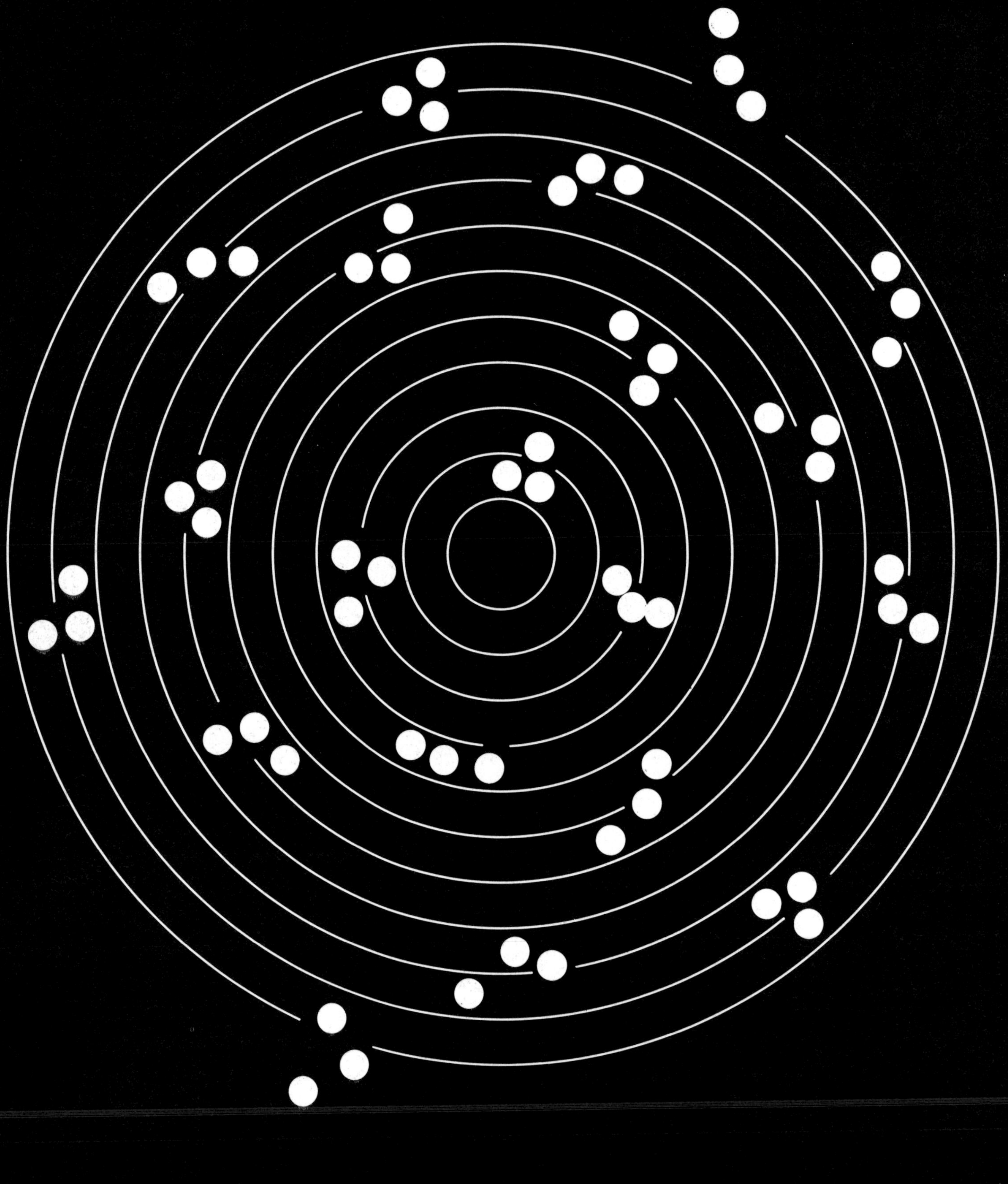

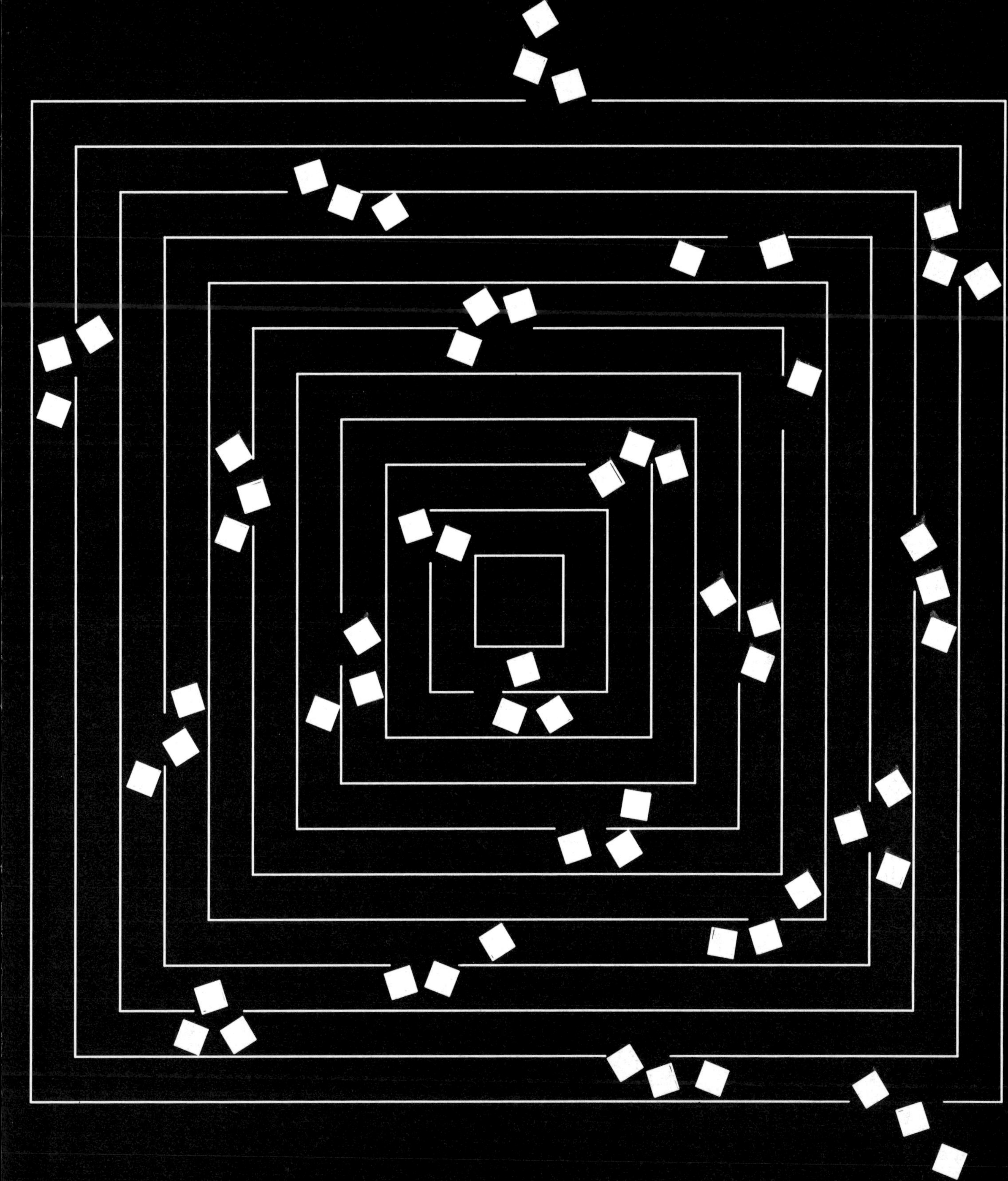

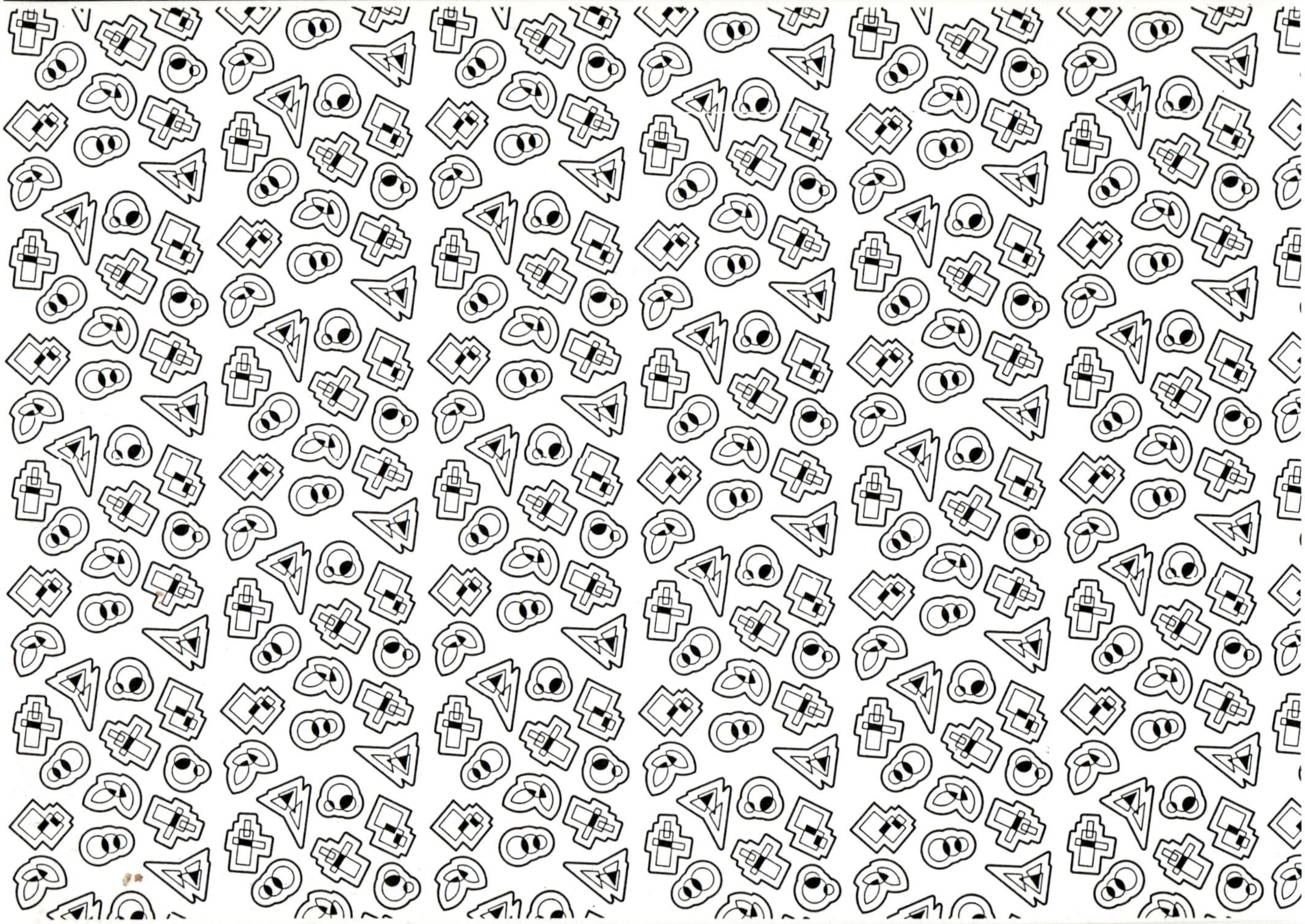

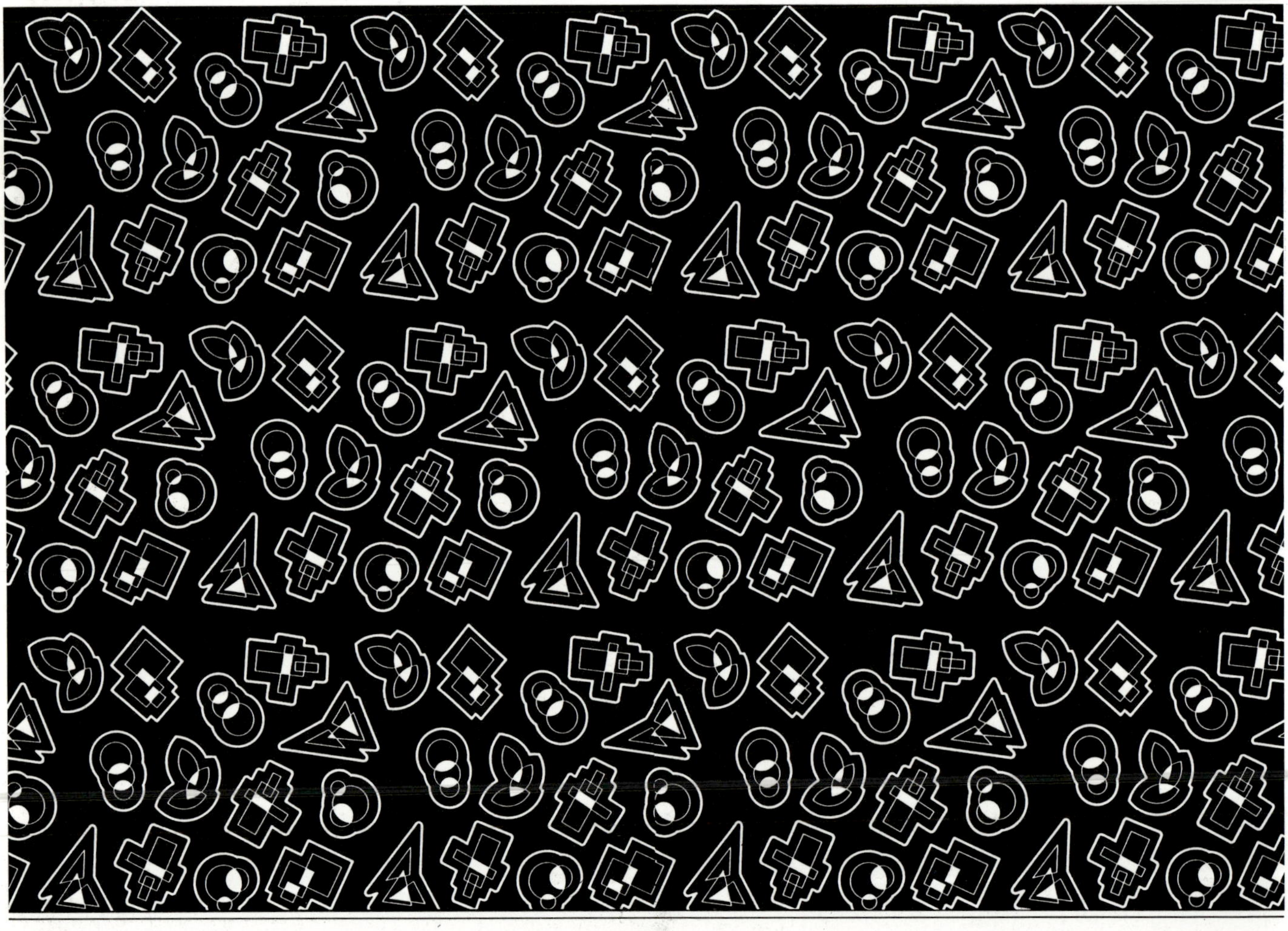

BASIC ELEMENTS BA19

54

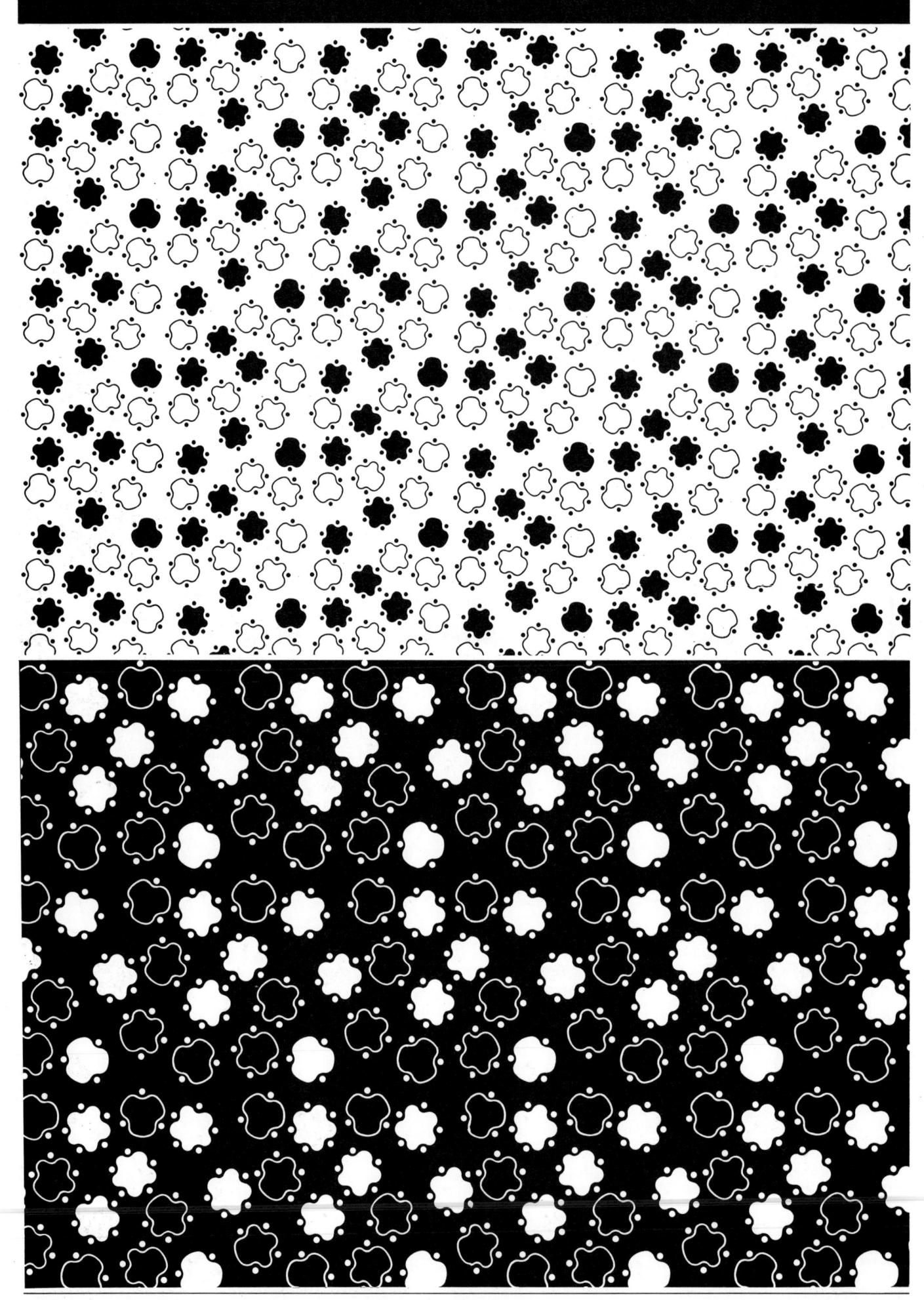

BASIC ELEMENTS   BA20

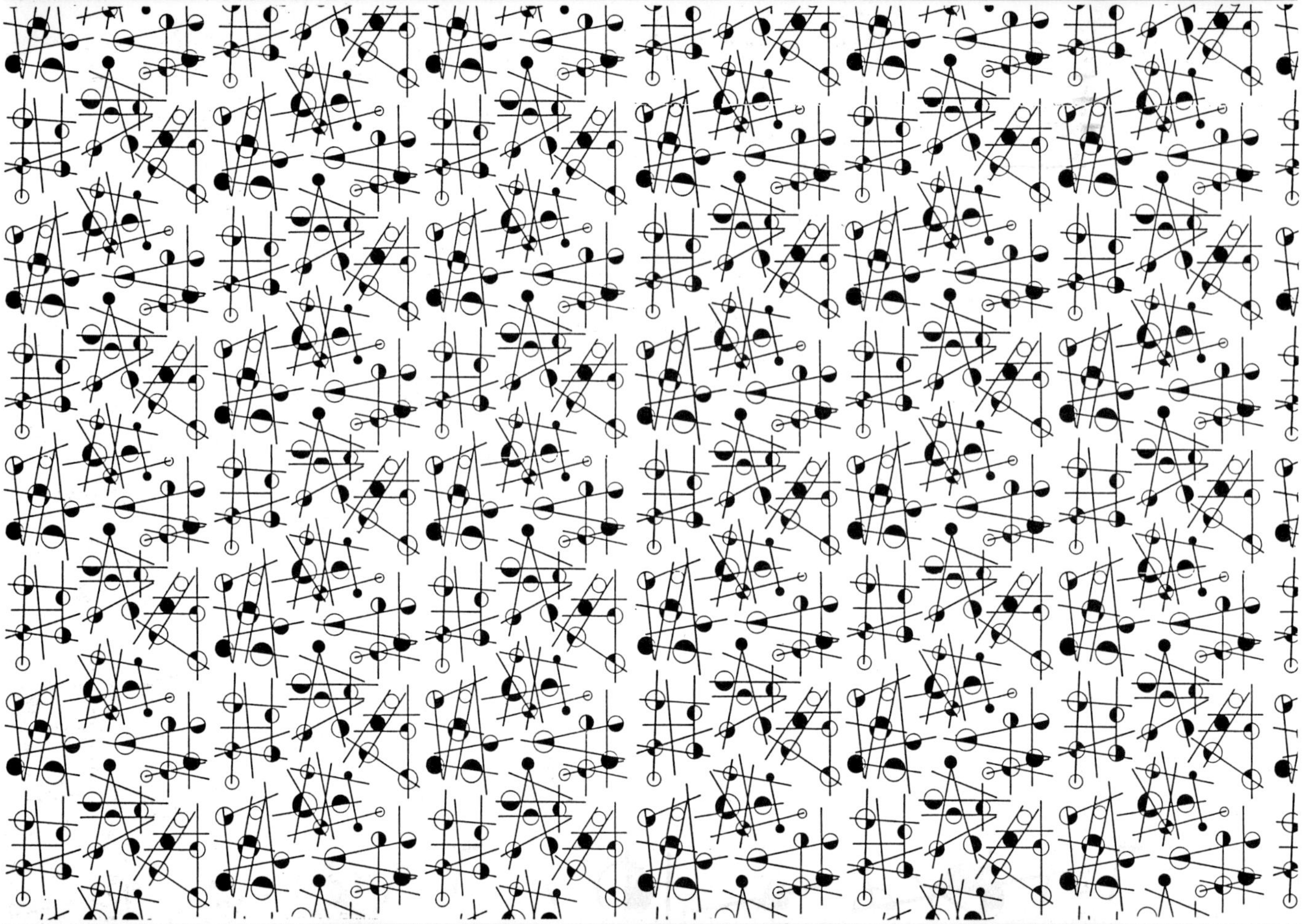

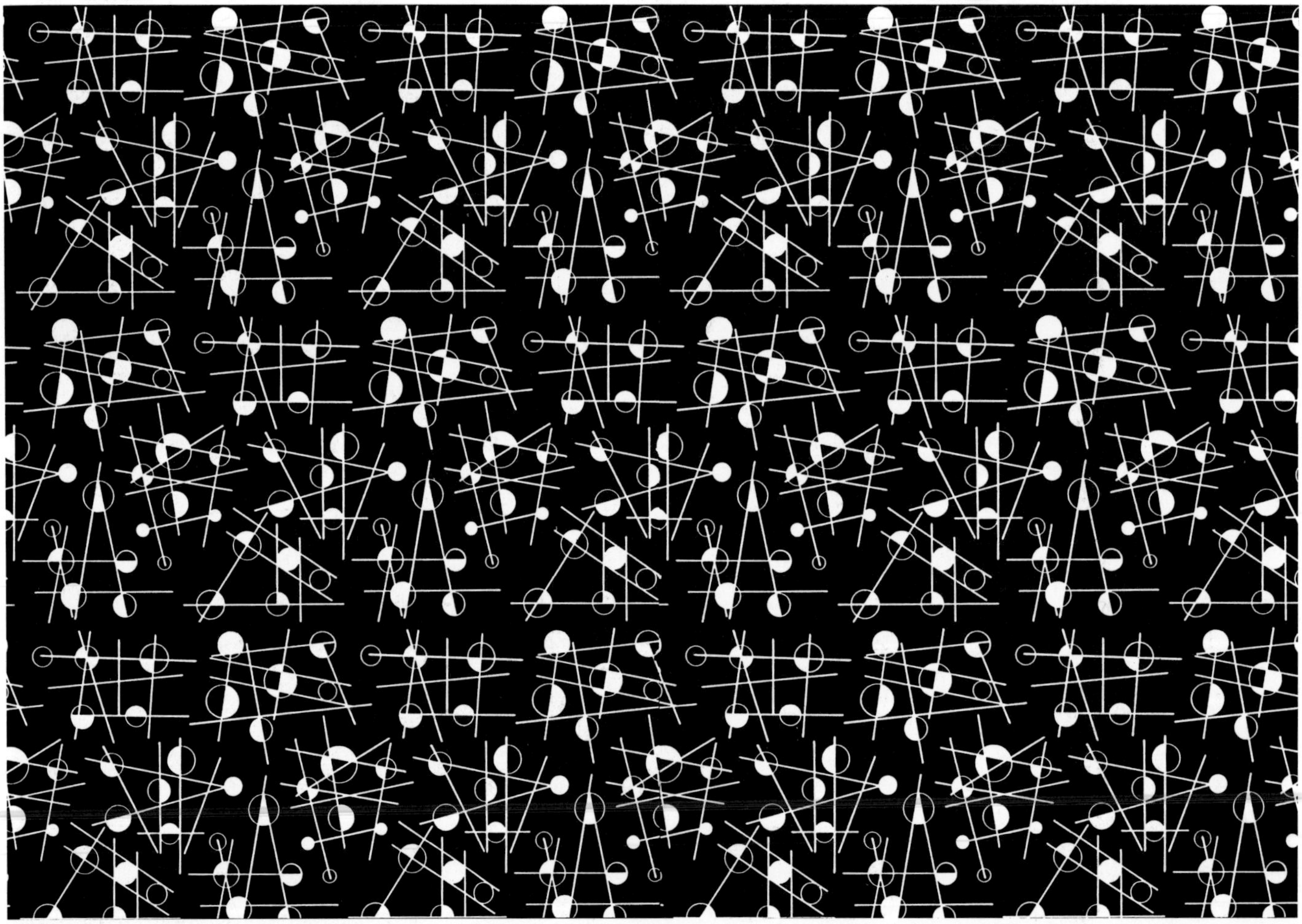

BASIC ELEMENTS BA21

58

BASIC ELEMENTS BA22

60

BASIC ELEMENTS BA23

62

BASIC ELEMENTS
BA24

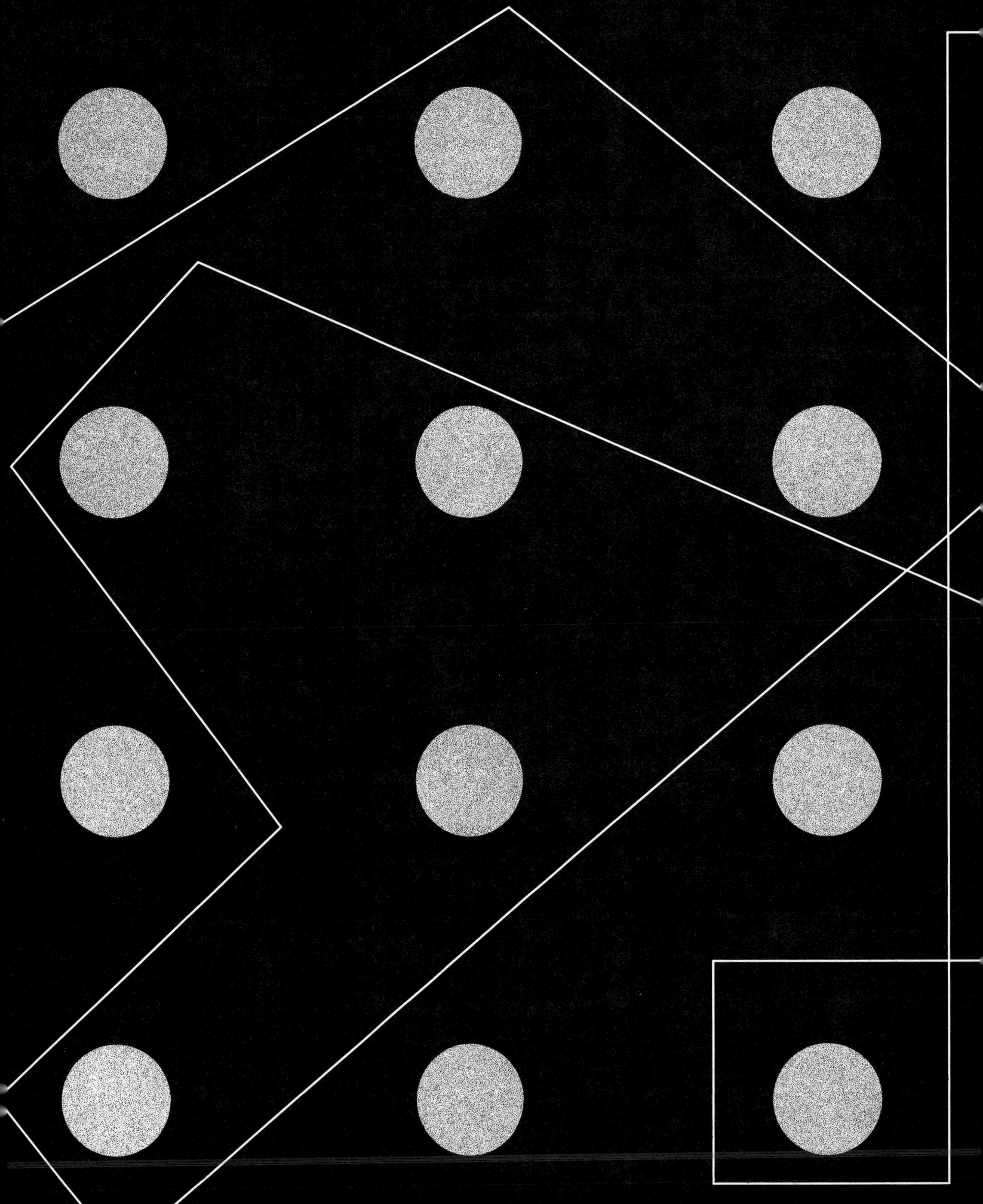

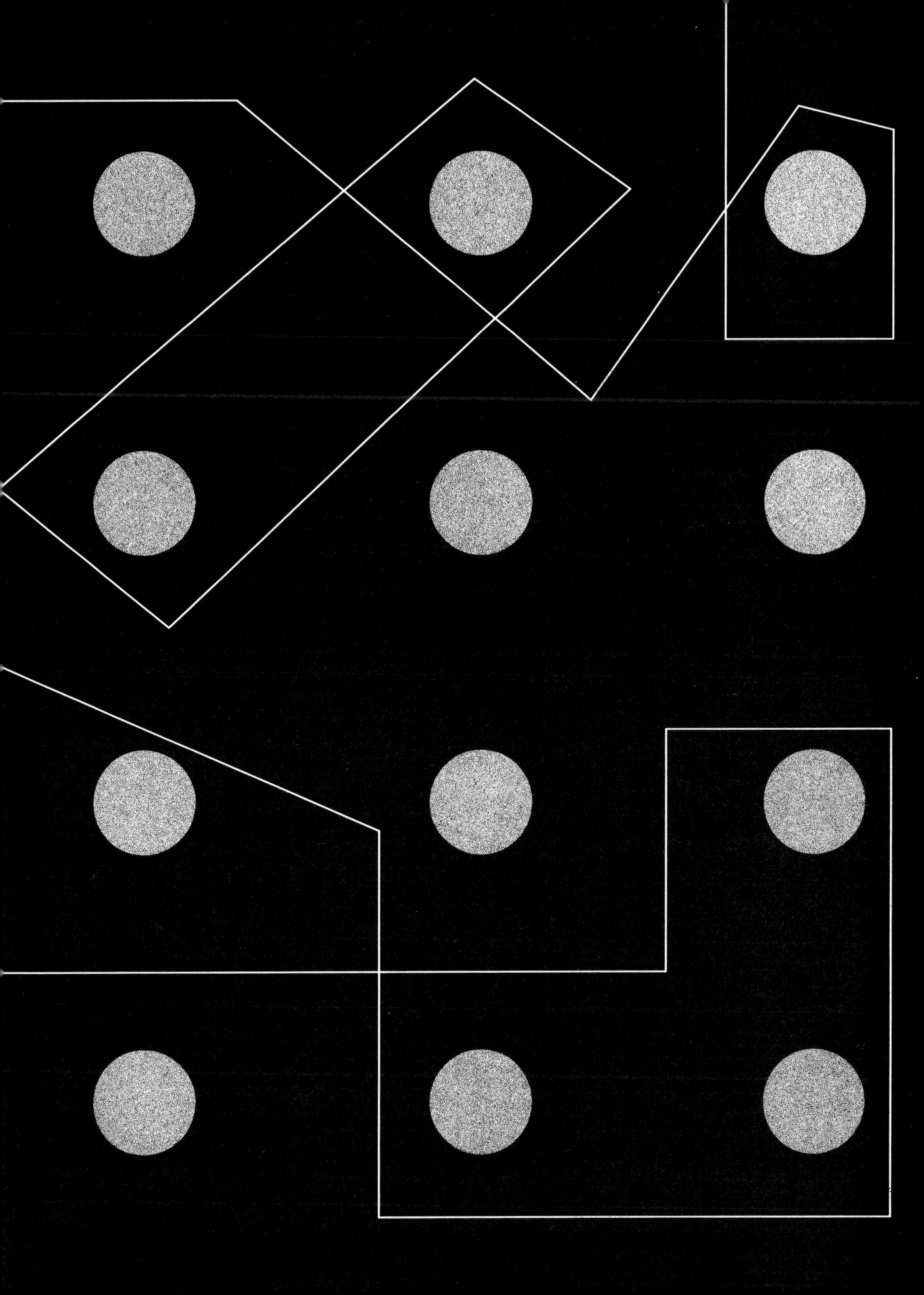

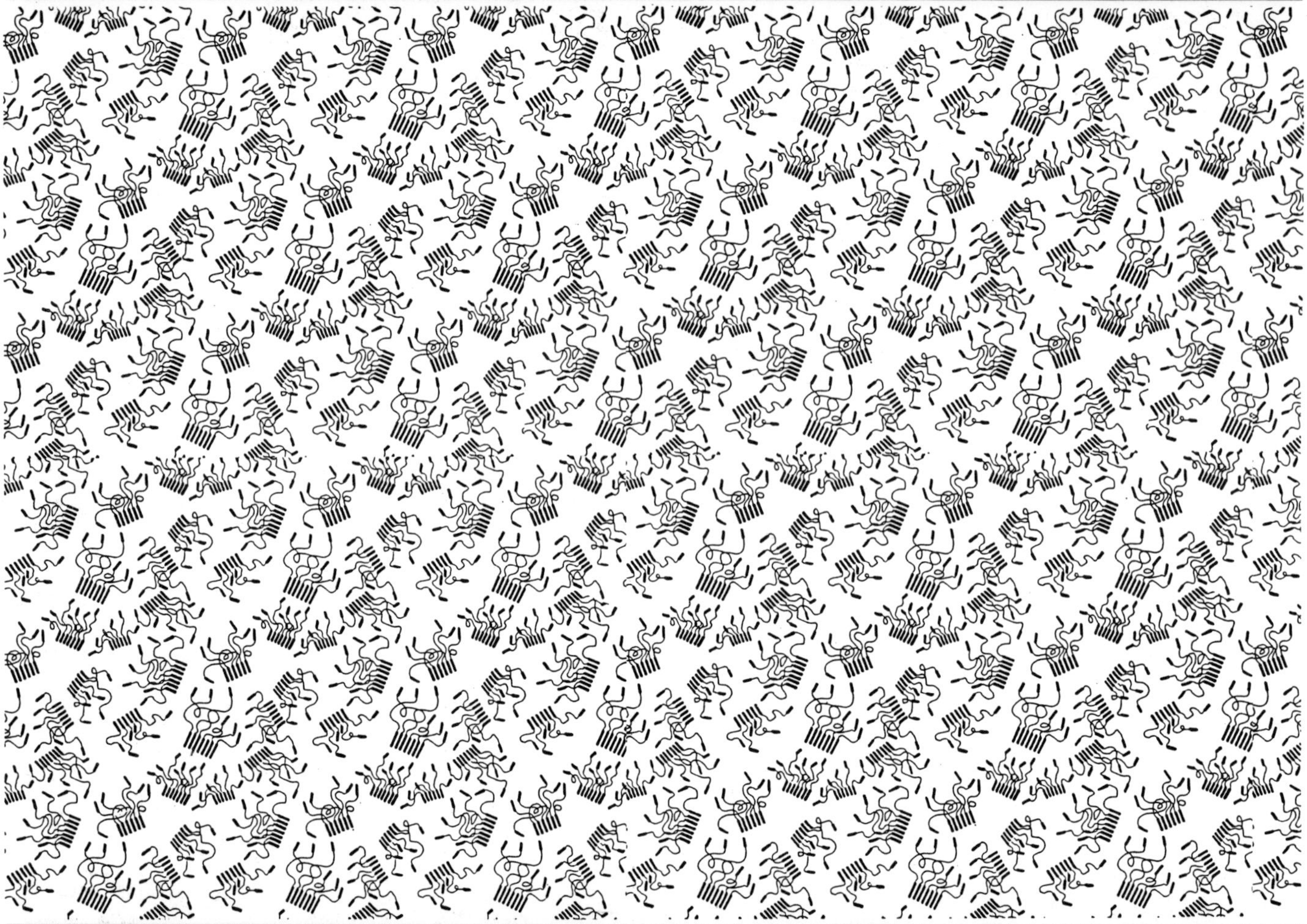

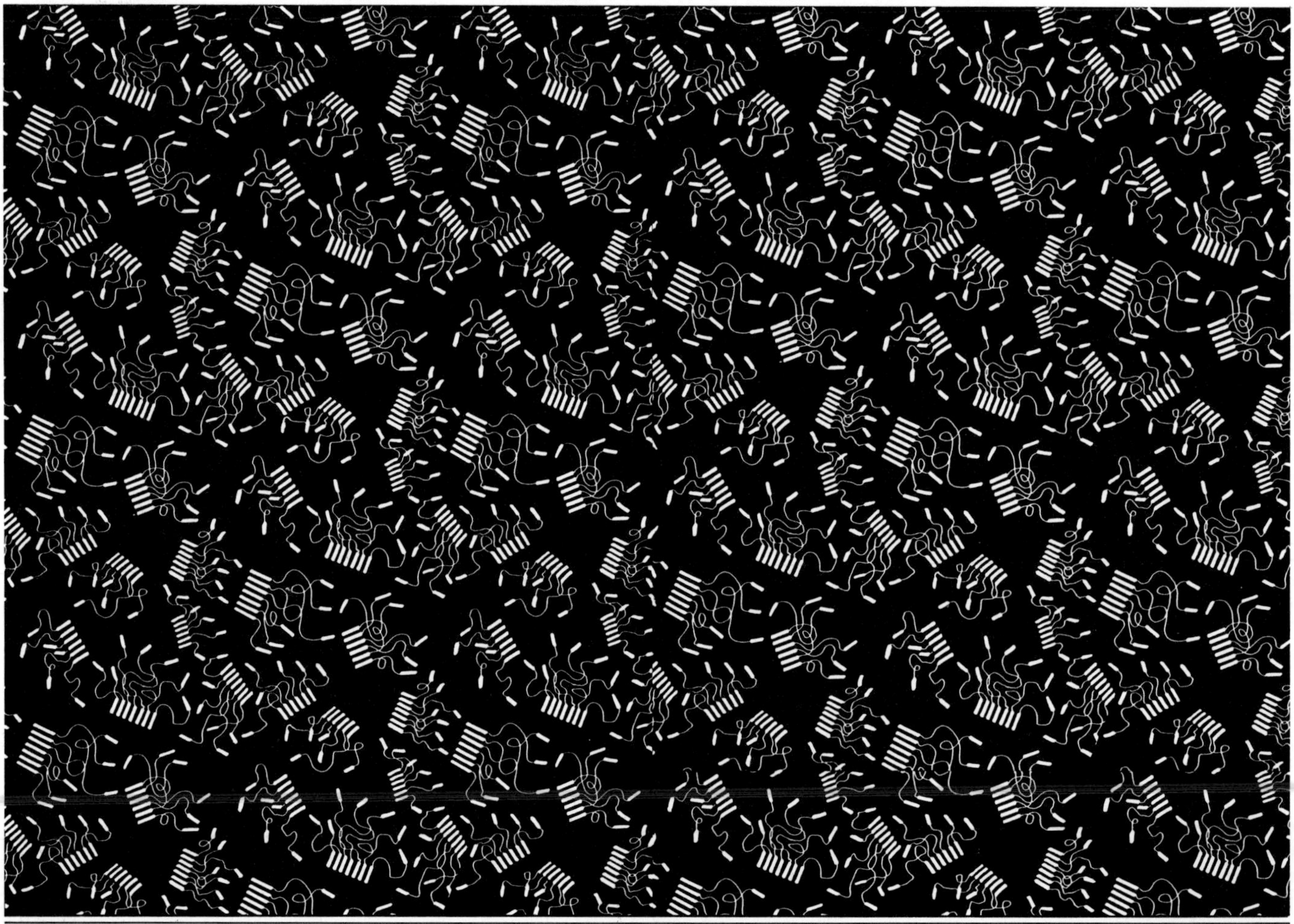

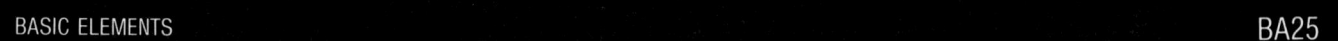

BASIC ELEMENTS BA25

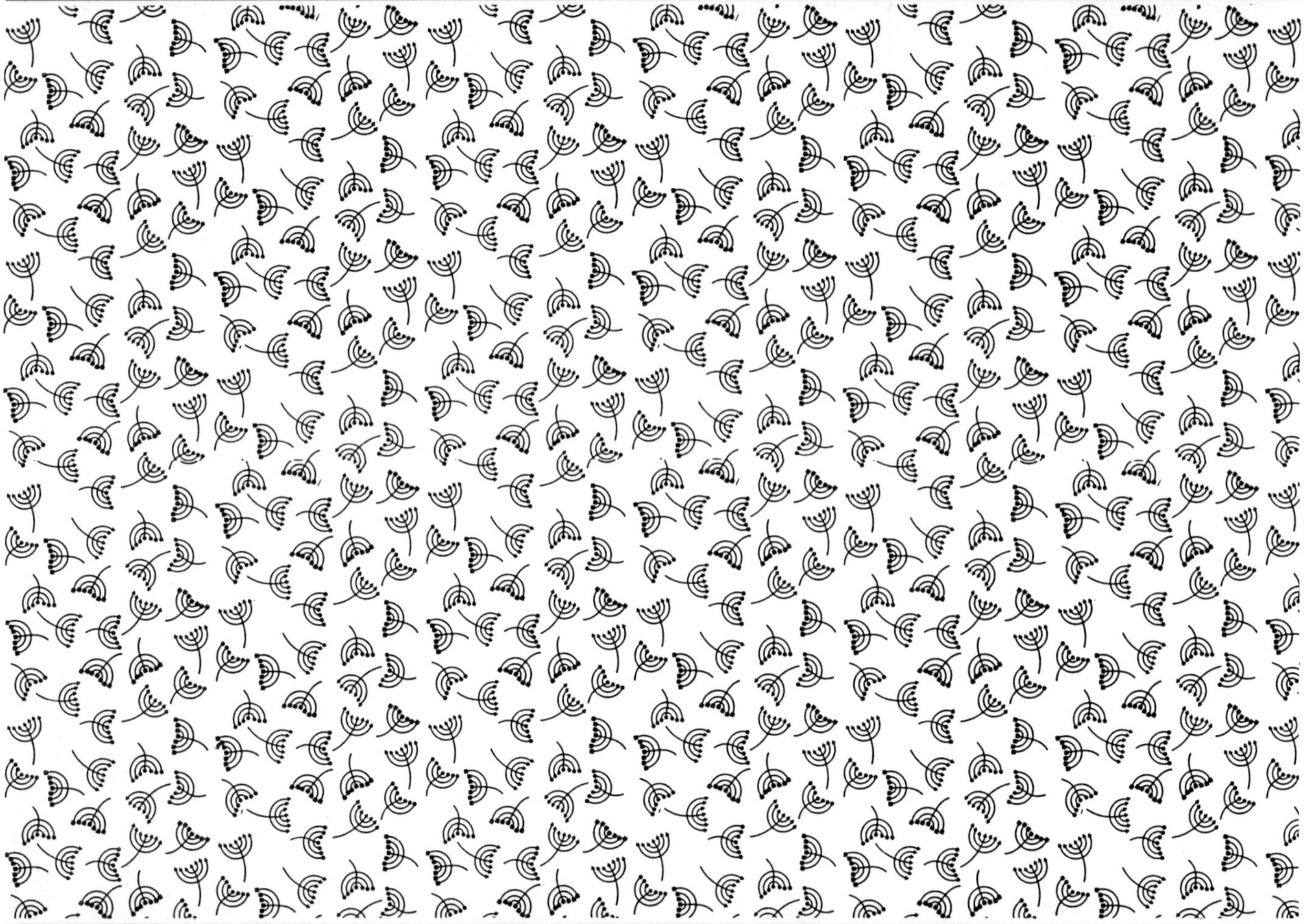

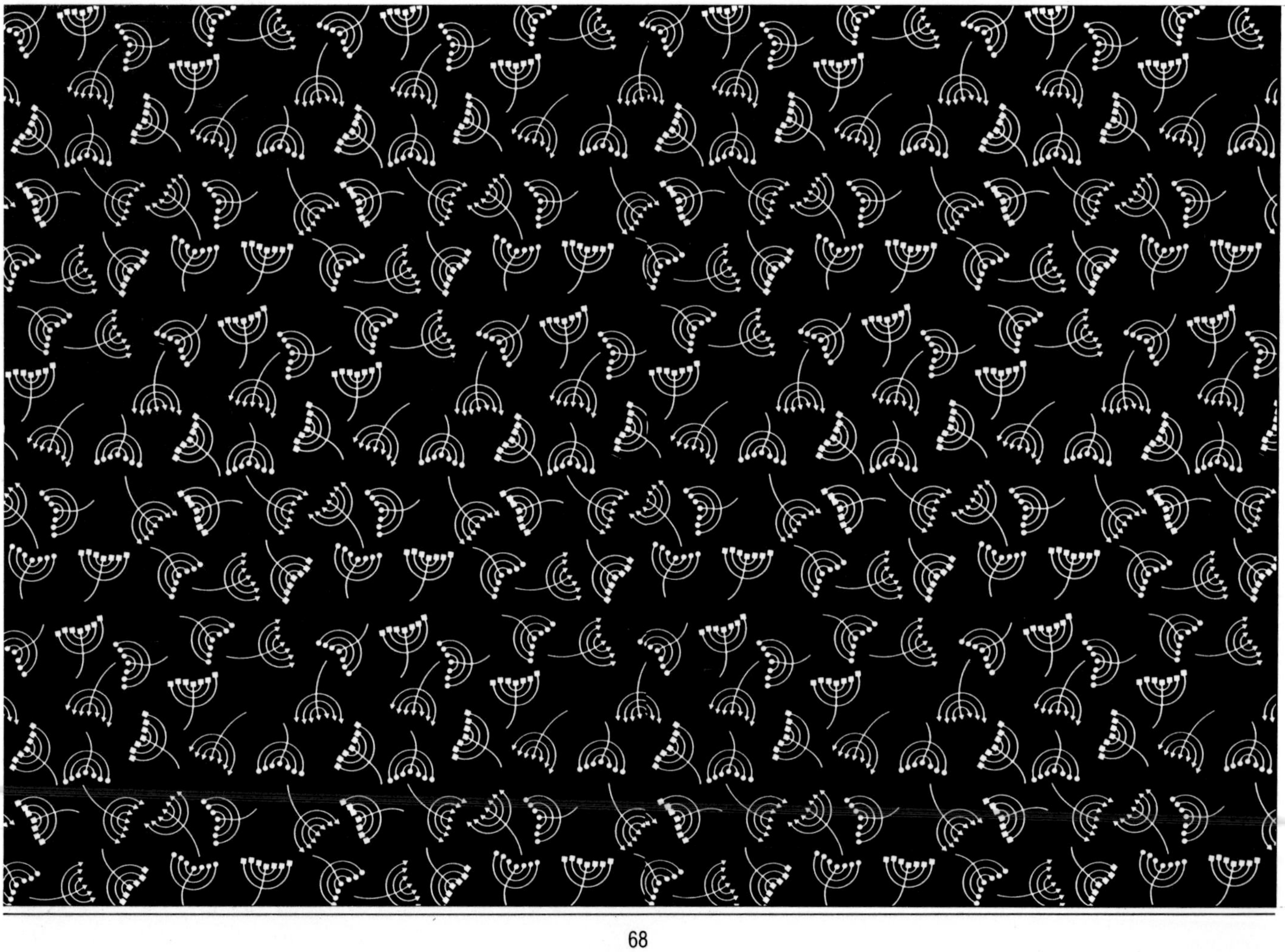

BASIC ELEMENTS

BA26

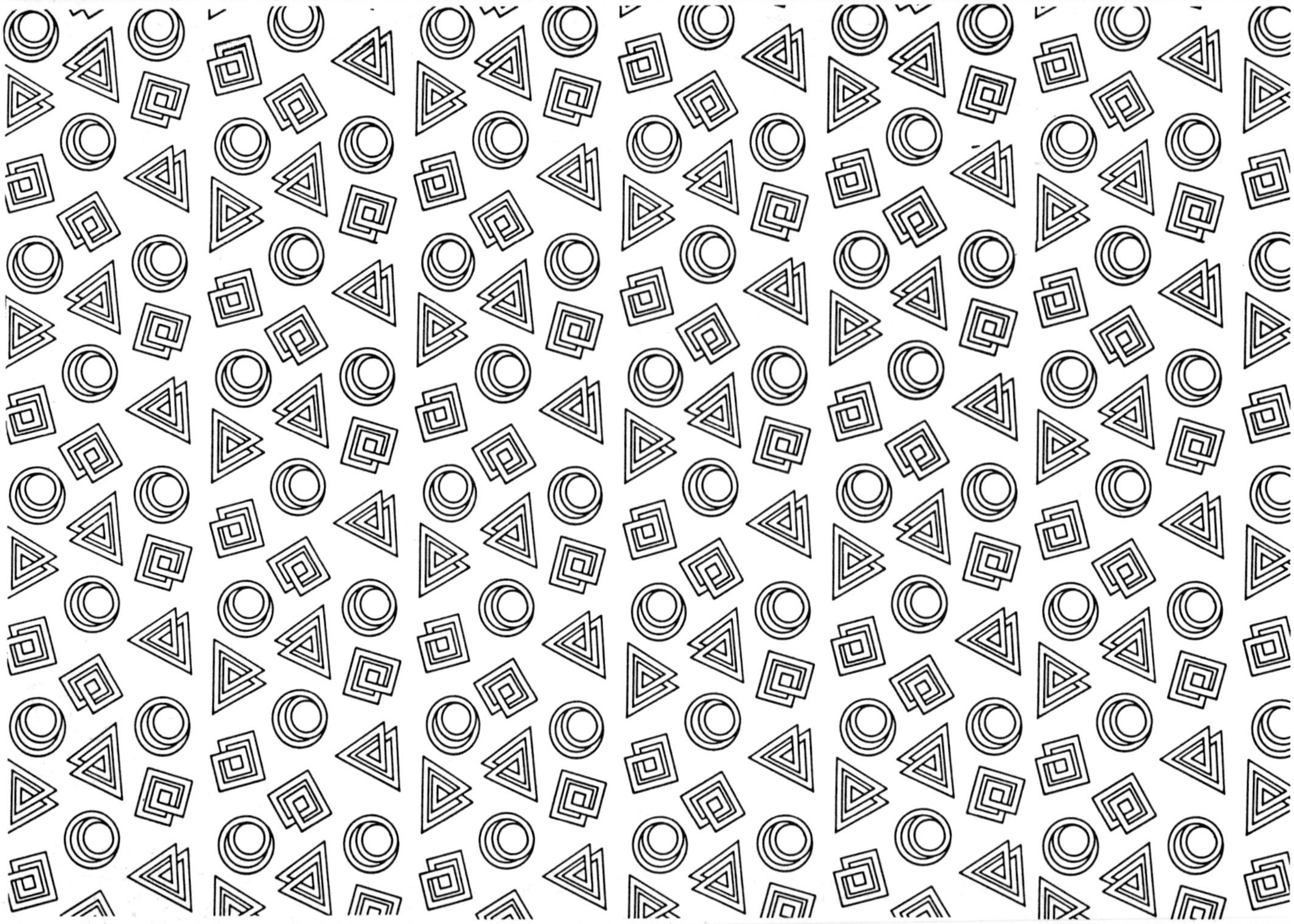

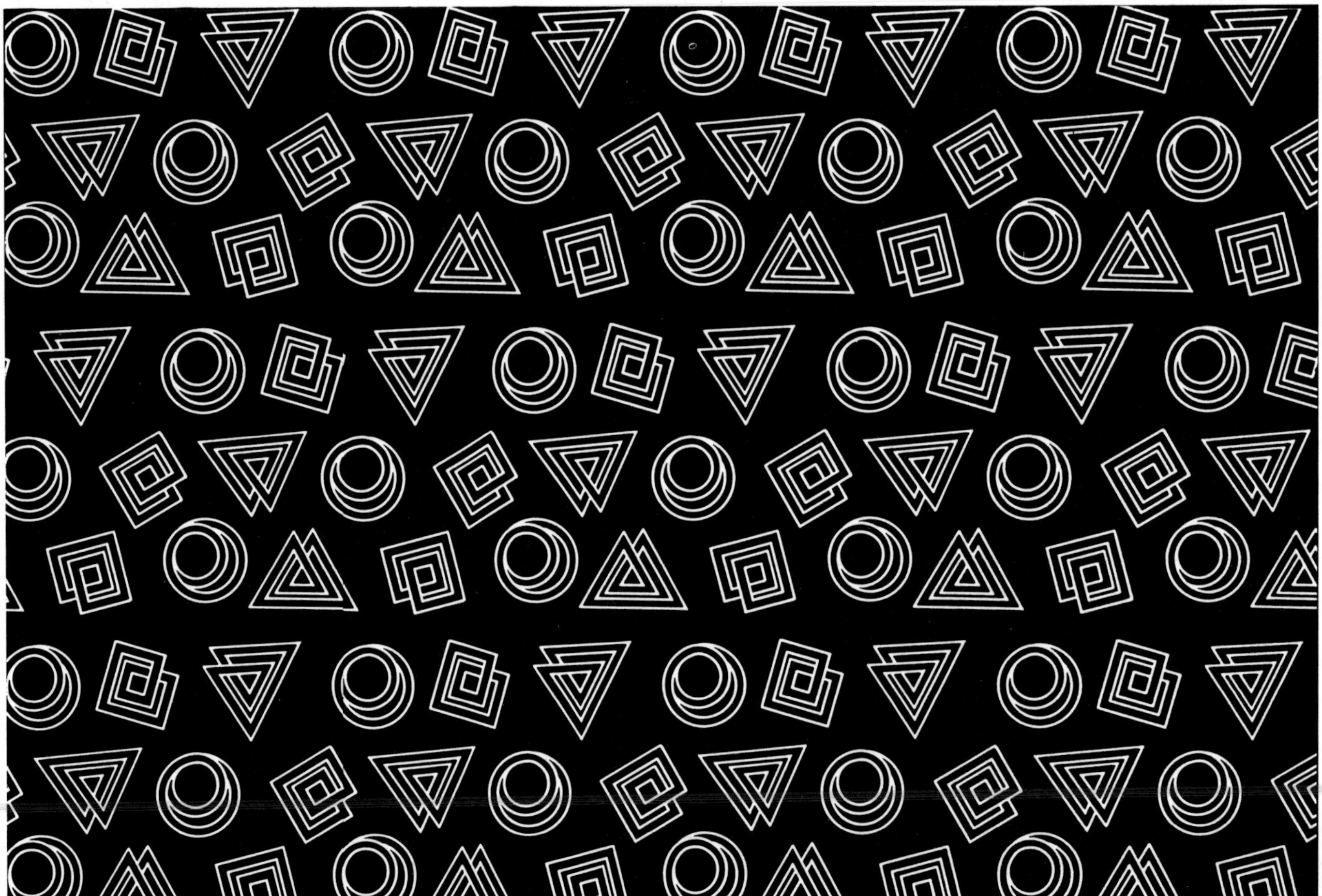

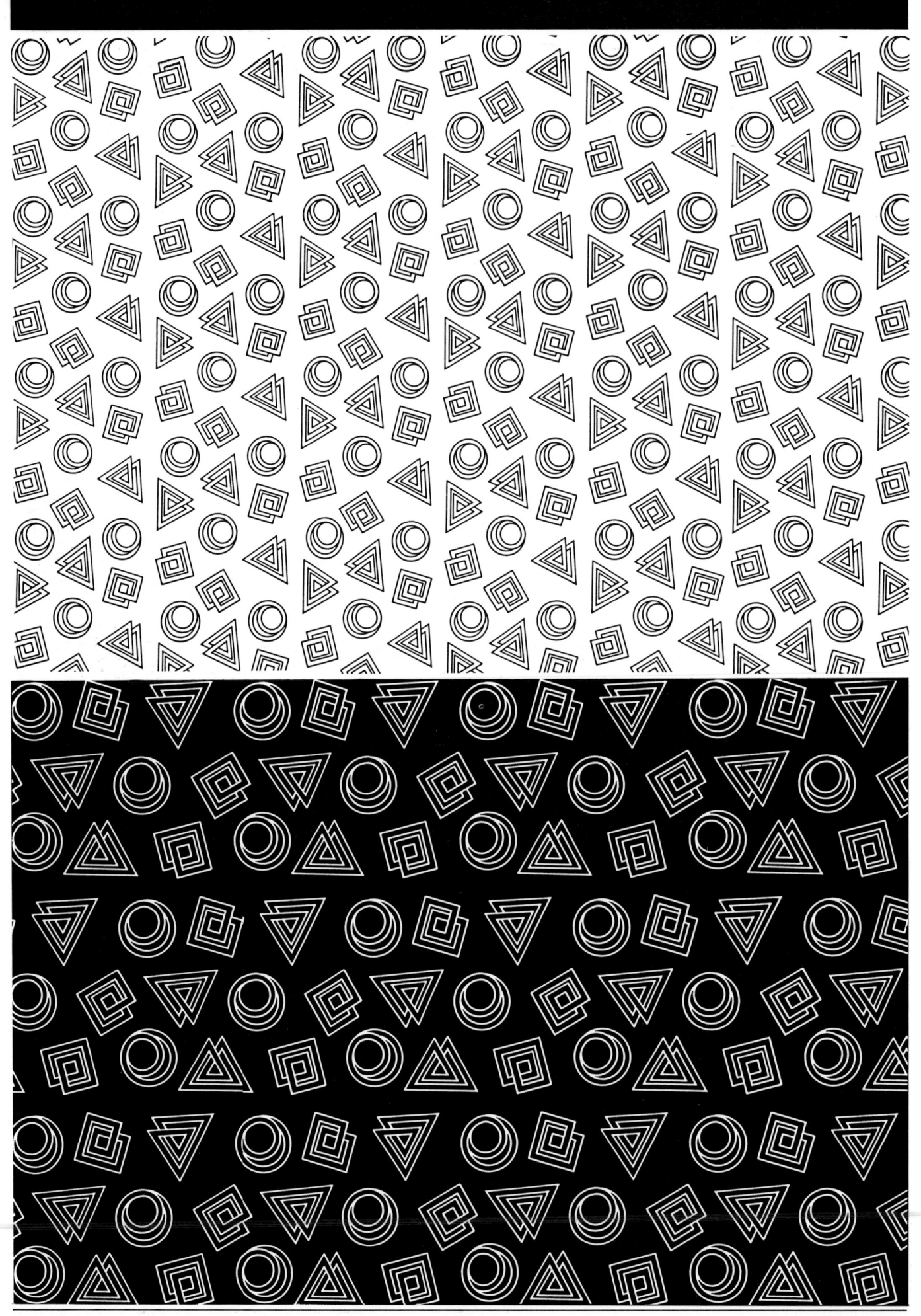

BASIC ELEMENTS BA27

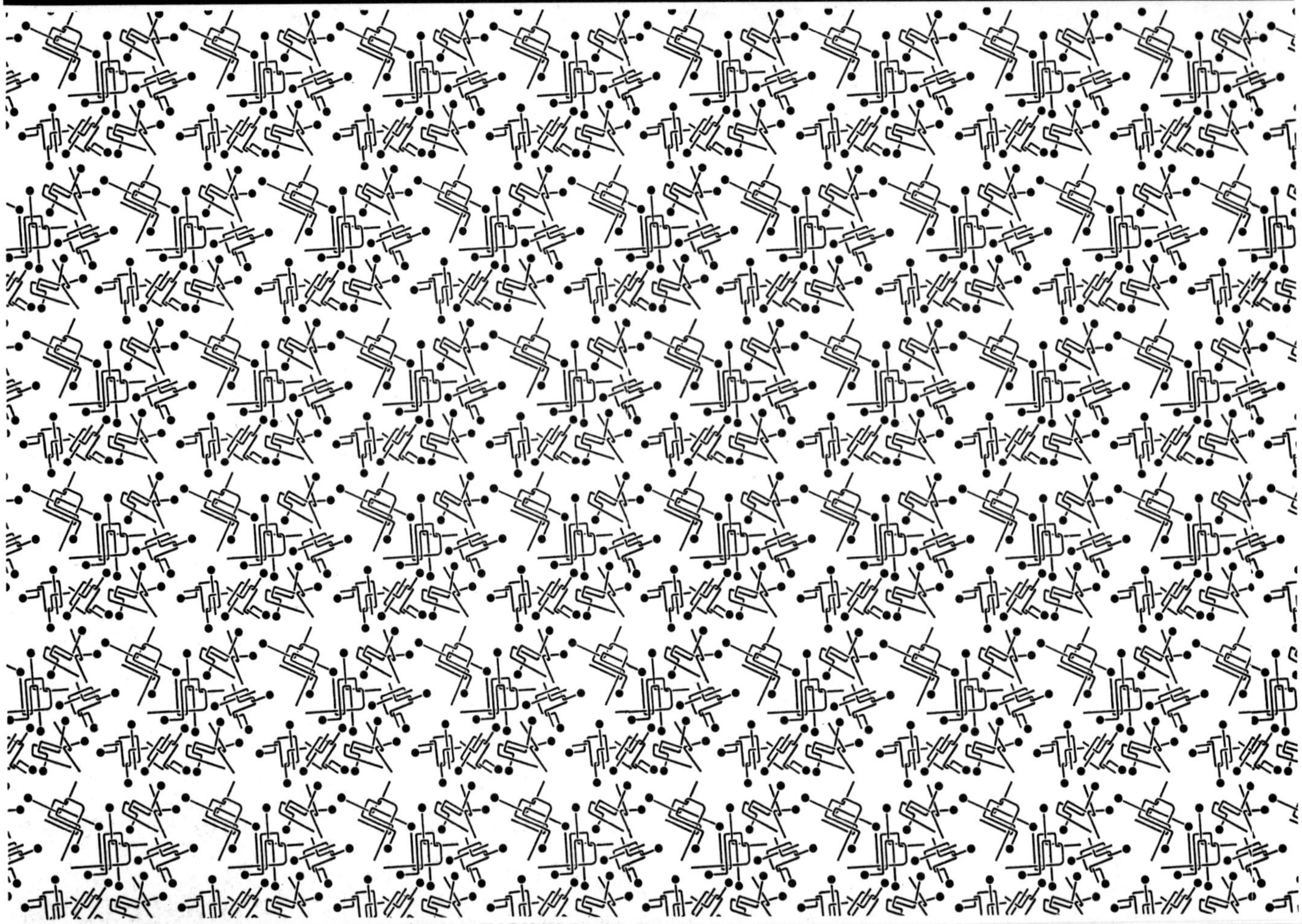

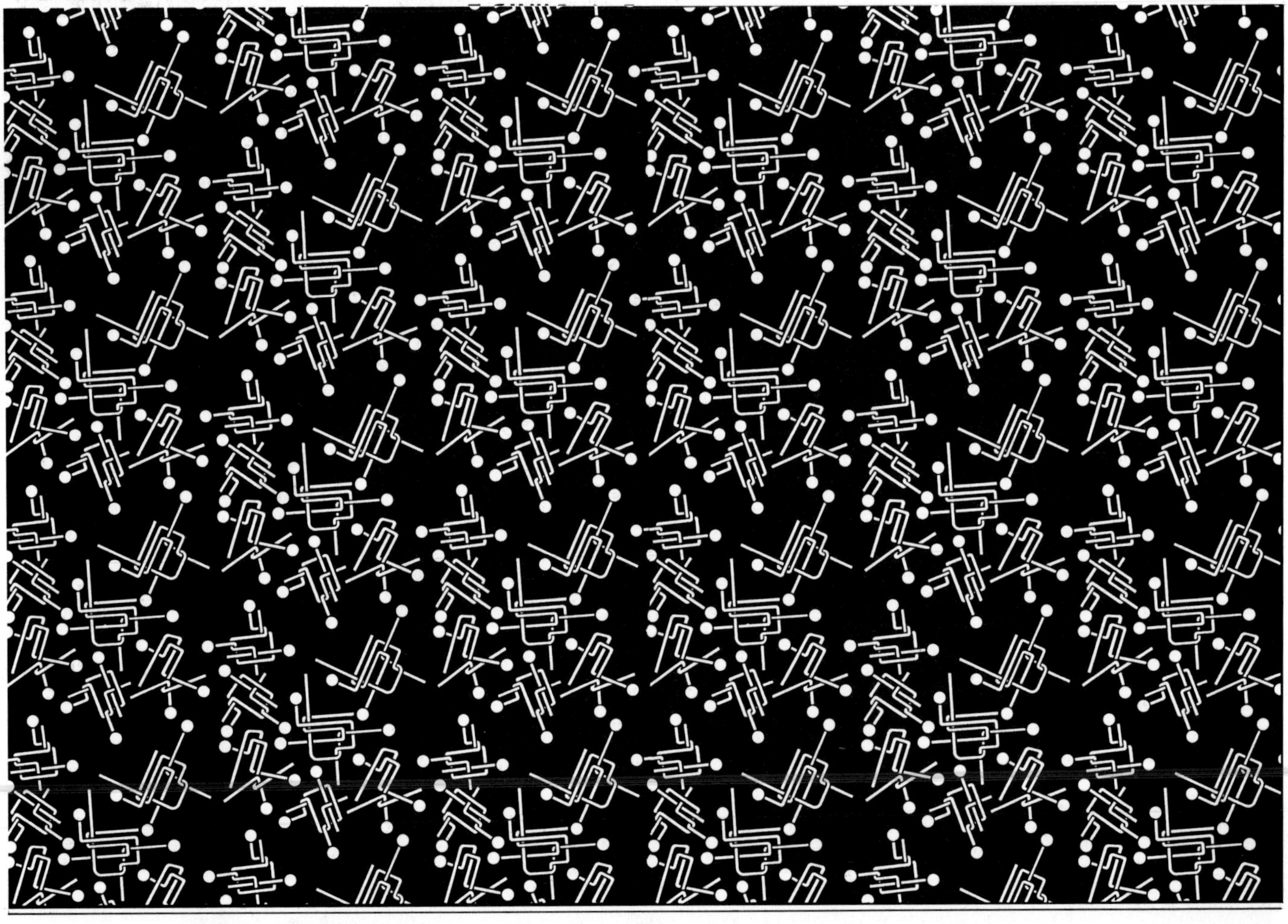

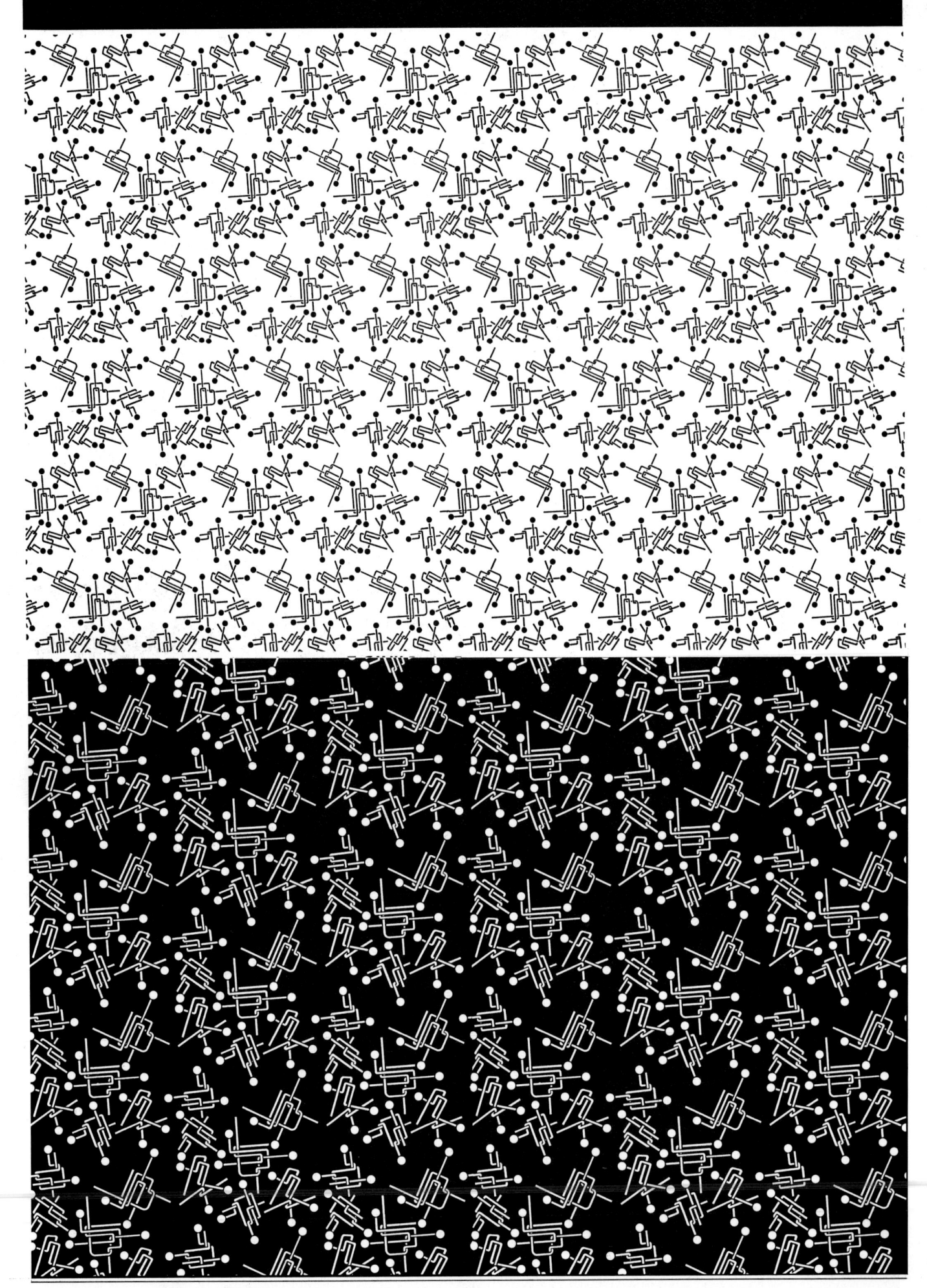

BASIC ELEMENTS BA28

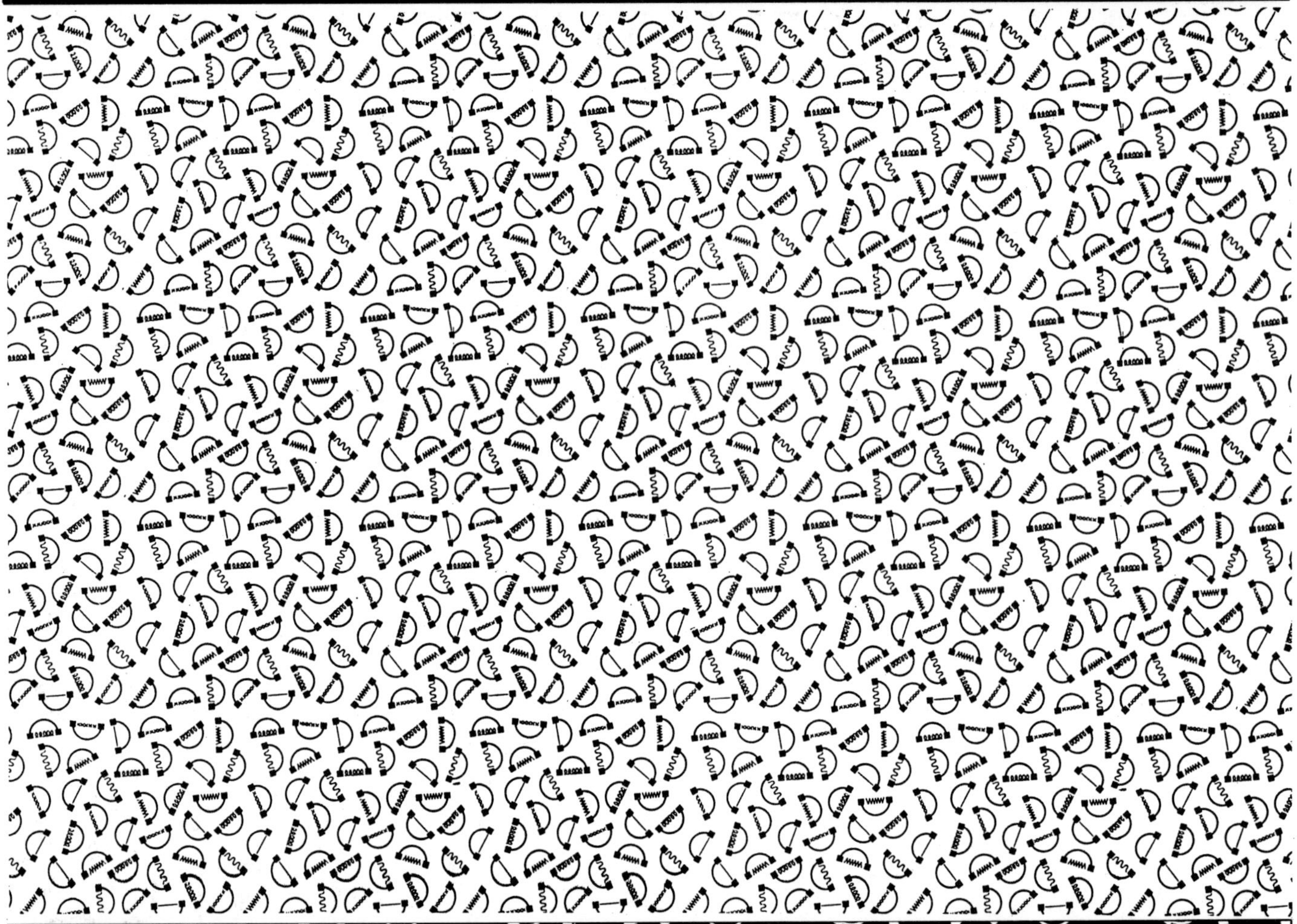

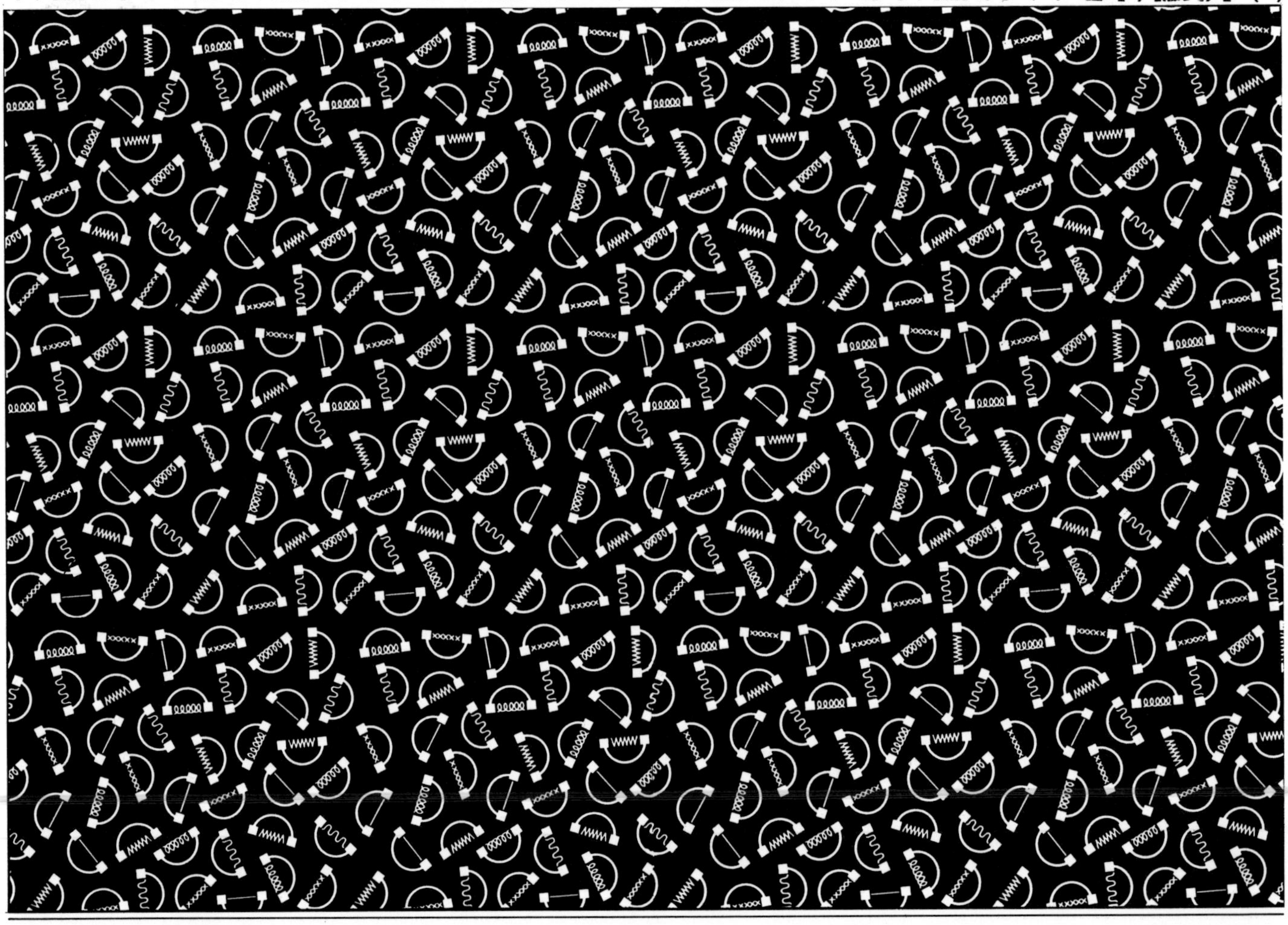

BASIC ELEMENTS BA29

76

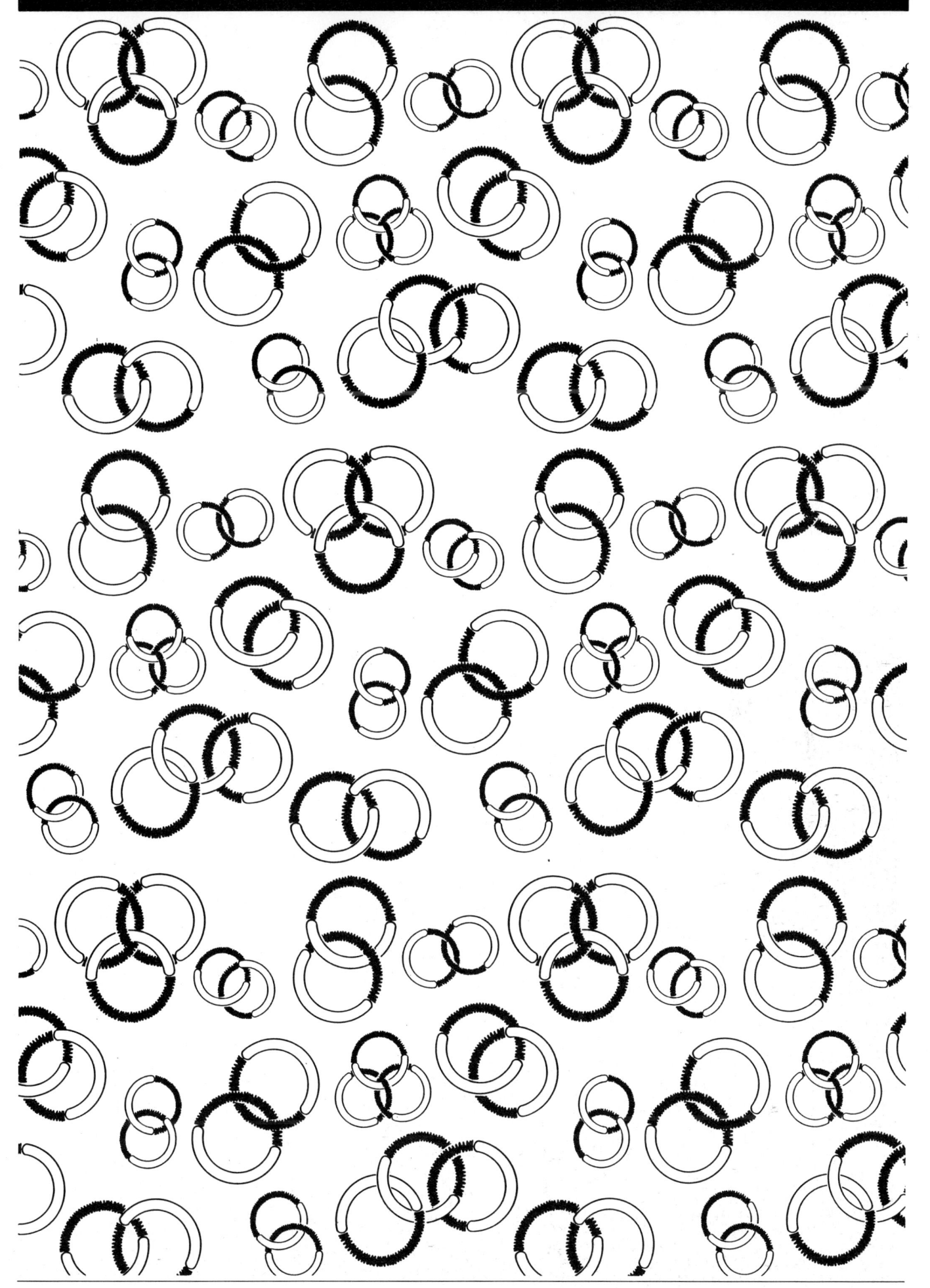

BASIC ELEMENTS　　　　　　　　　　　　　　　　　　　　　　　　　　　　　　　　BA30

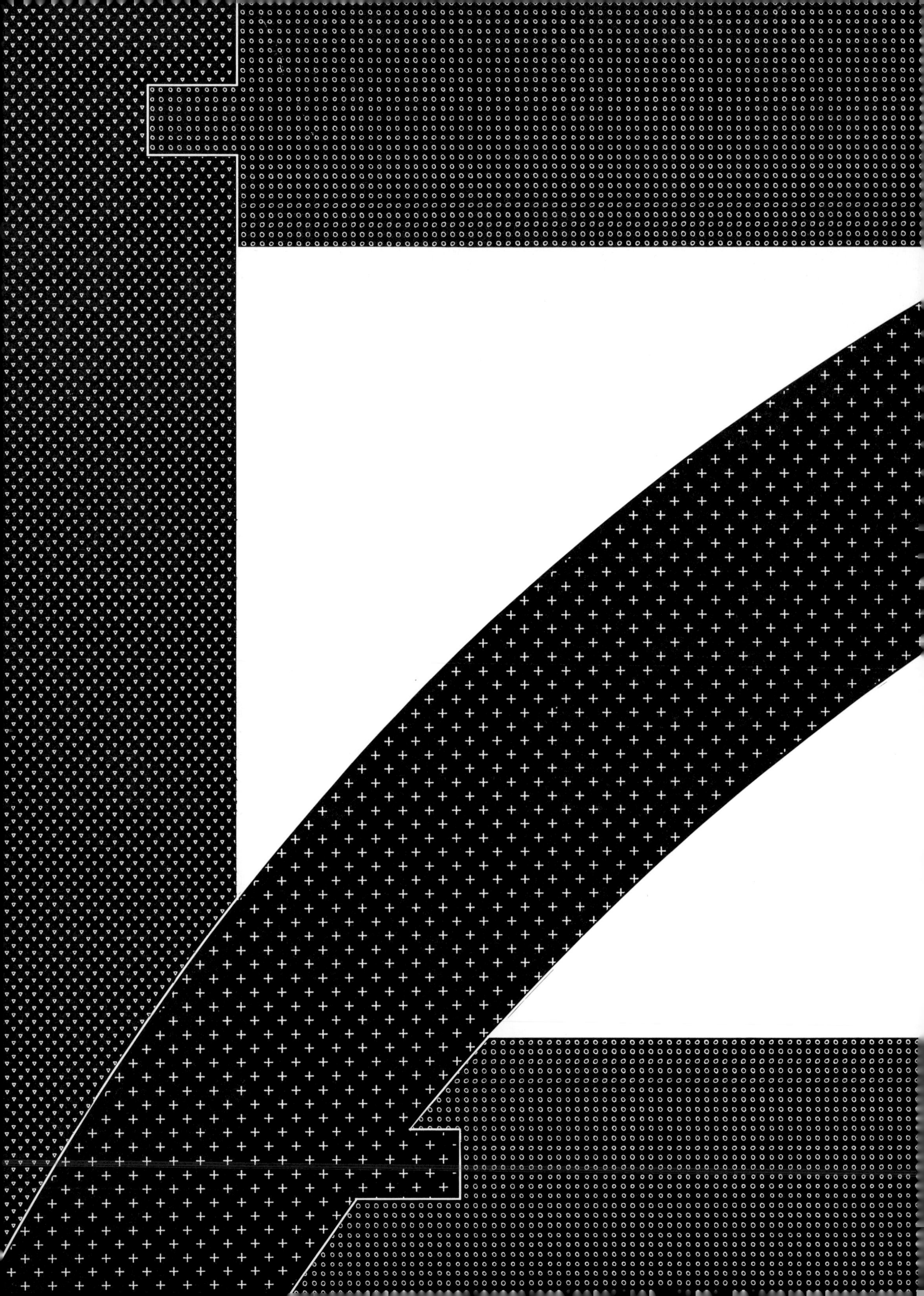

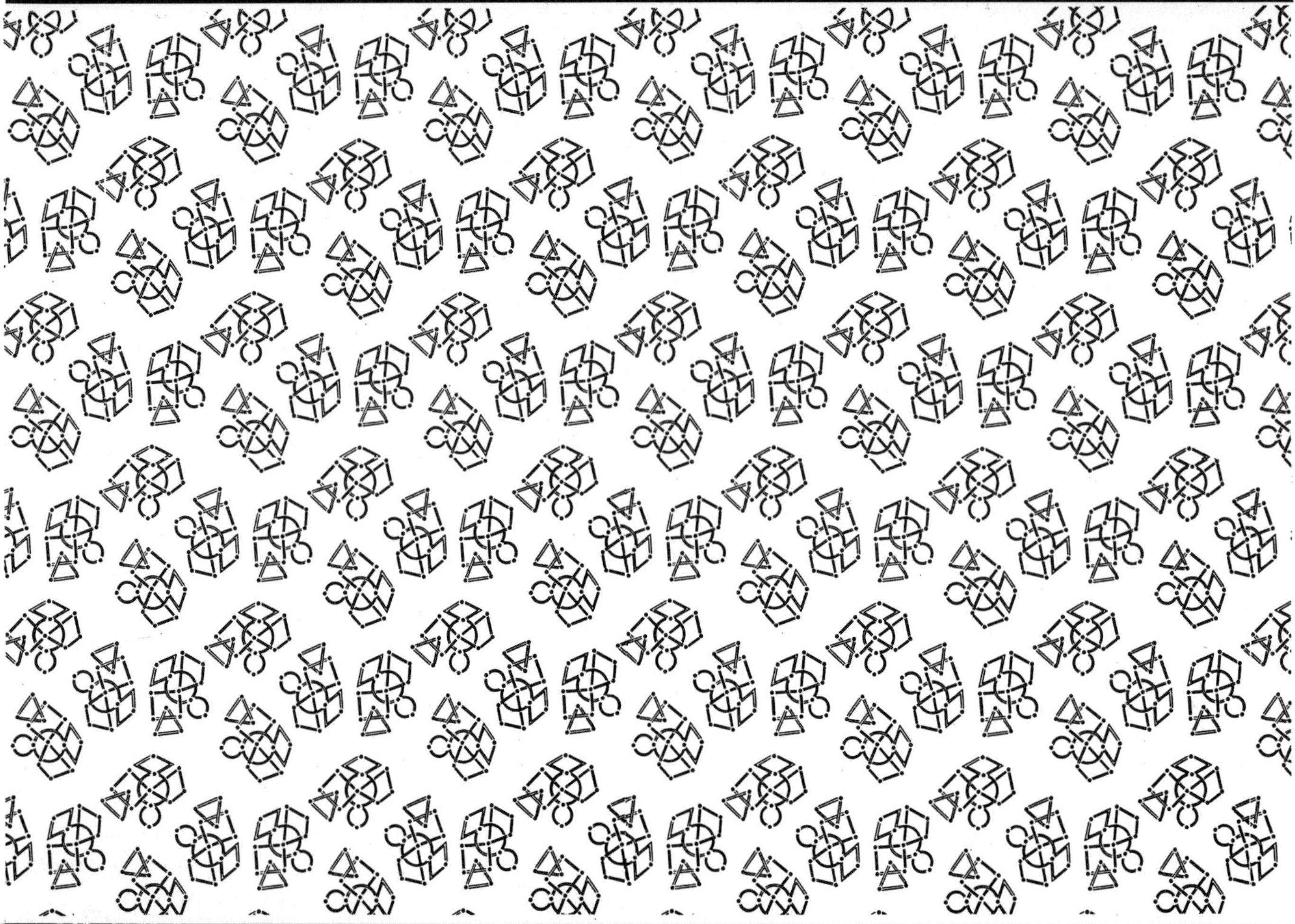

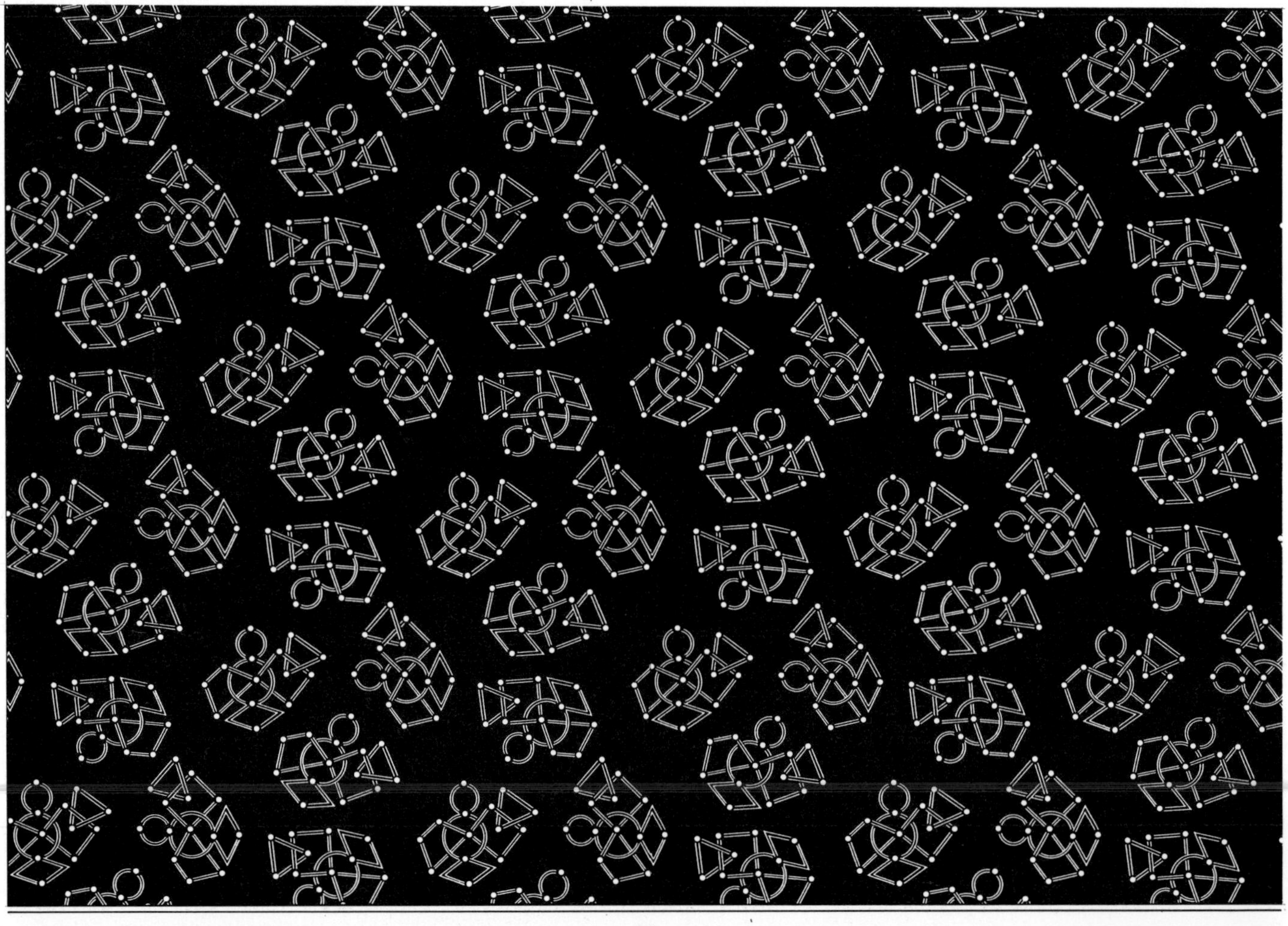

BASIC ELEMENTS
BA31

82

BASIC ELEMENTS BA32

84

BASIC ELEMENTS BA33

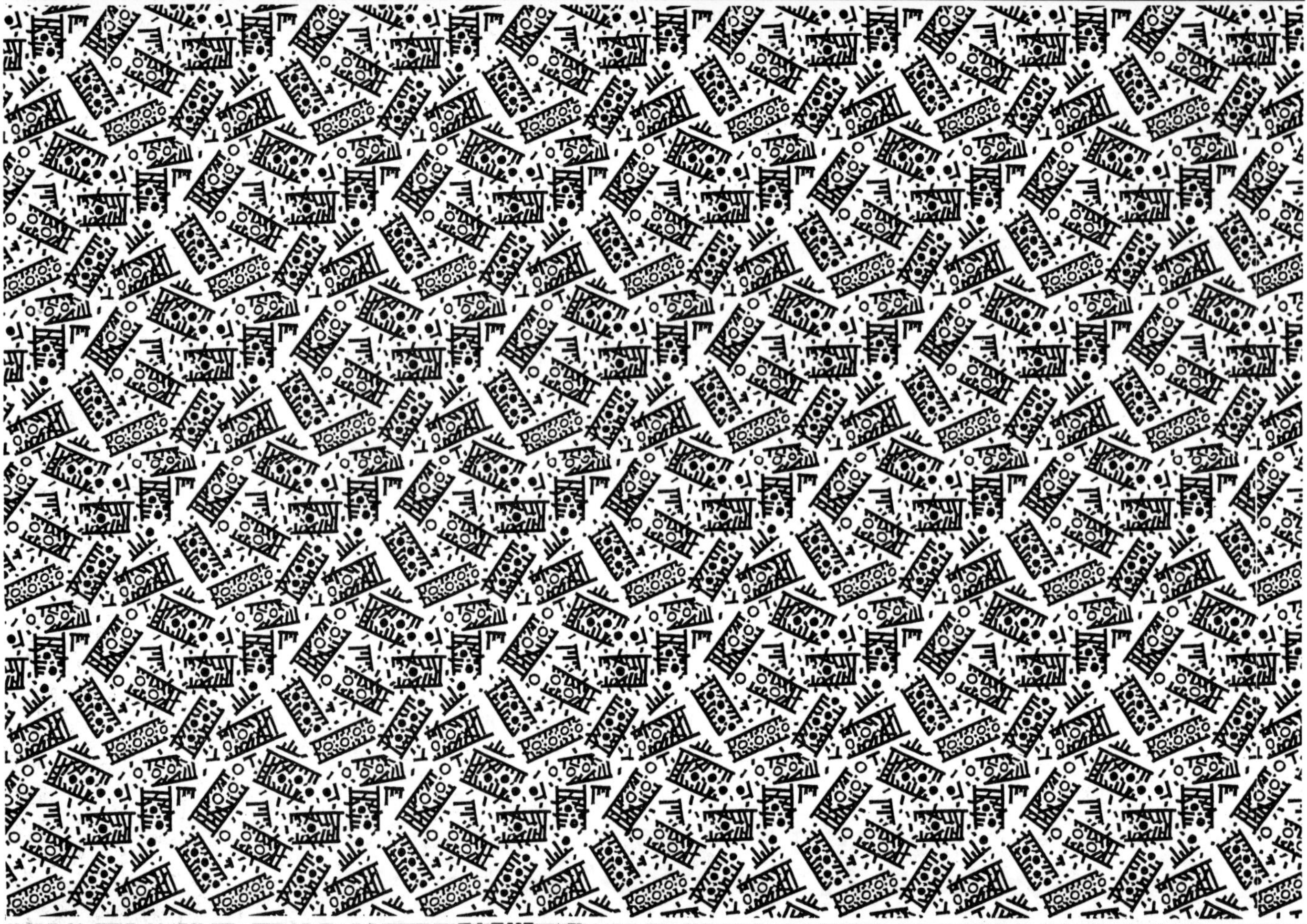

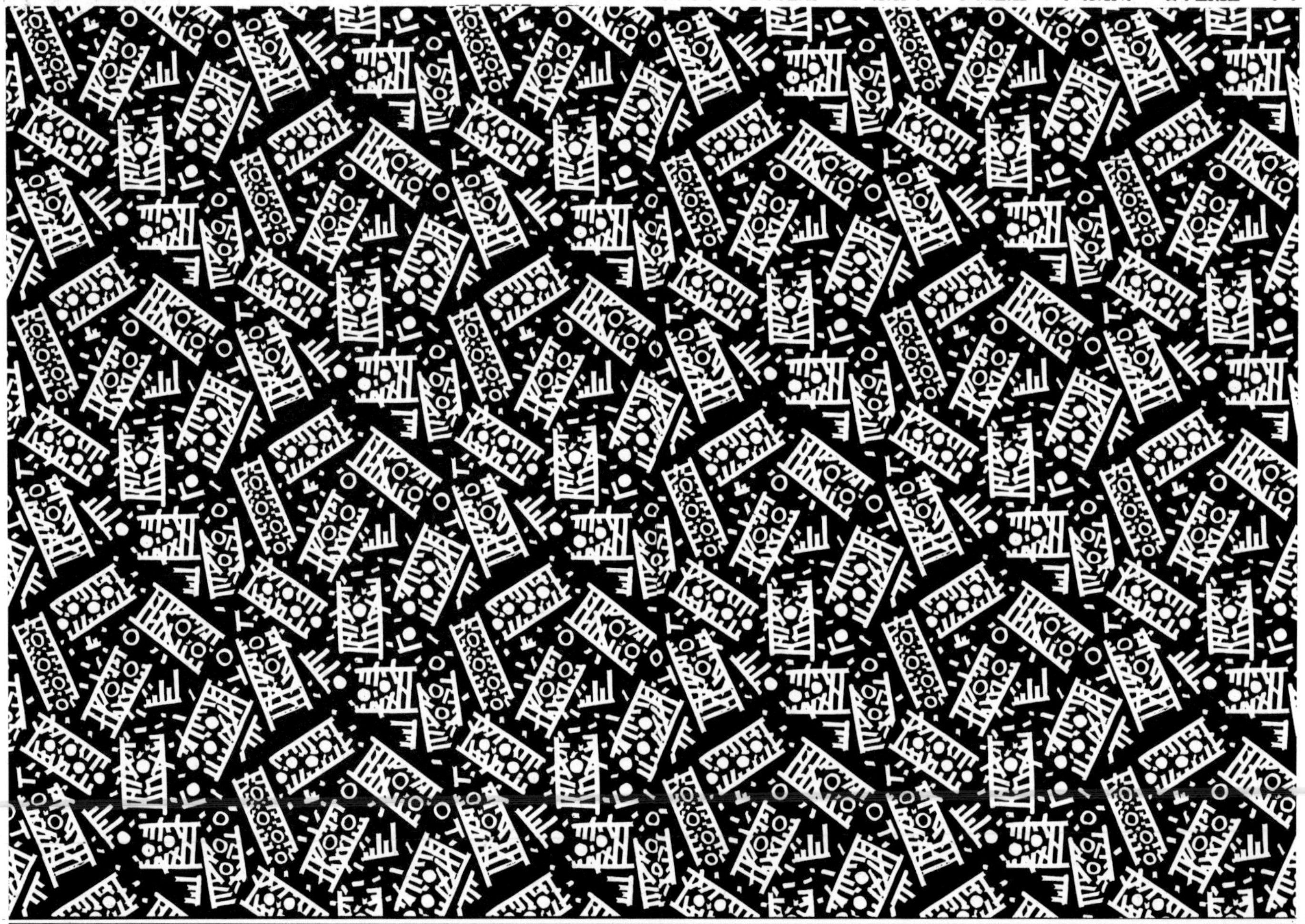

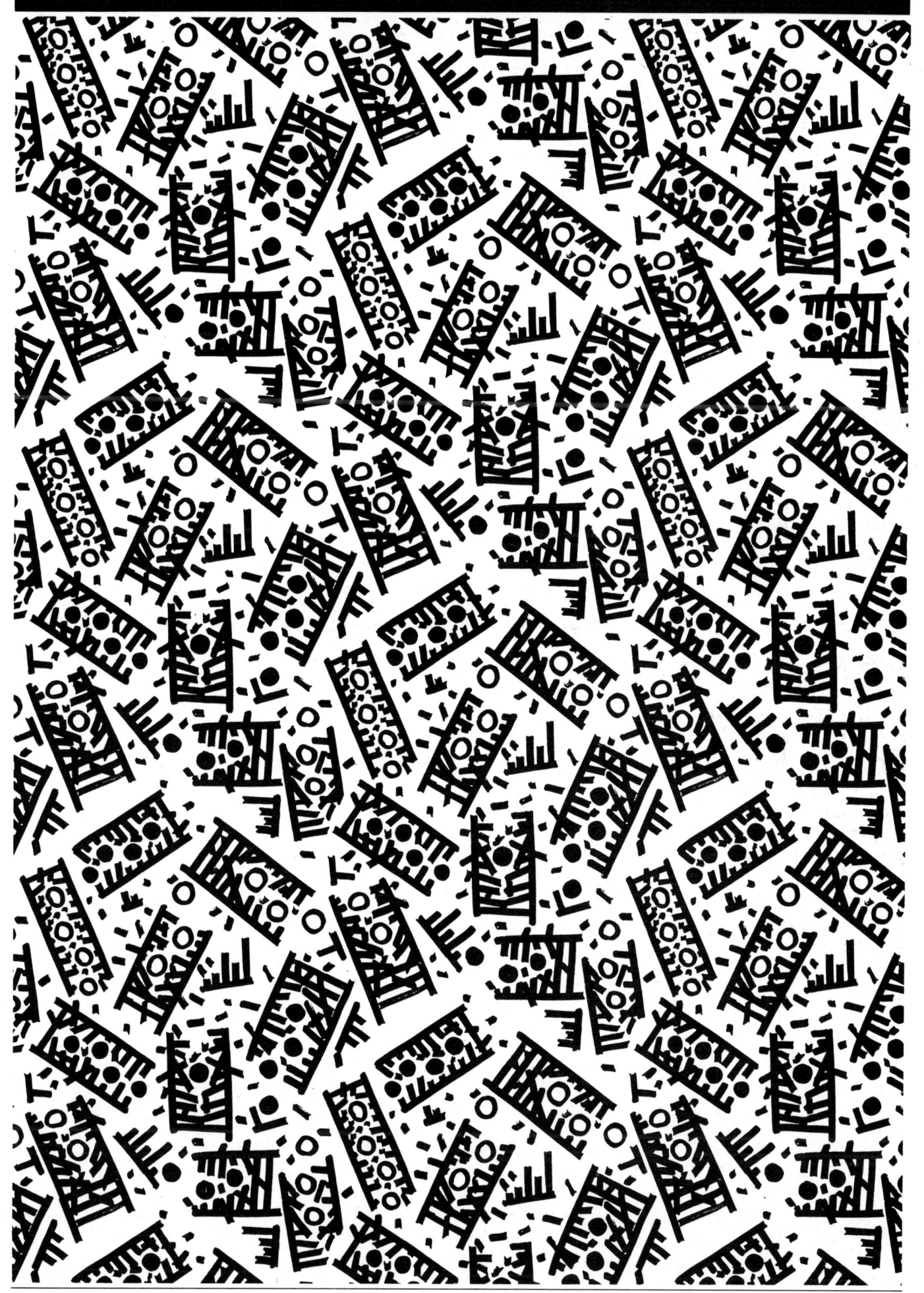

BASIC ELEMENTS BA34

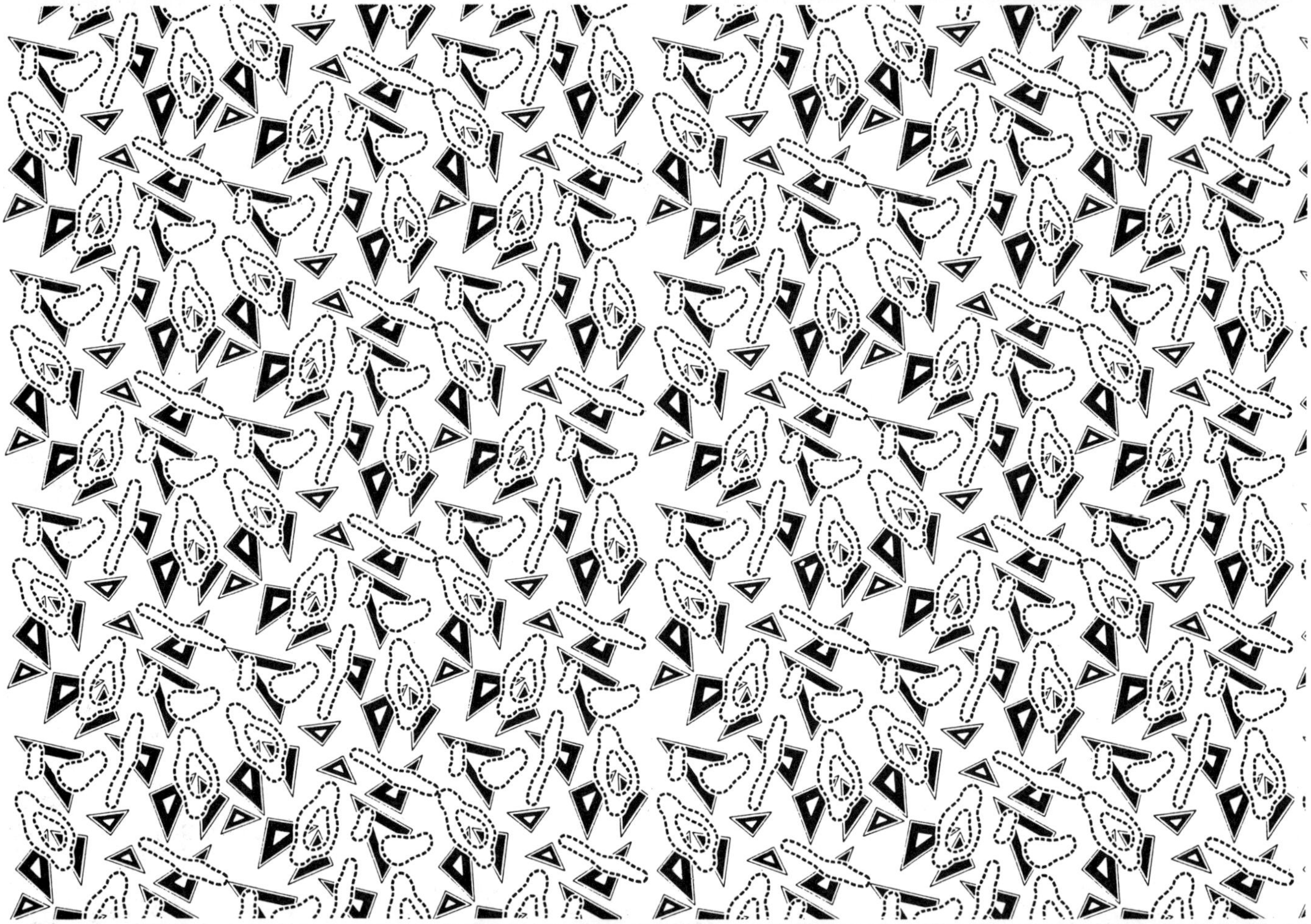

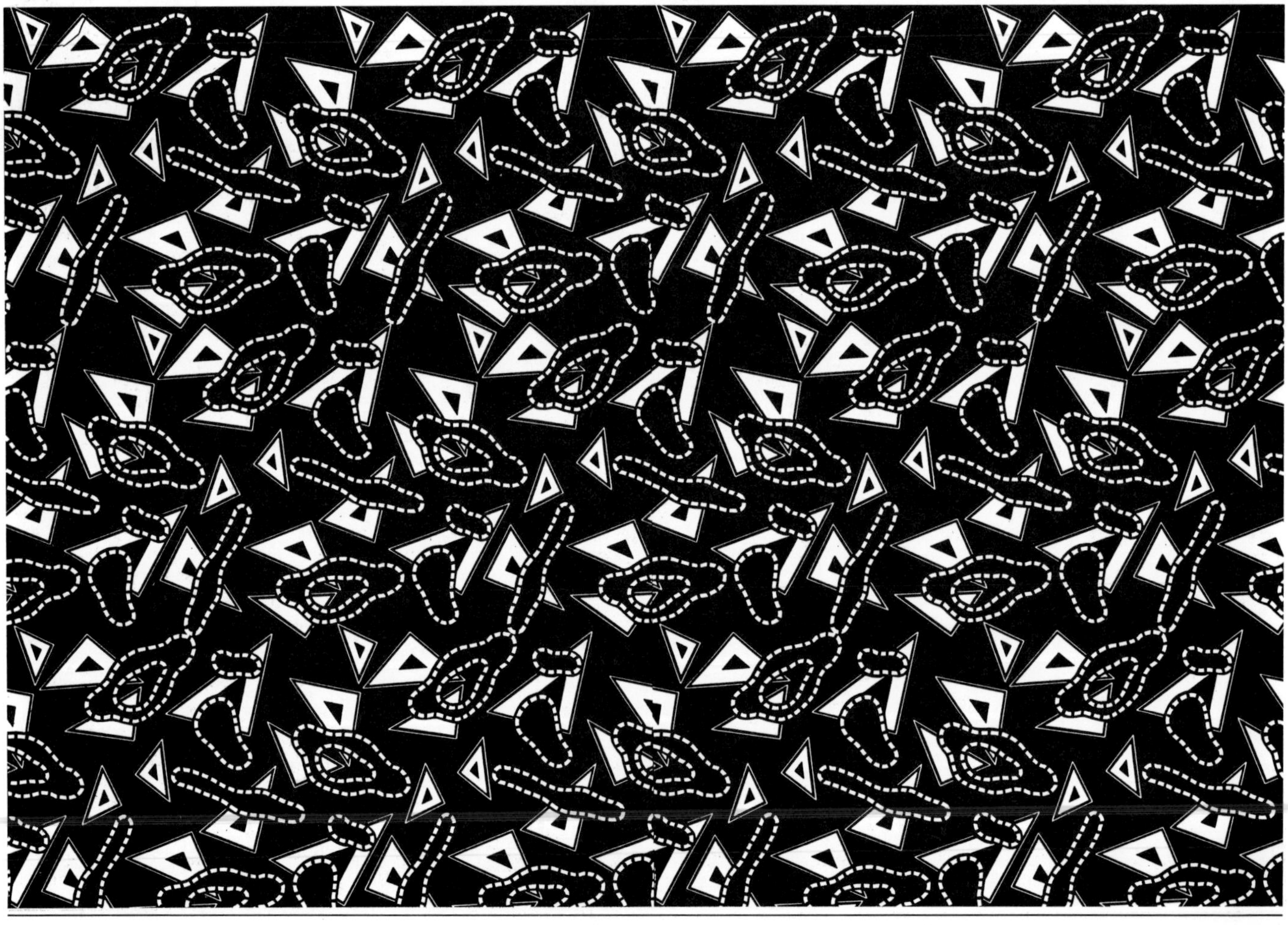

BASIC ELEMENTS

BA35

90

BASIC ELEMENTS

BA36

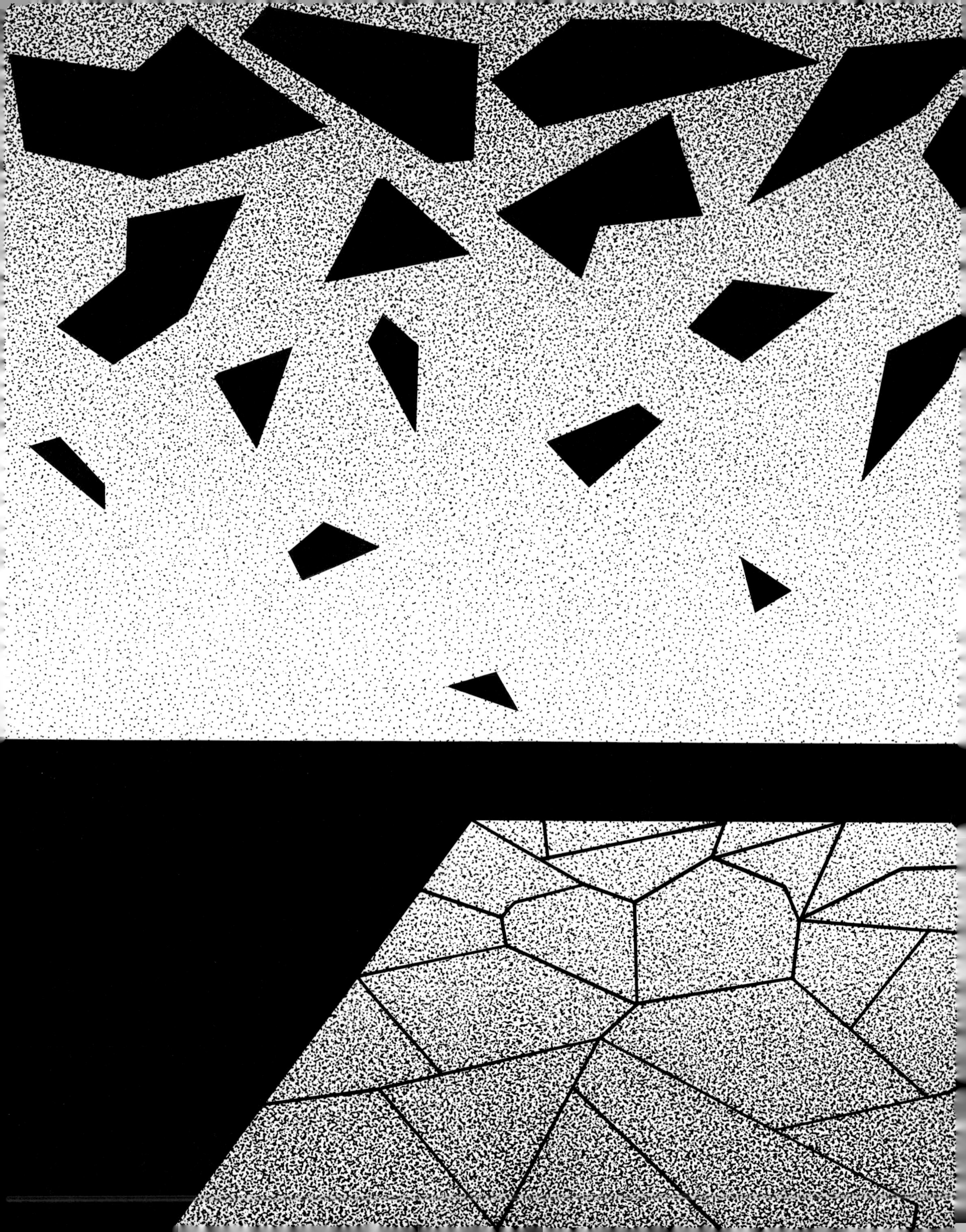

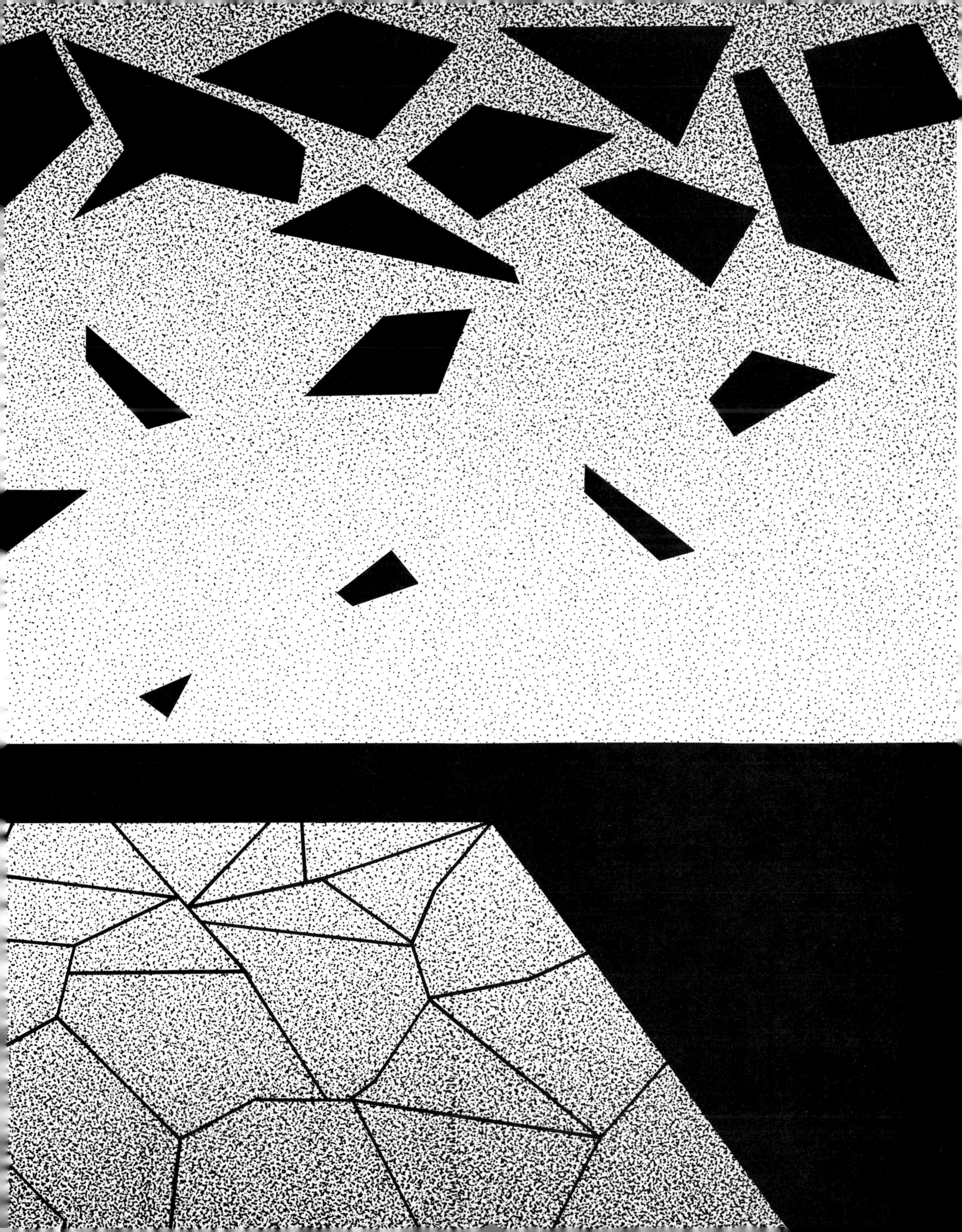

94

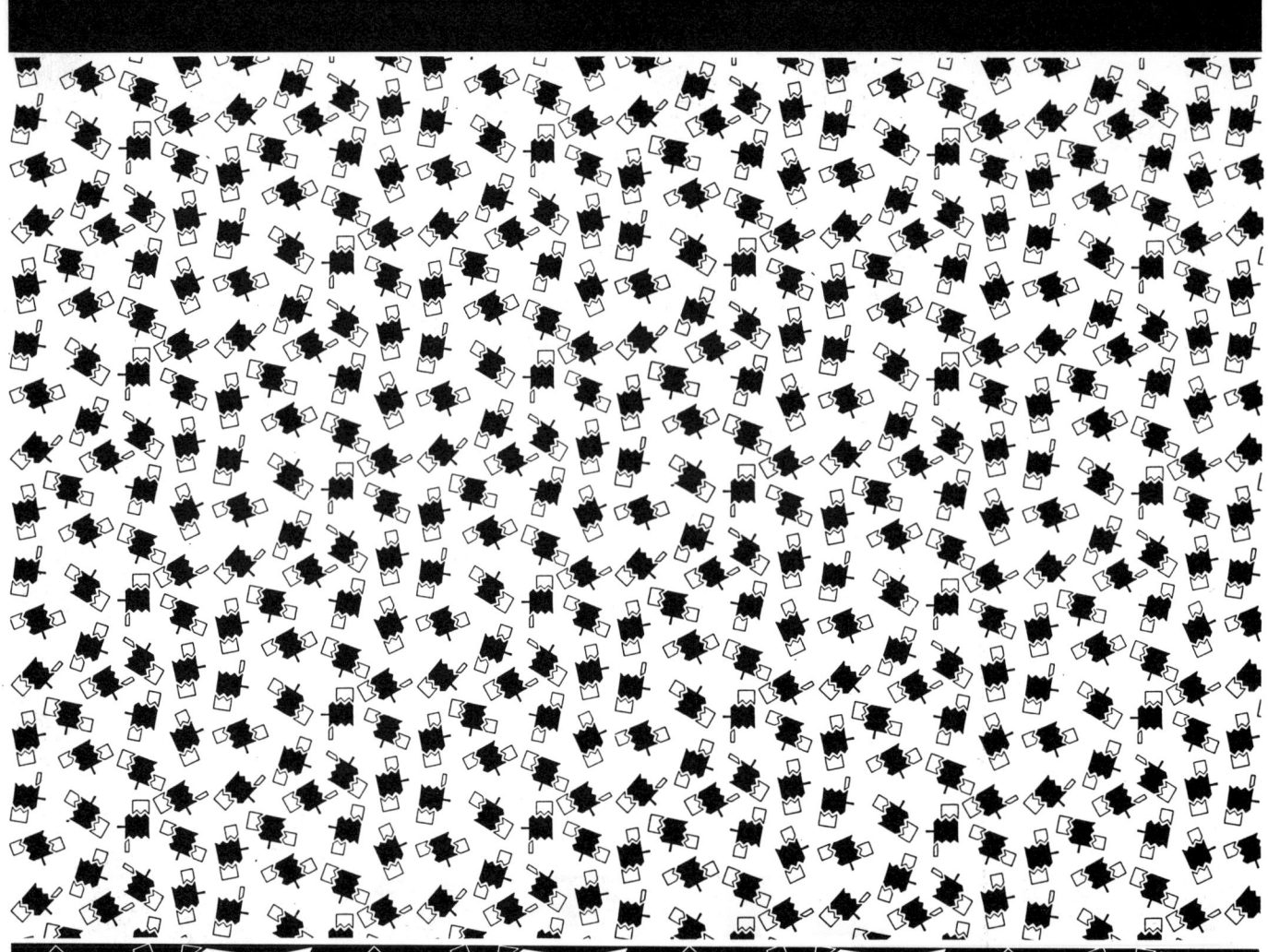

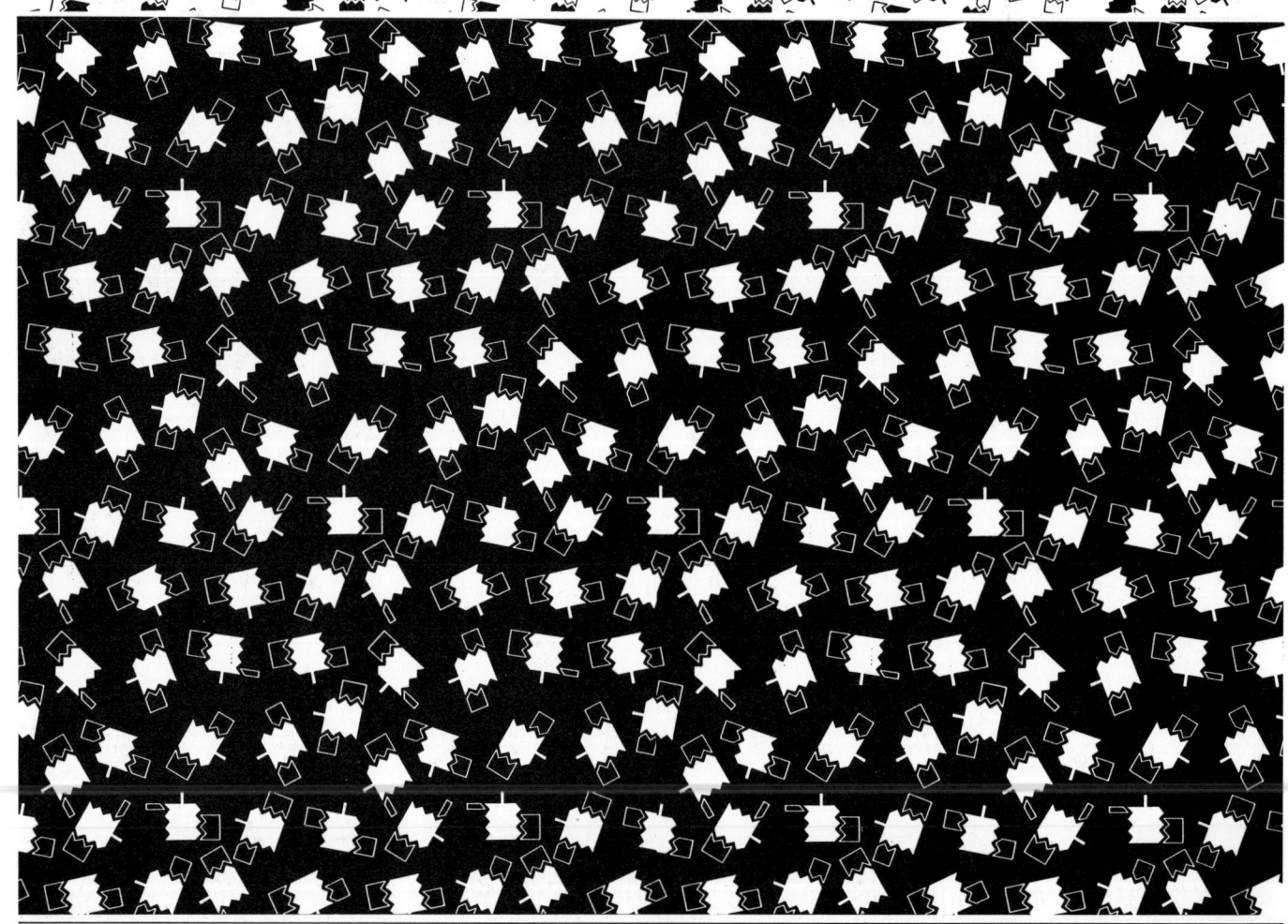

BASIC ELEMENTS   BA37

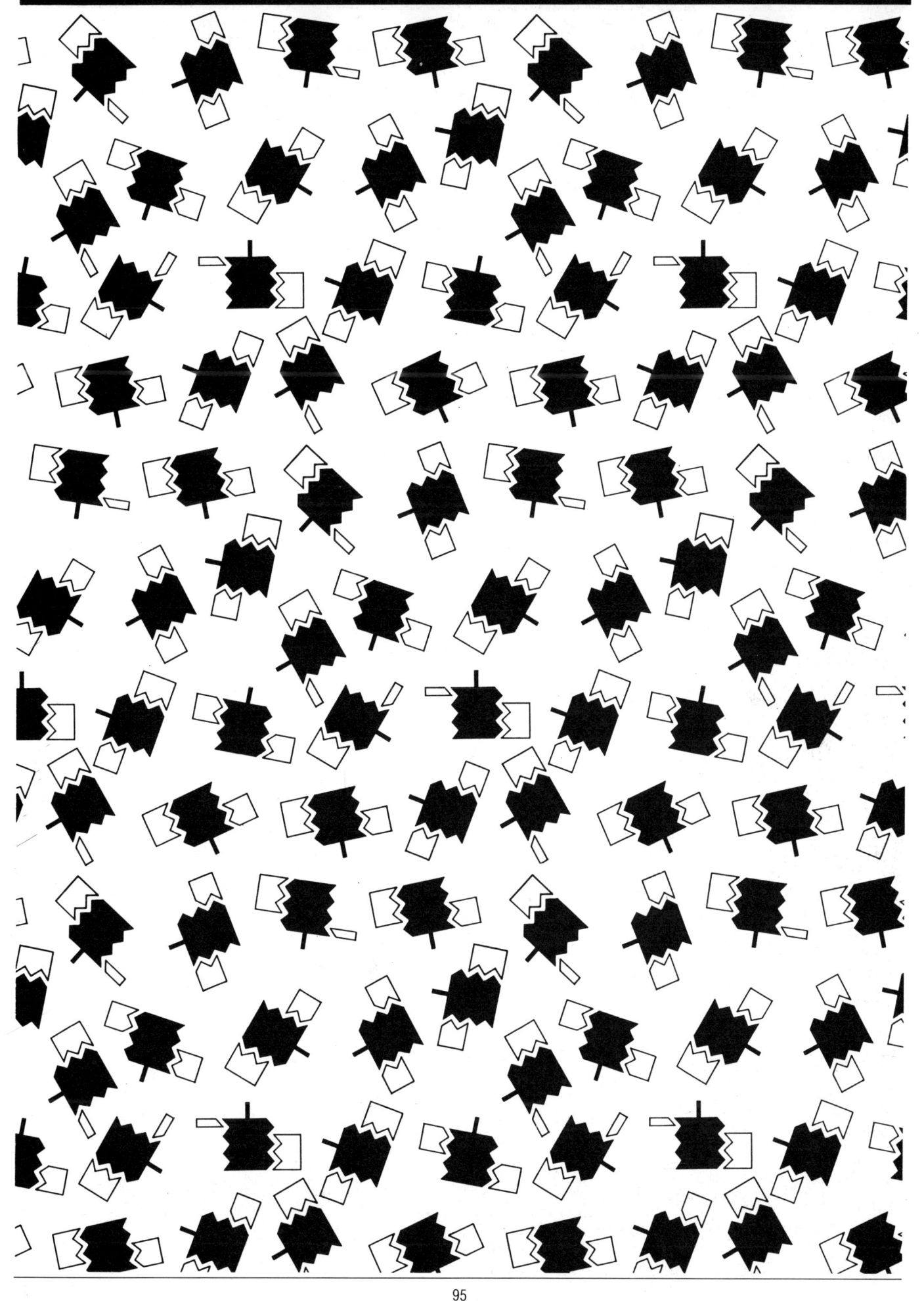

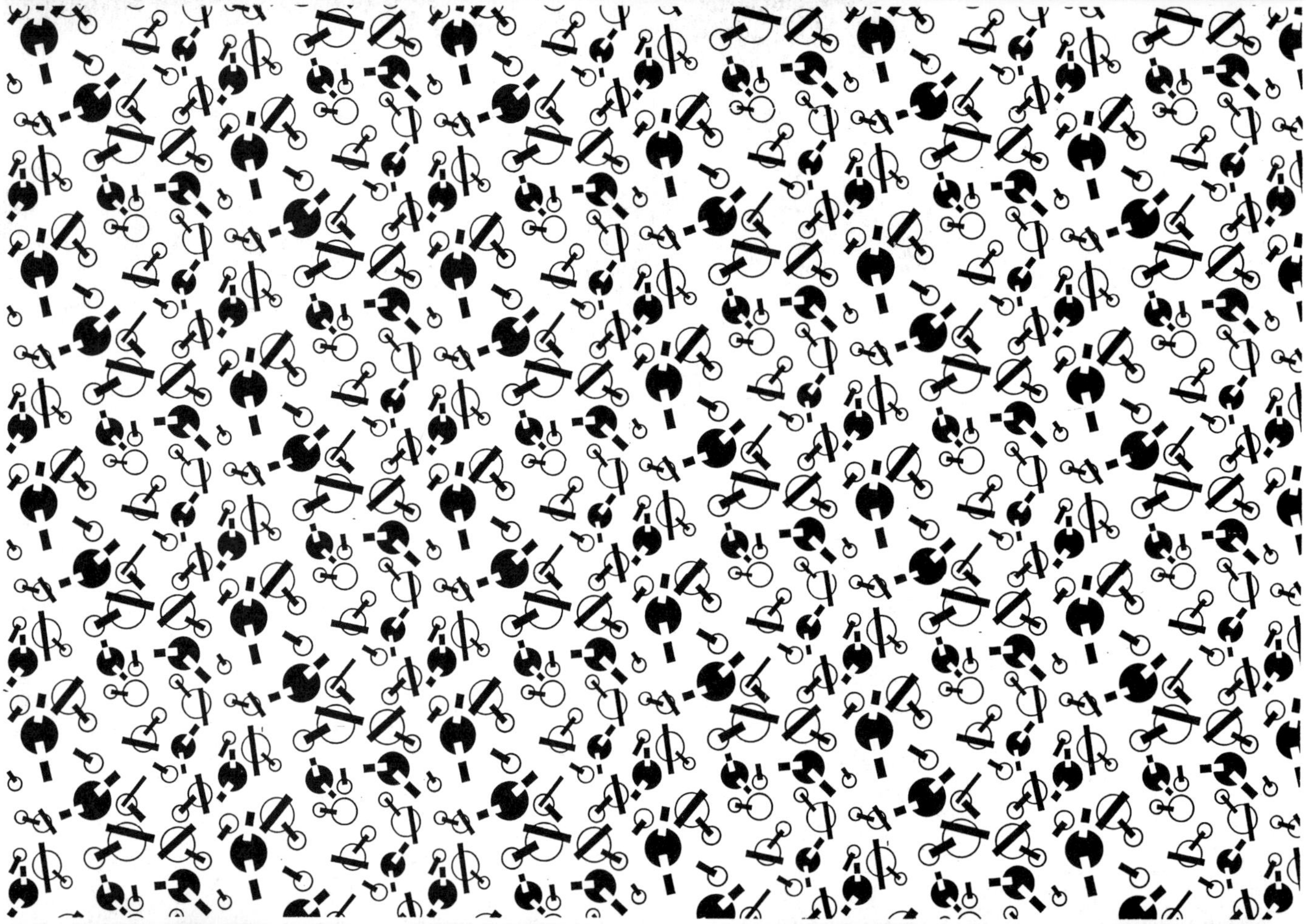

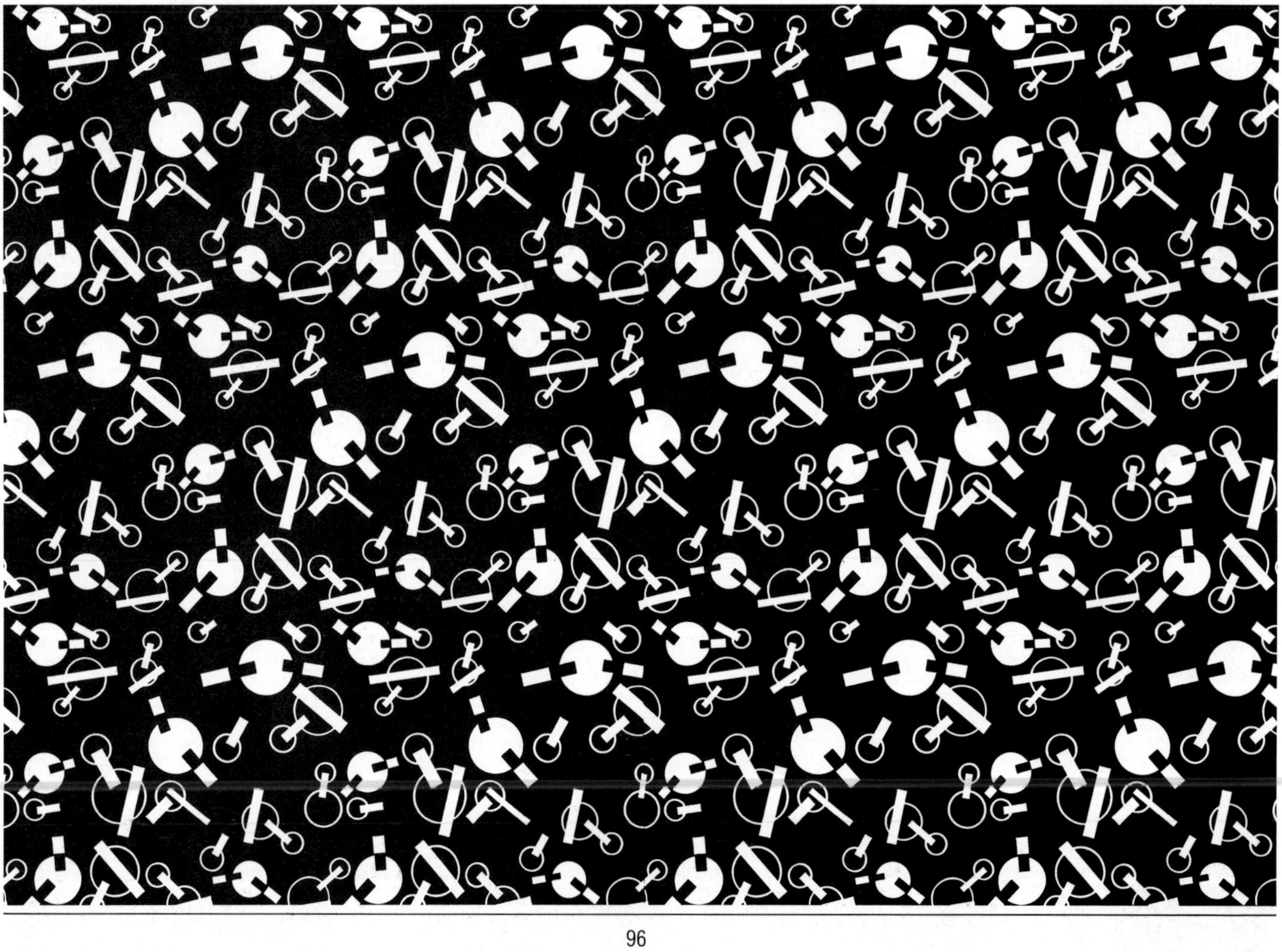

BASIC ELEMENTS BA38

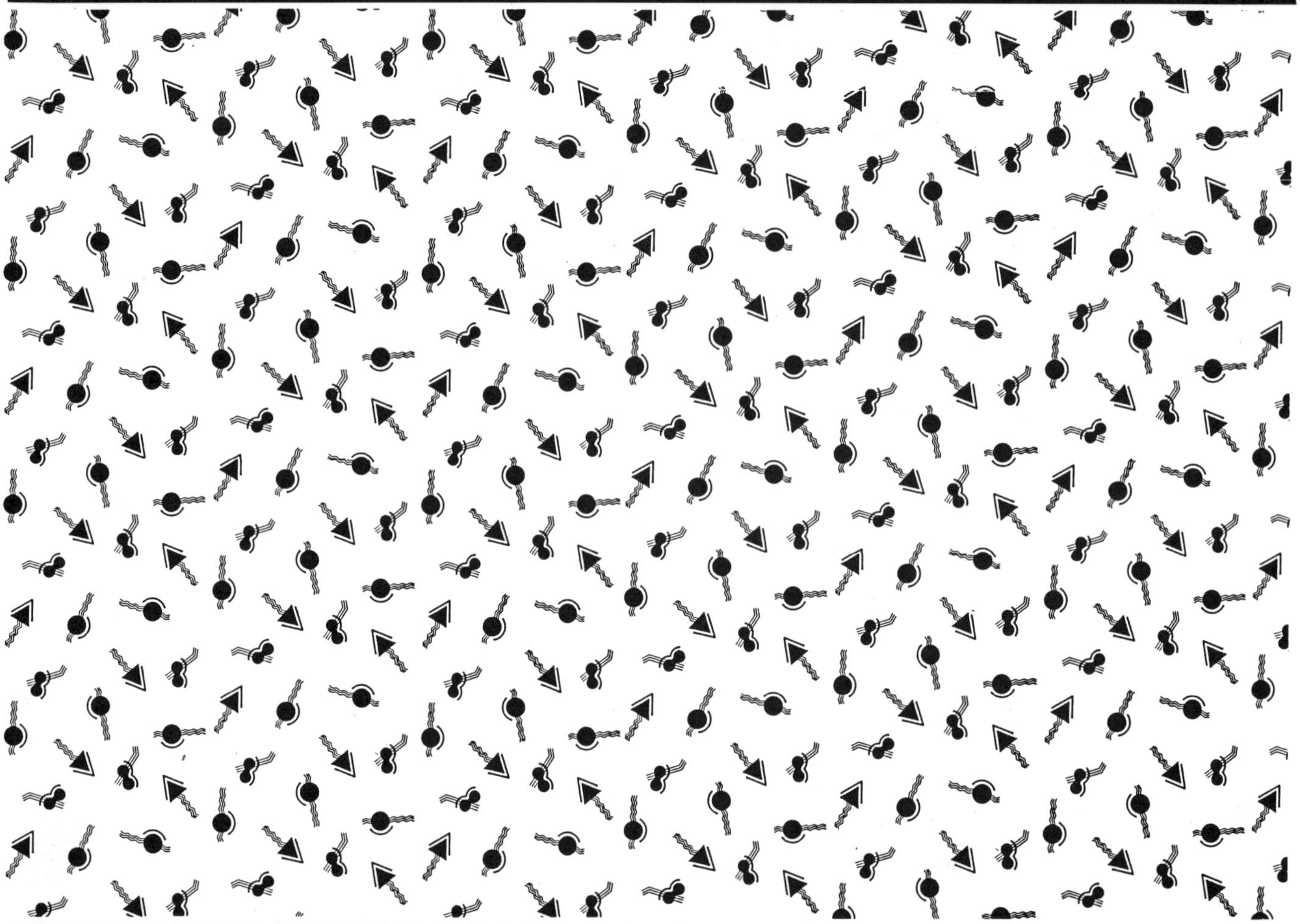

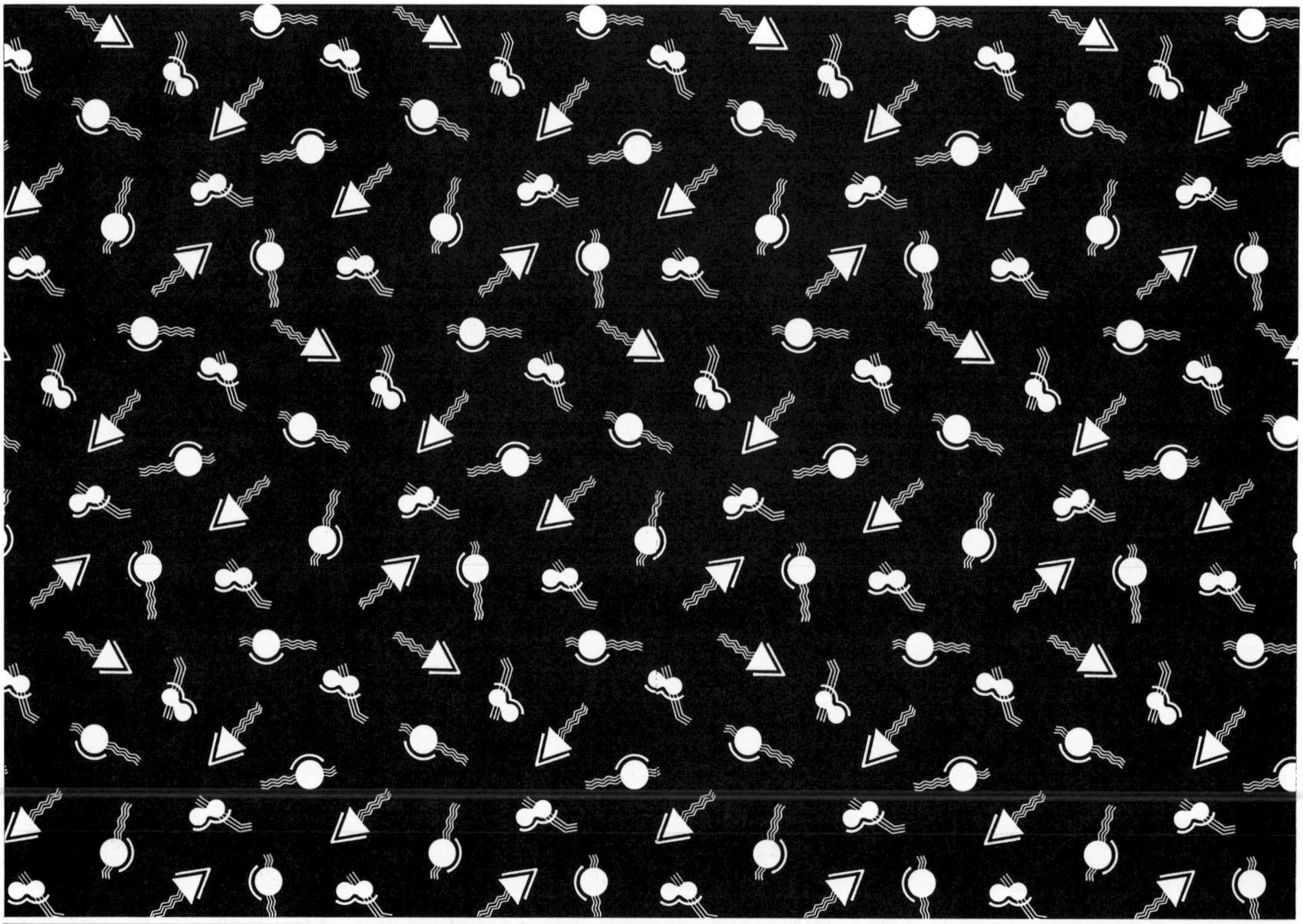

BASIC ELEMENTS BA39

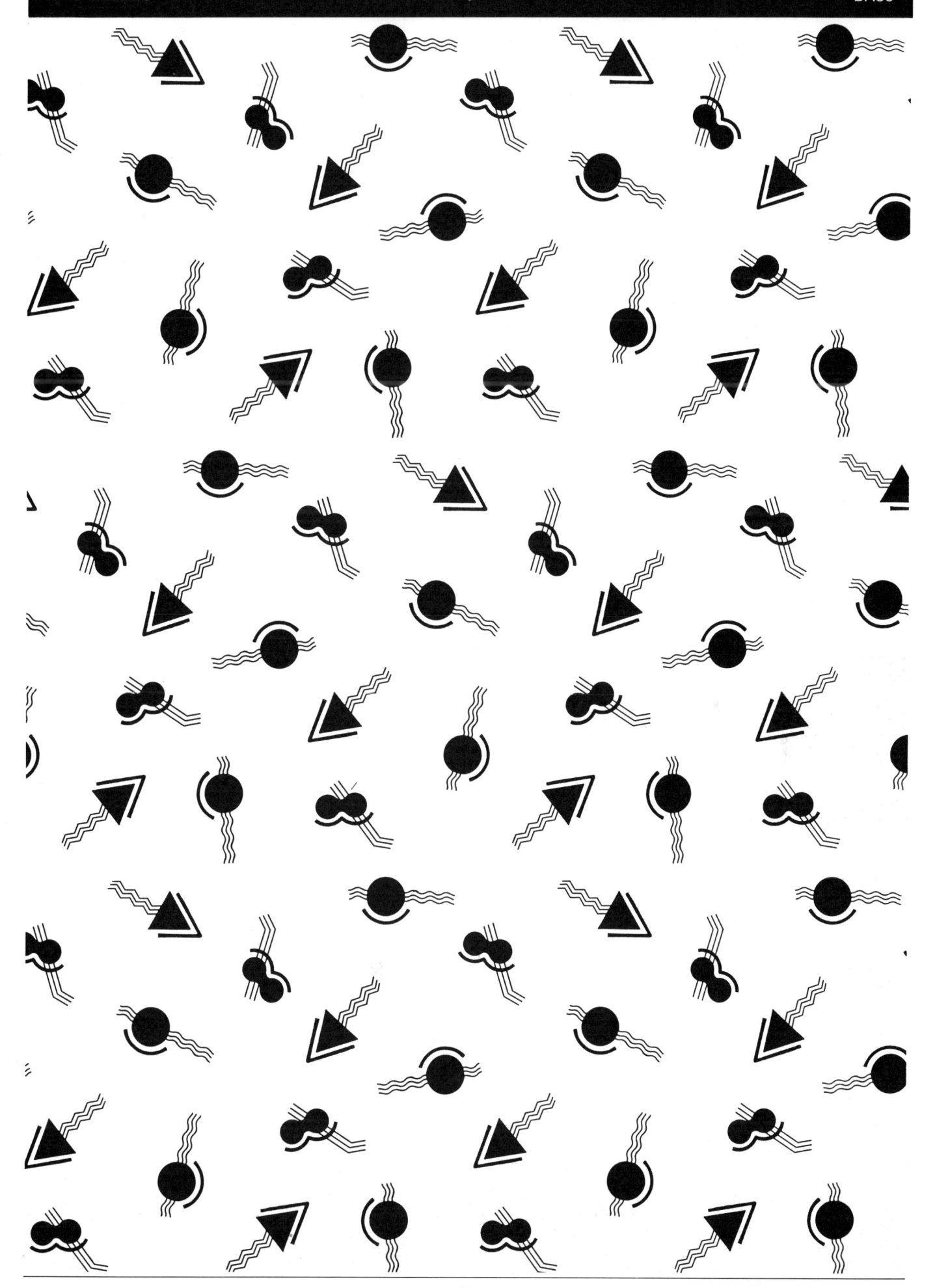

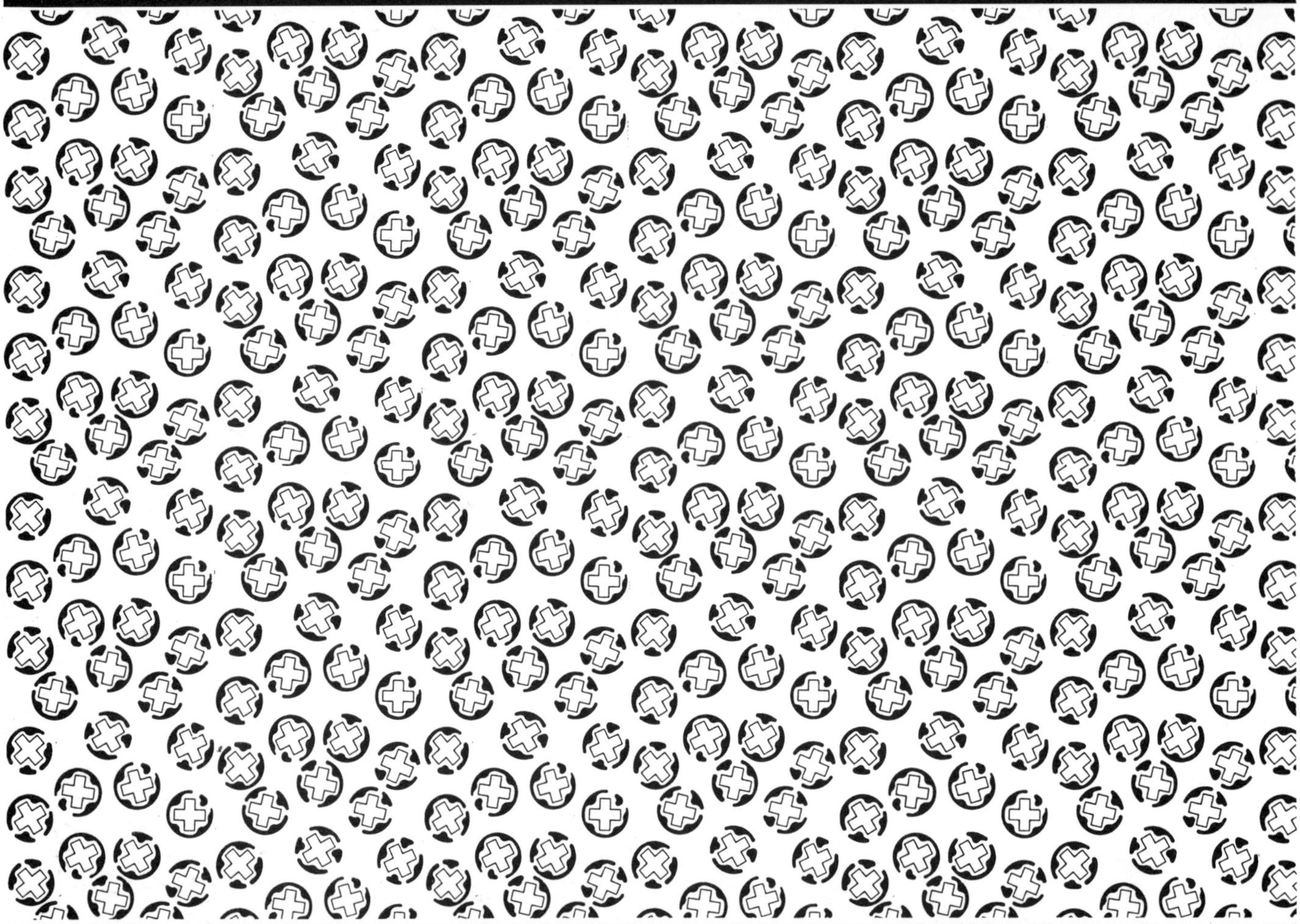

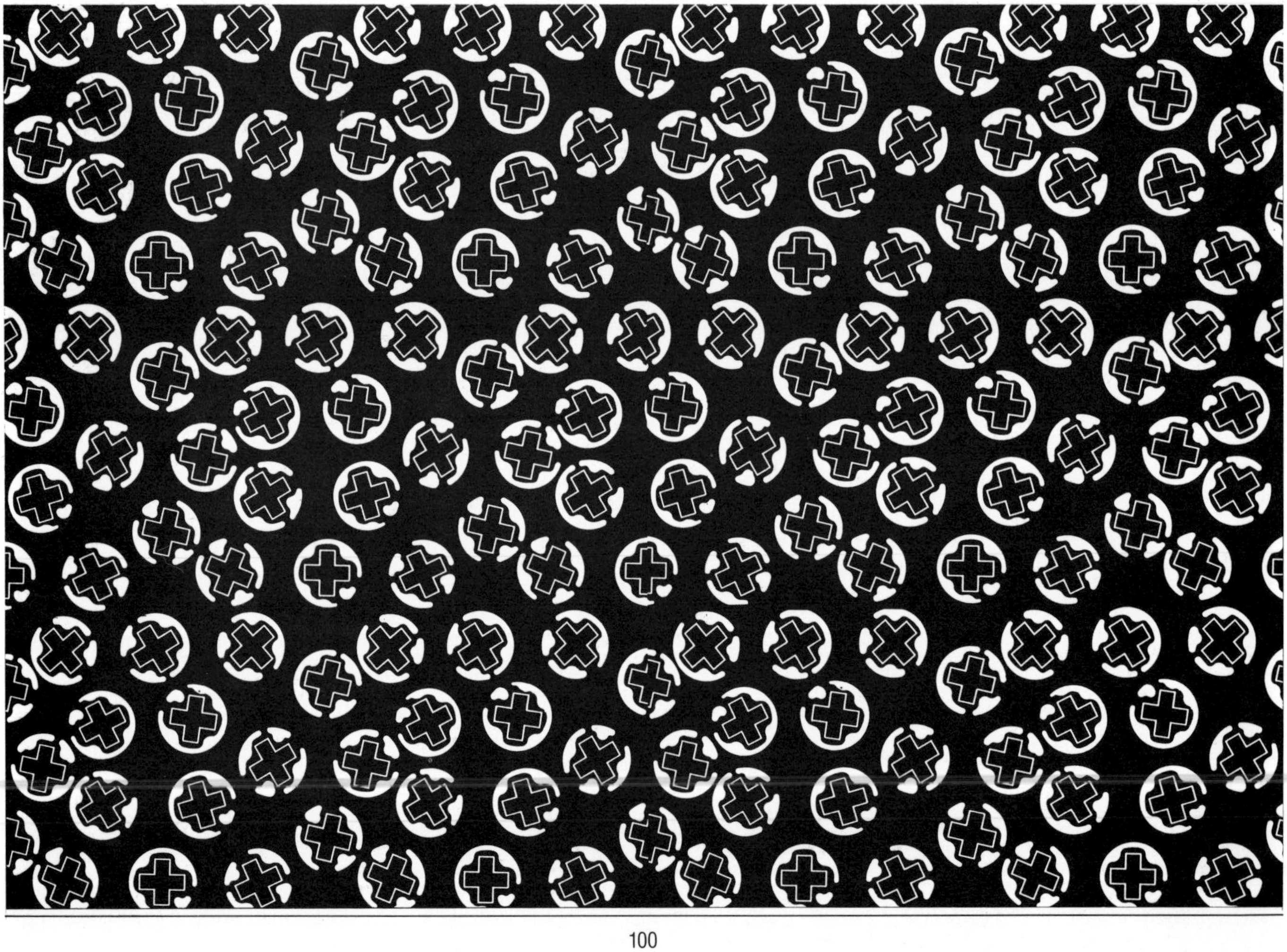

BASIC ELEMENTS BA40

102

BASIC ELEMENTS

BA41

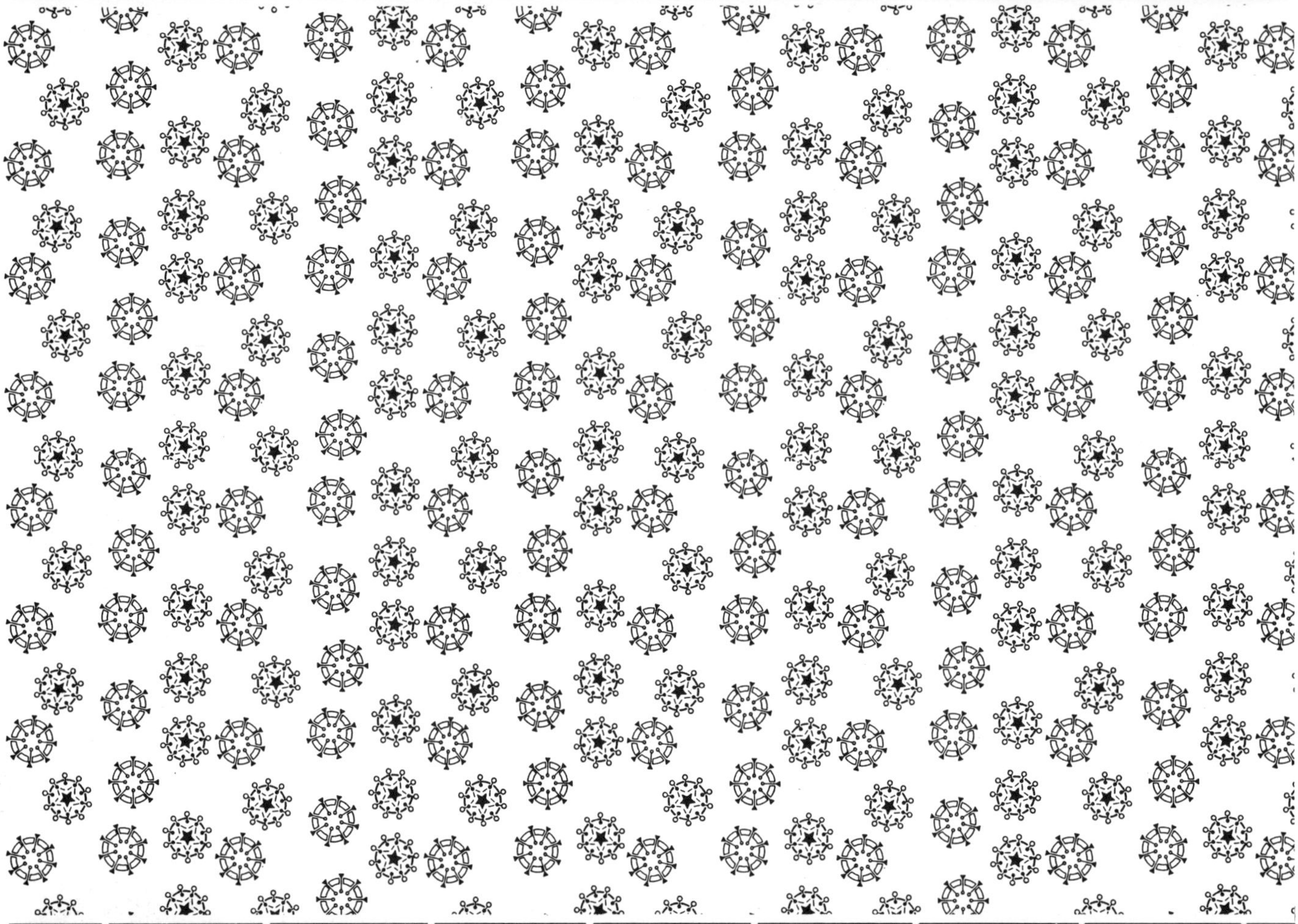

BASIC ELEMENTS BA42

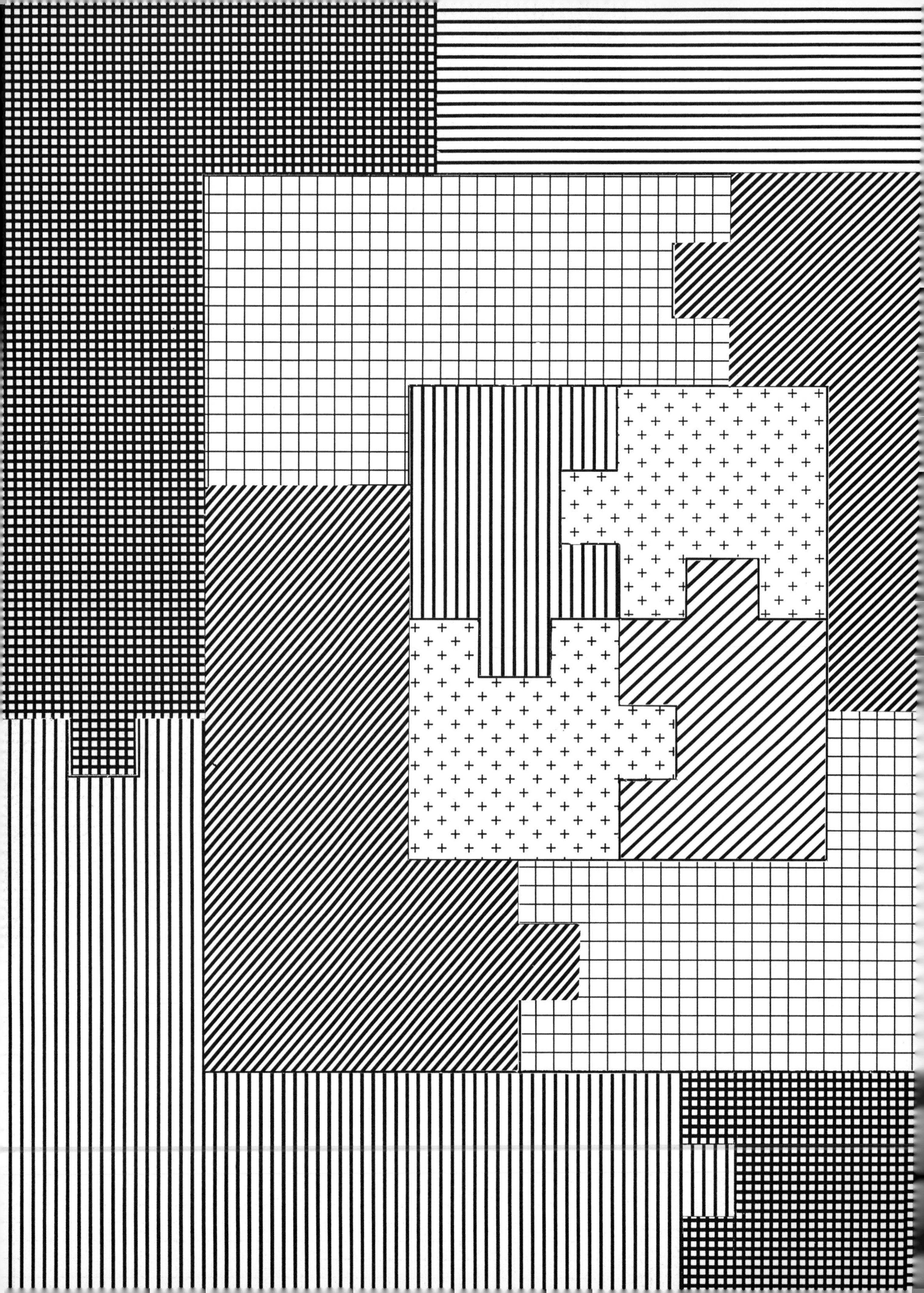

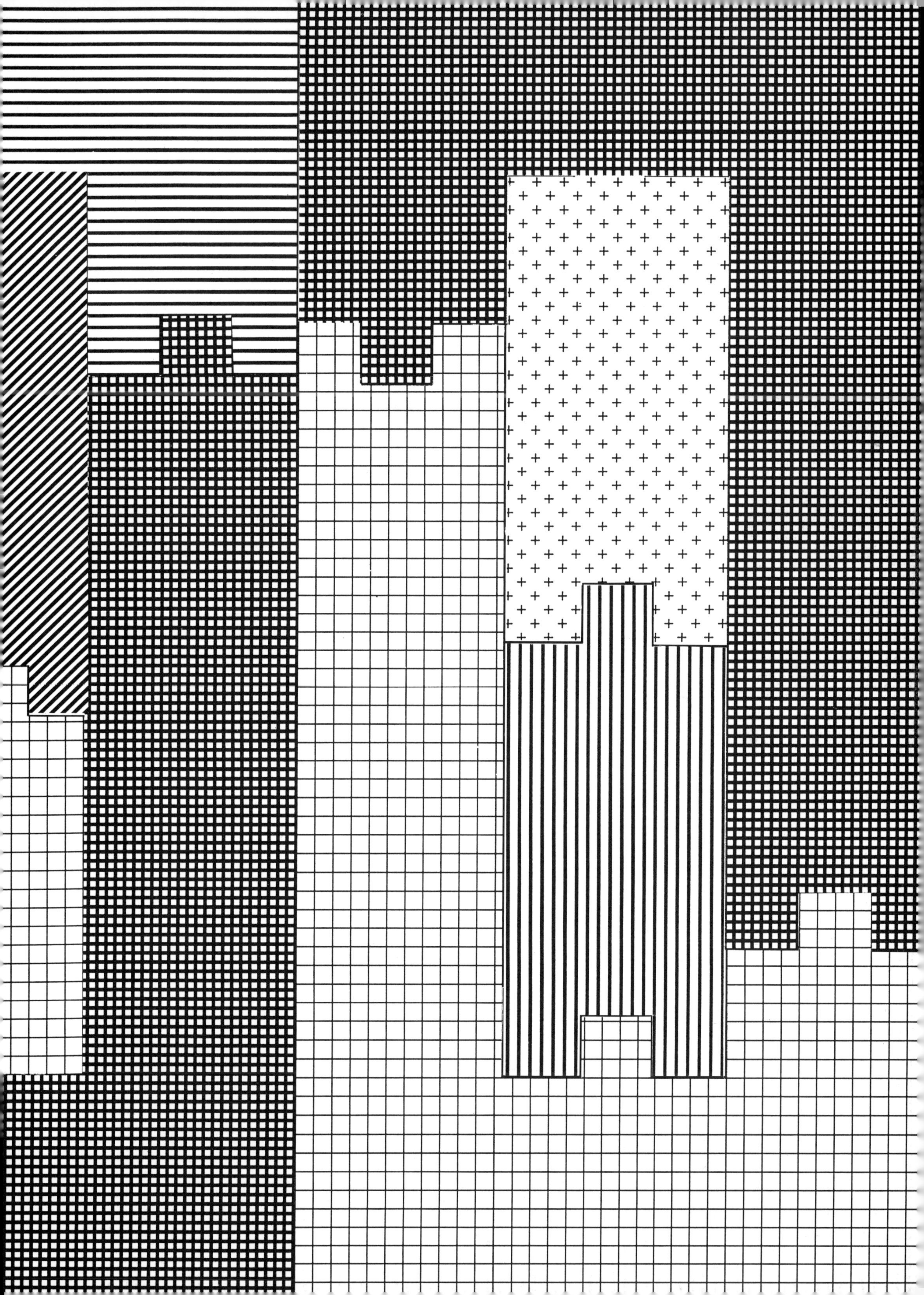

108

BASIC ELEMENTS BA43

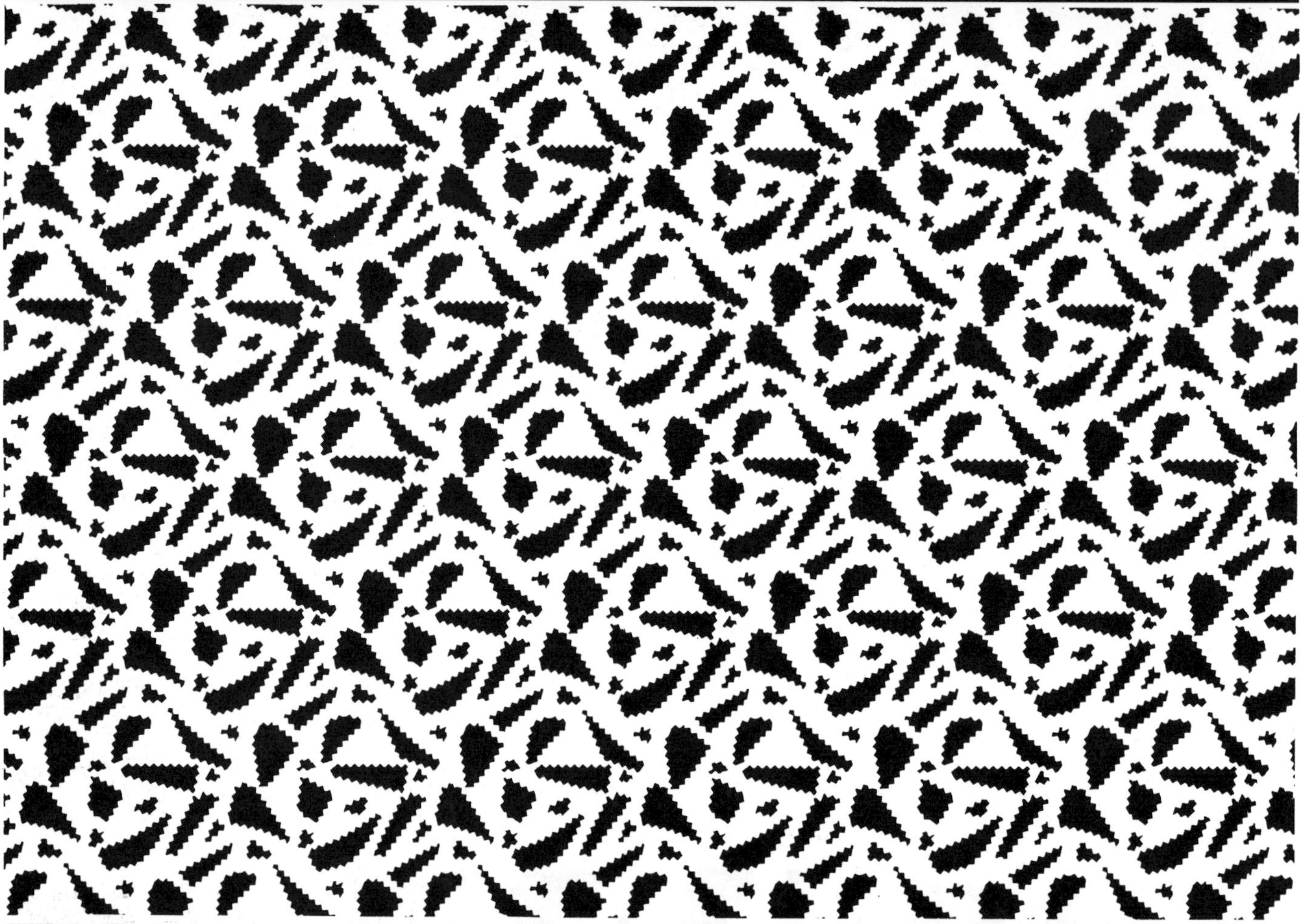

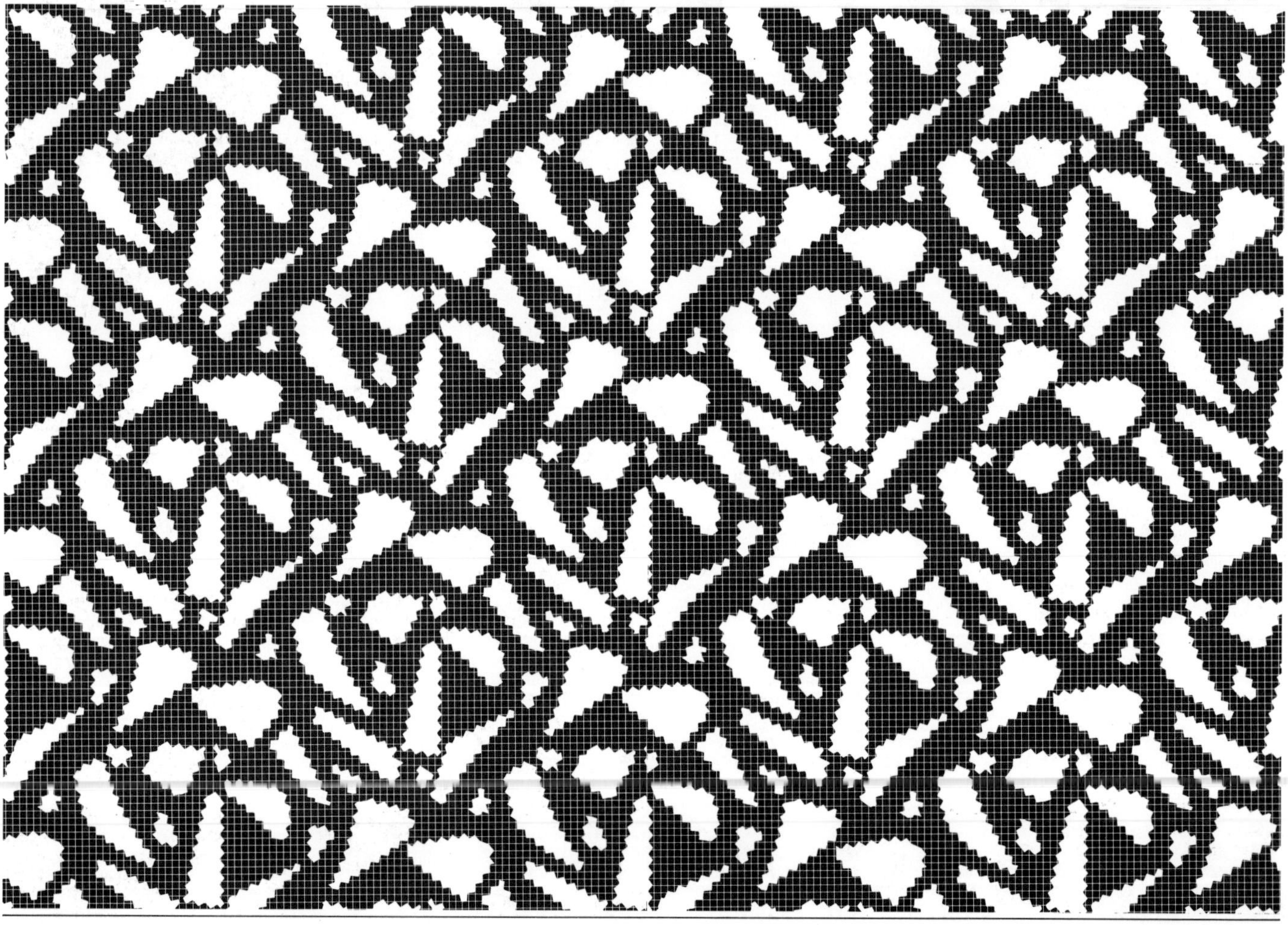

BASIC ELEMENTS BA44

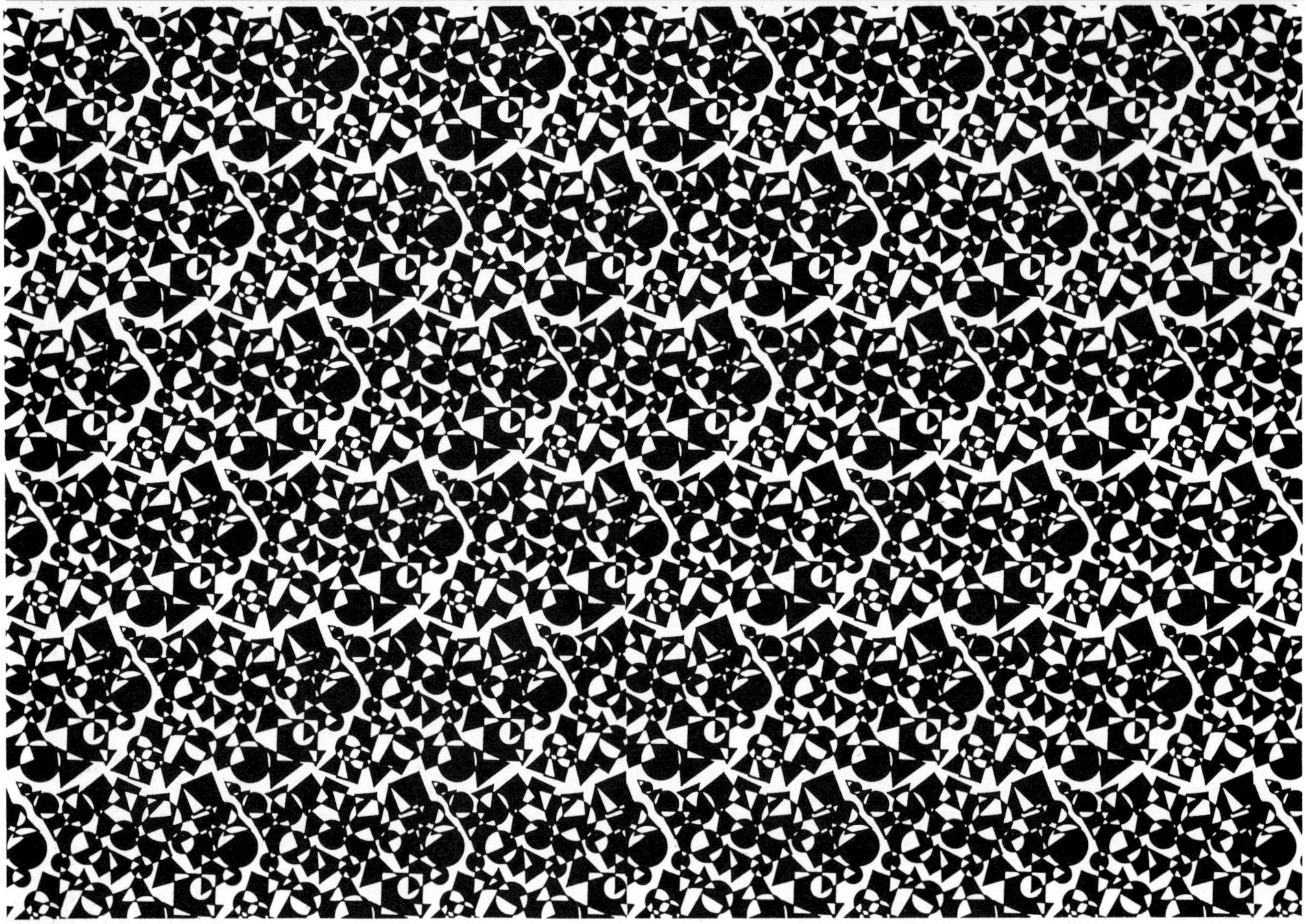

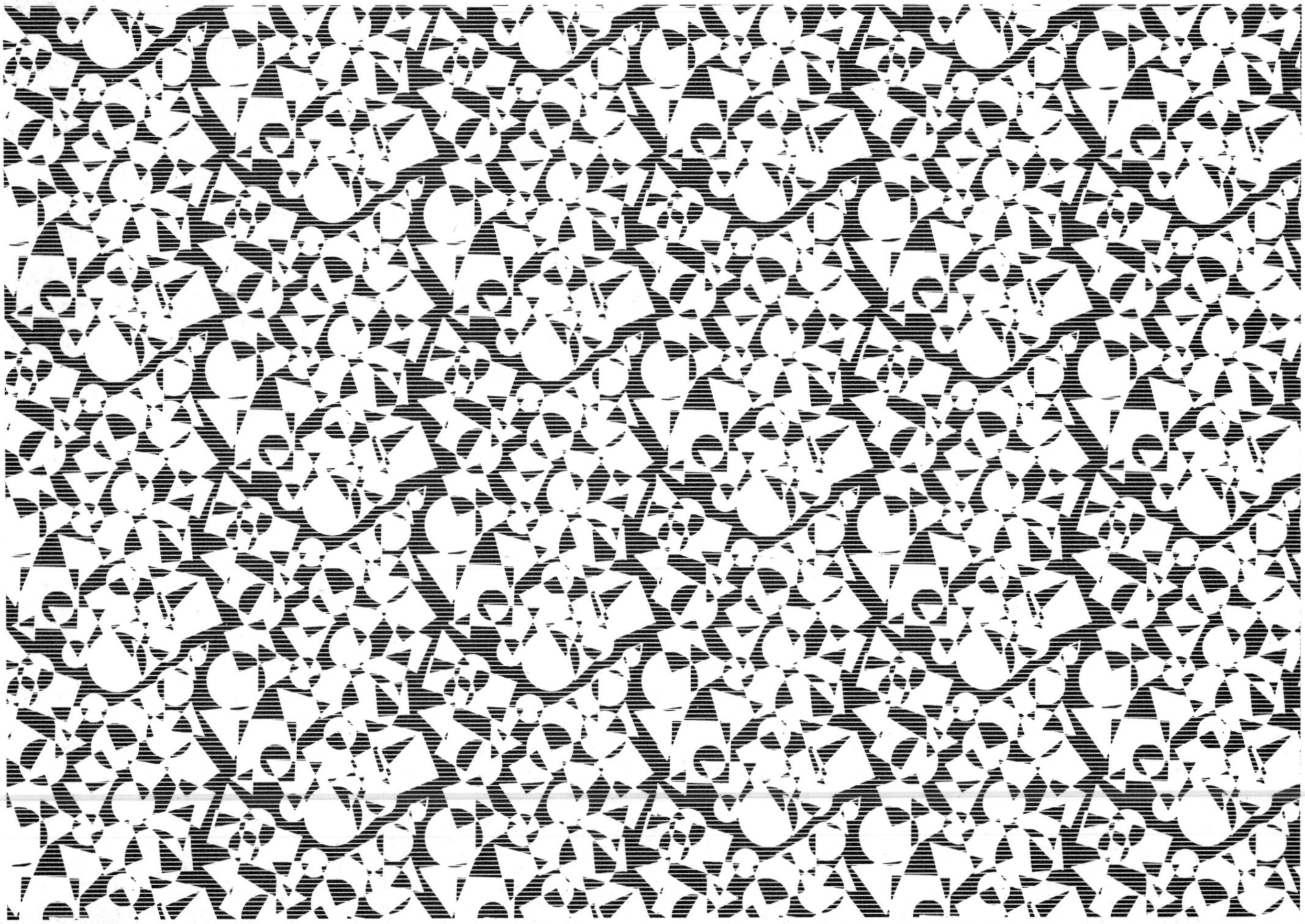

BASIC ELEMENTS

BA45

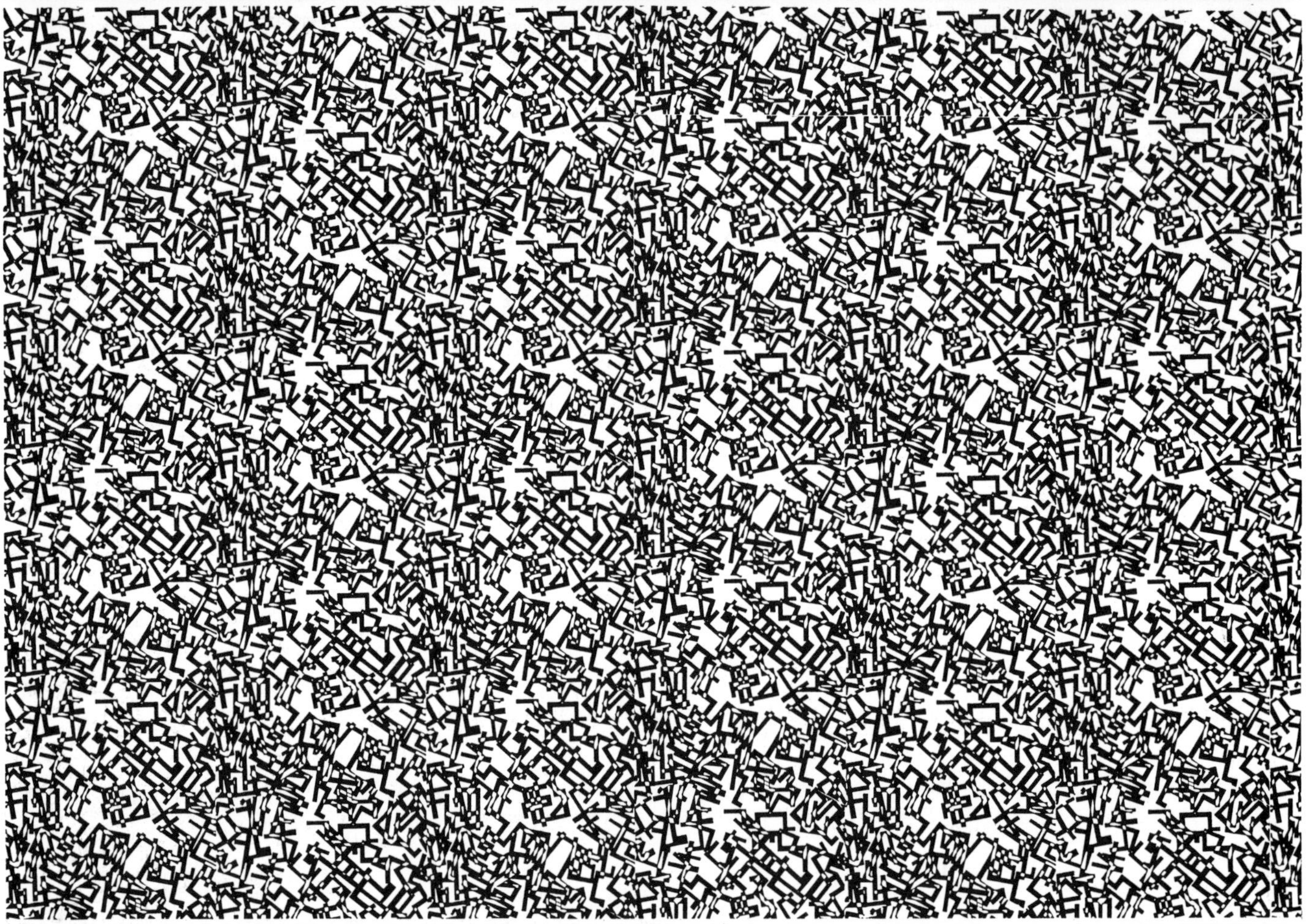

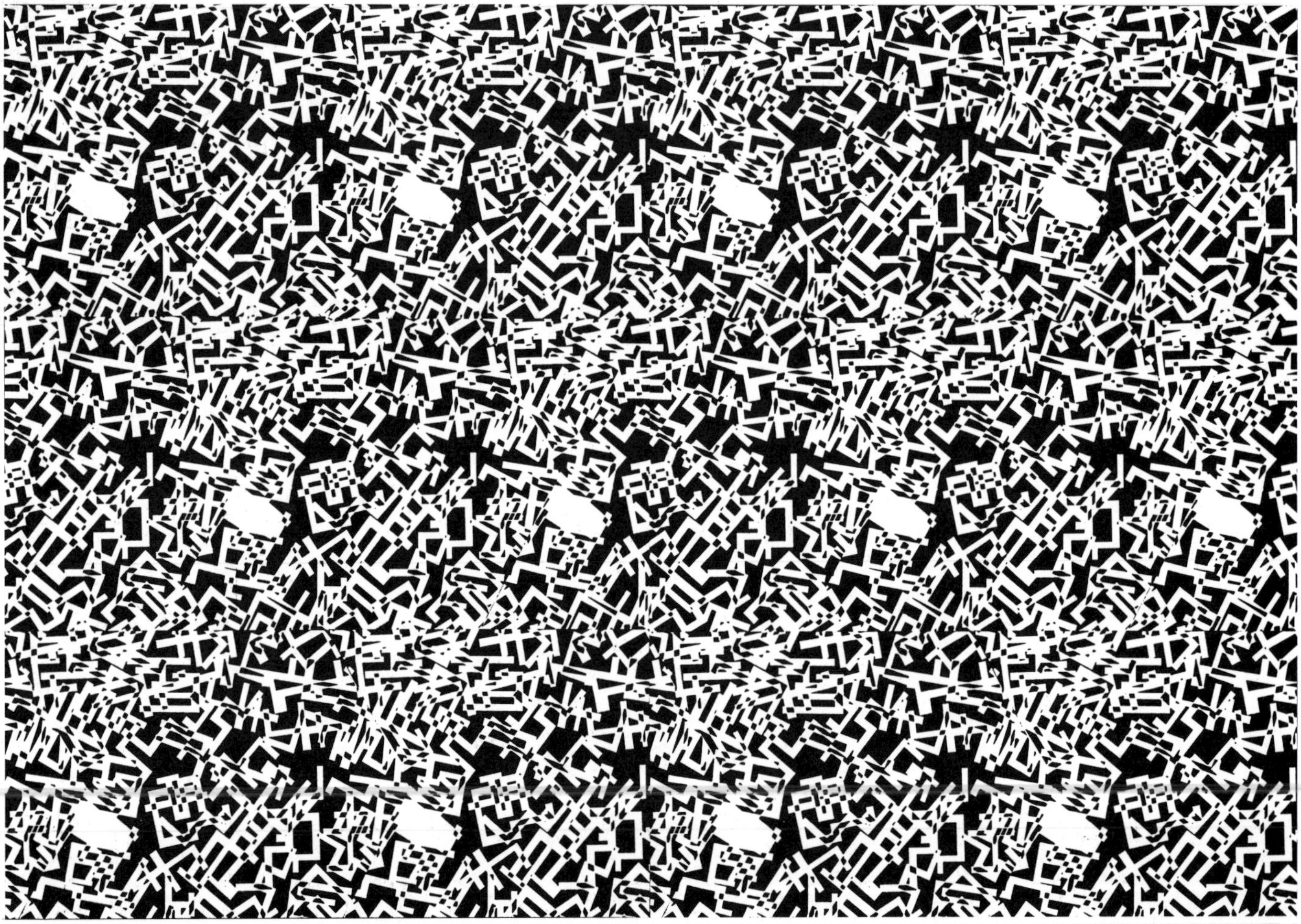

BASIC ELEMENTS BA46

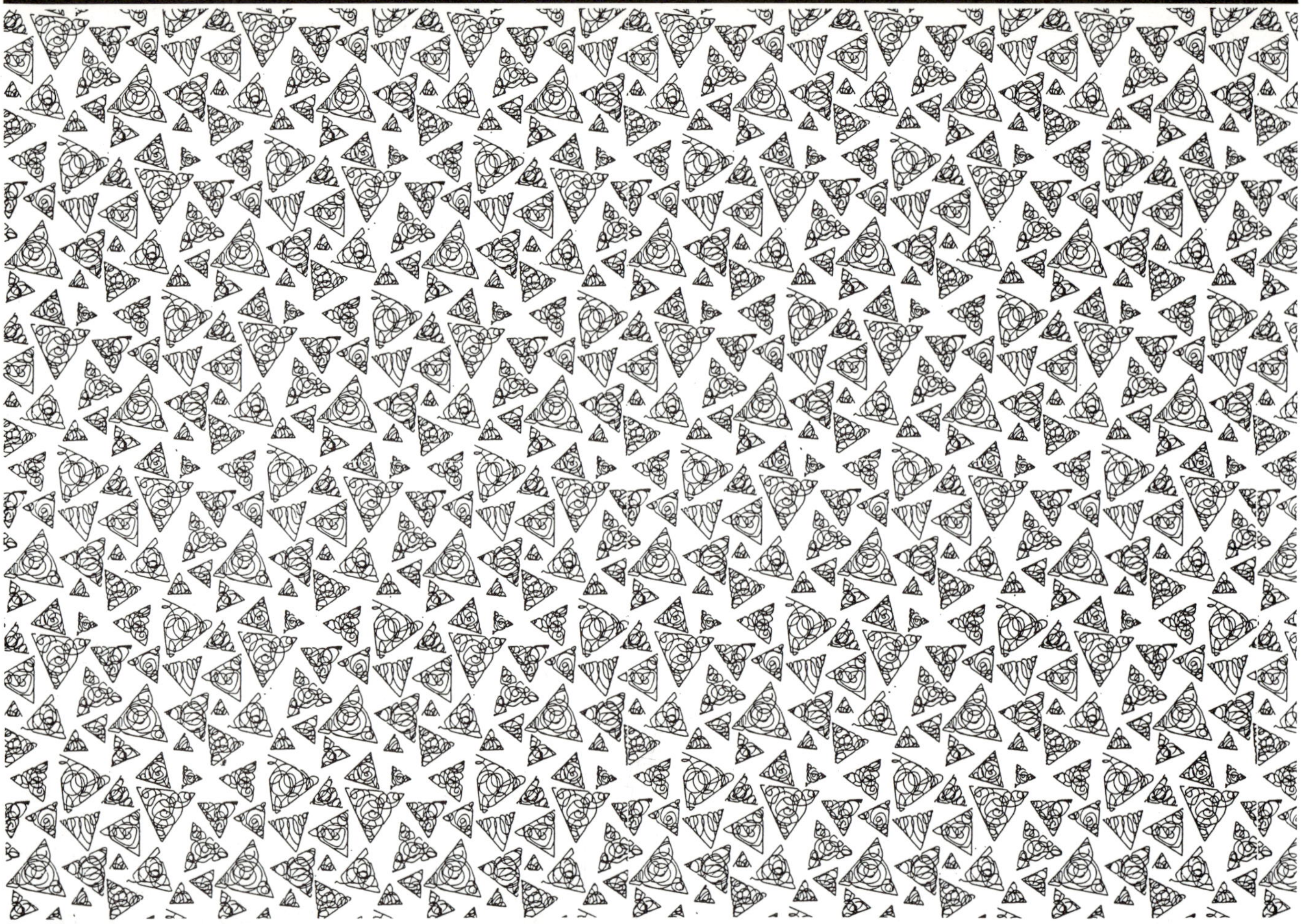

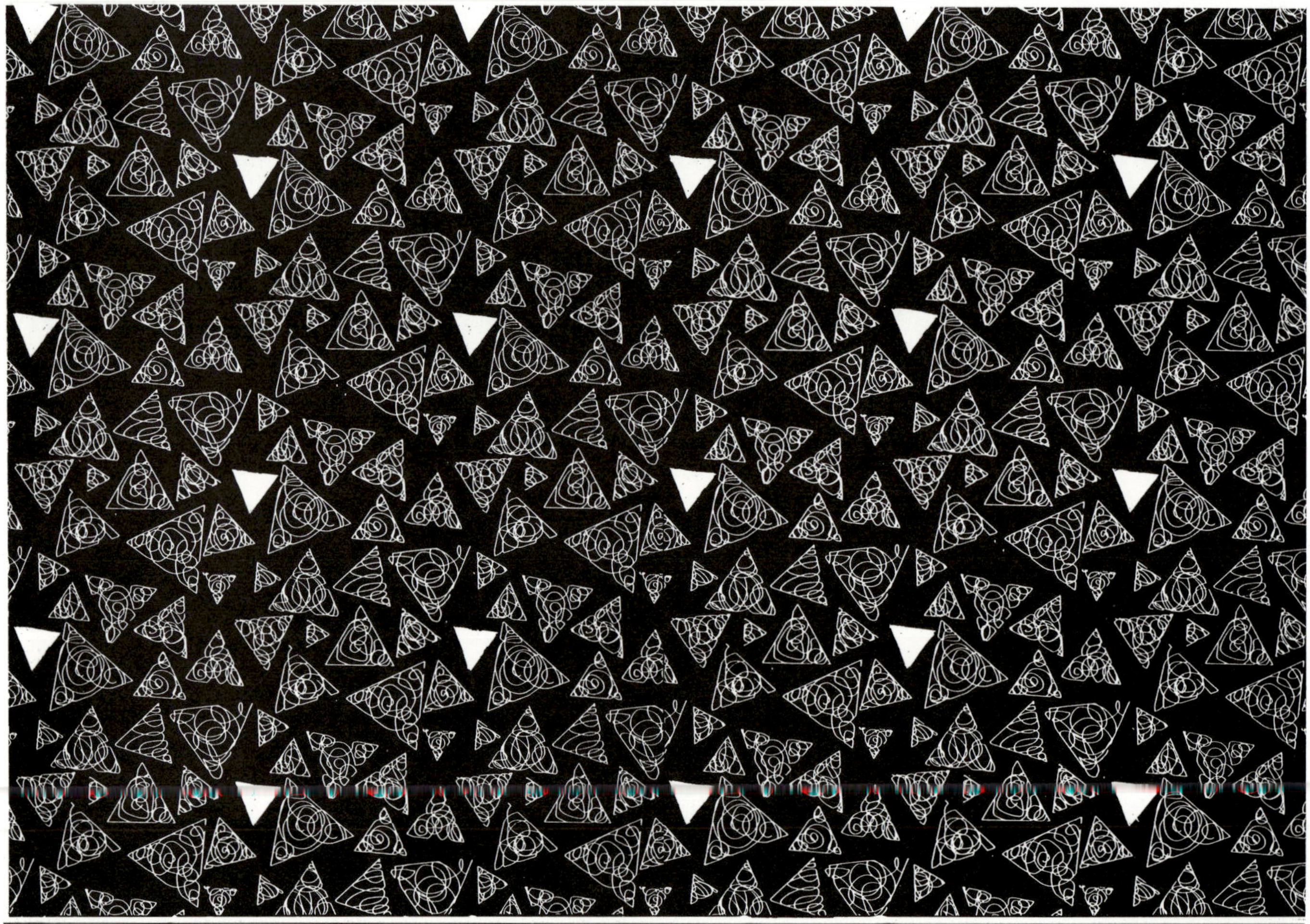

BASIC ELEMENTS

BA47

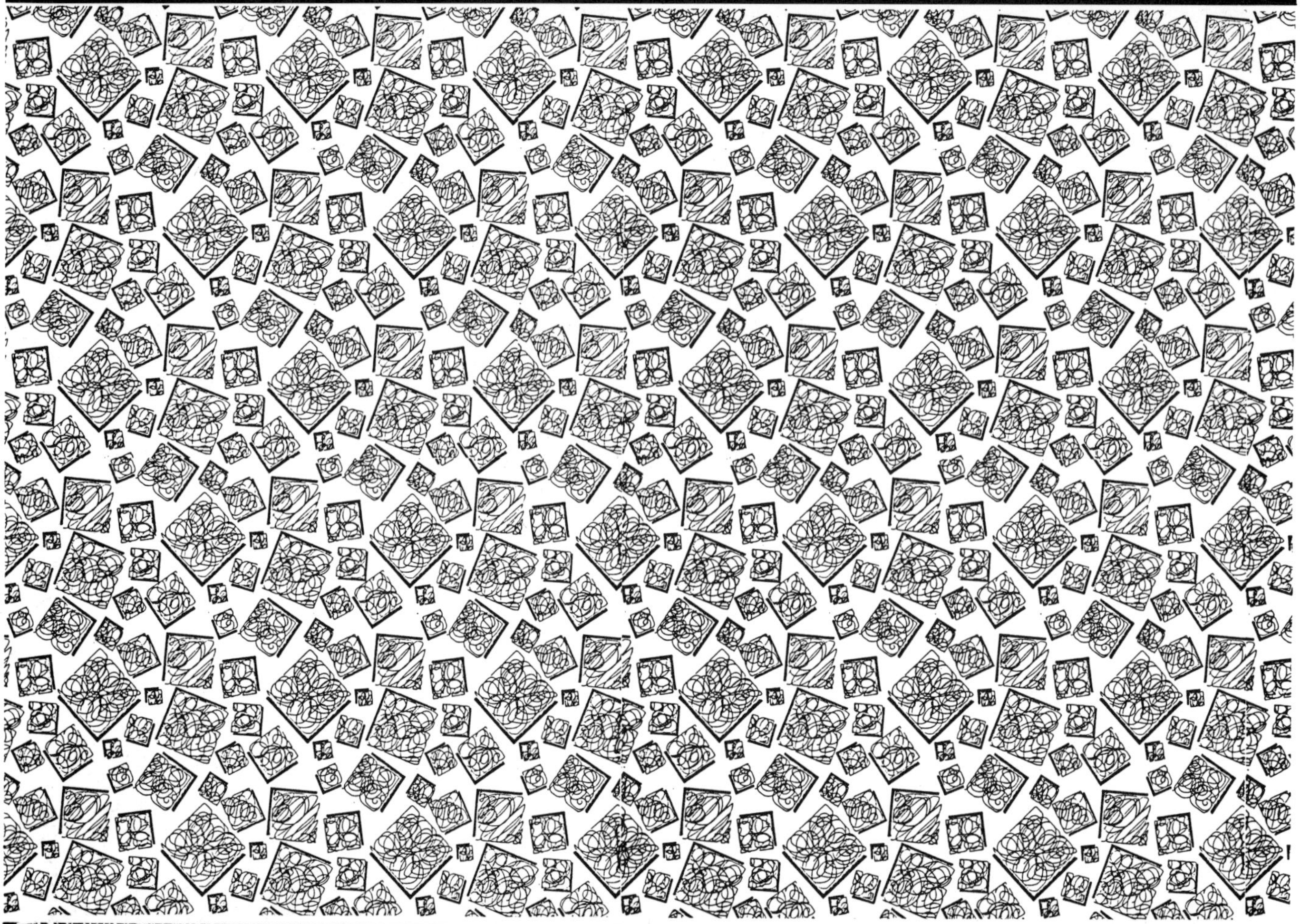

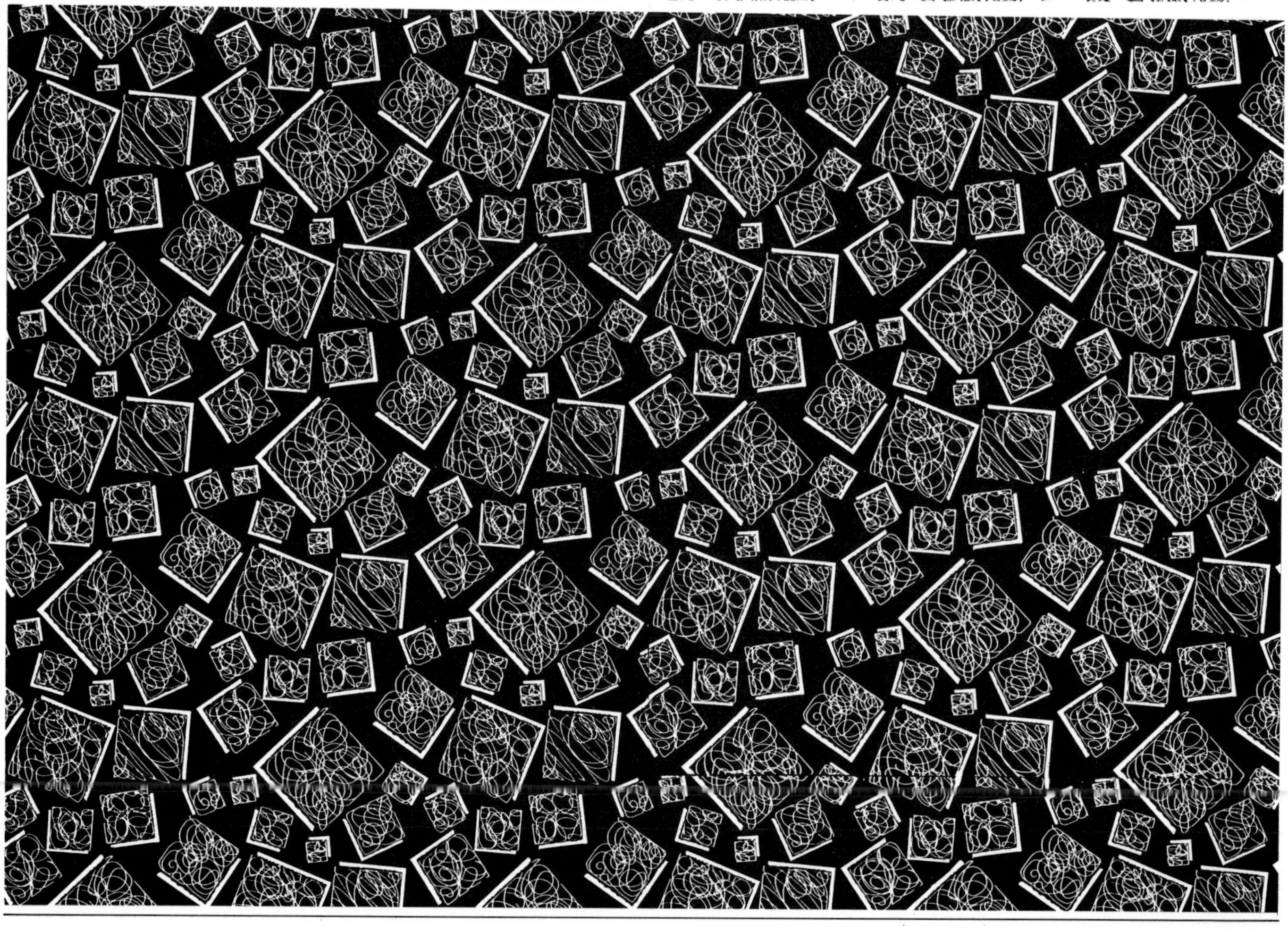

BASIC ELEMENTS BA48

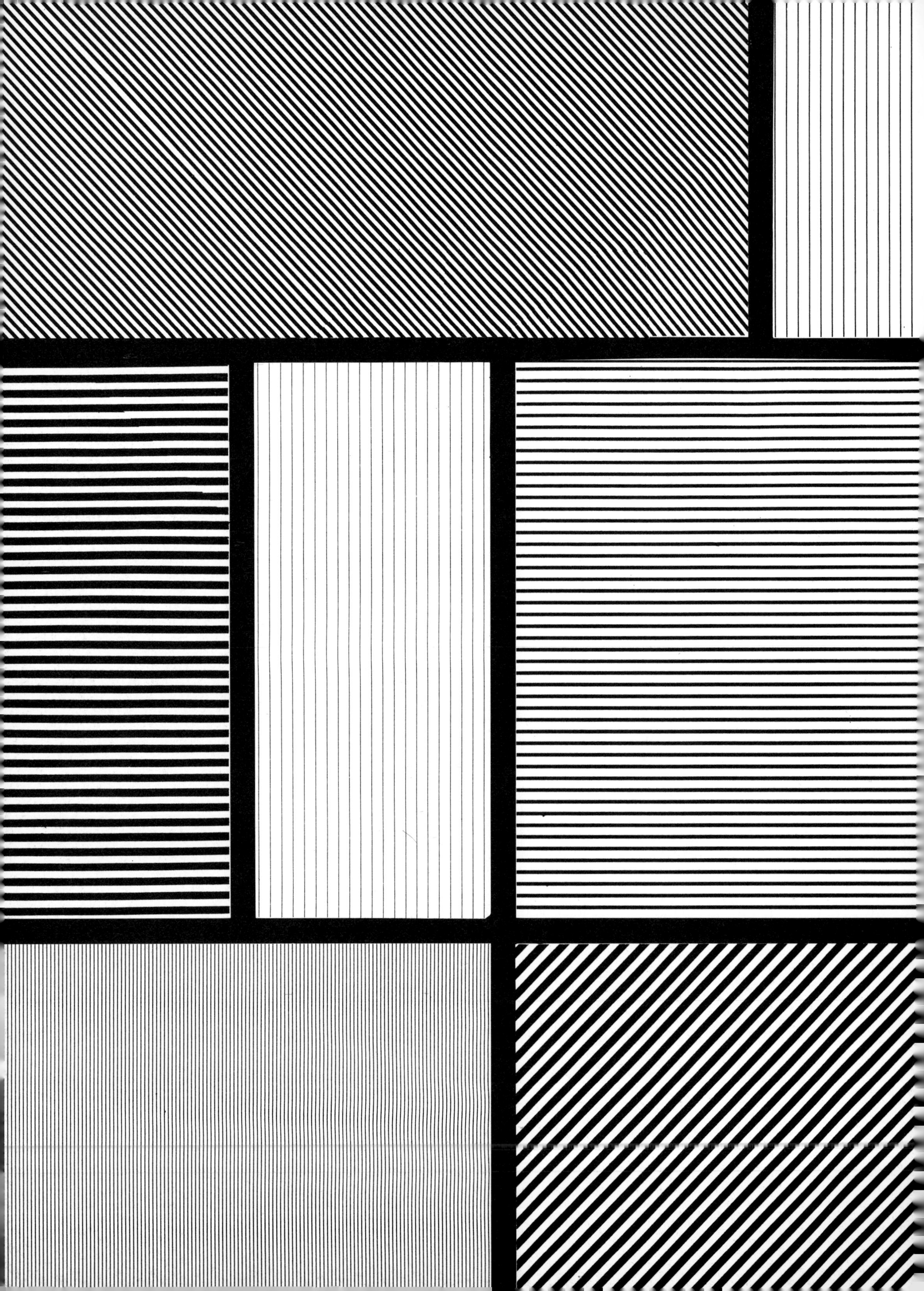

122

BASIC ELEMENTS BA49

124

BASIC ELEMENTS BA50

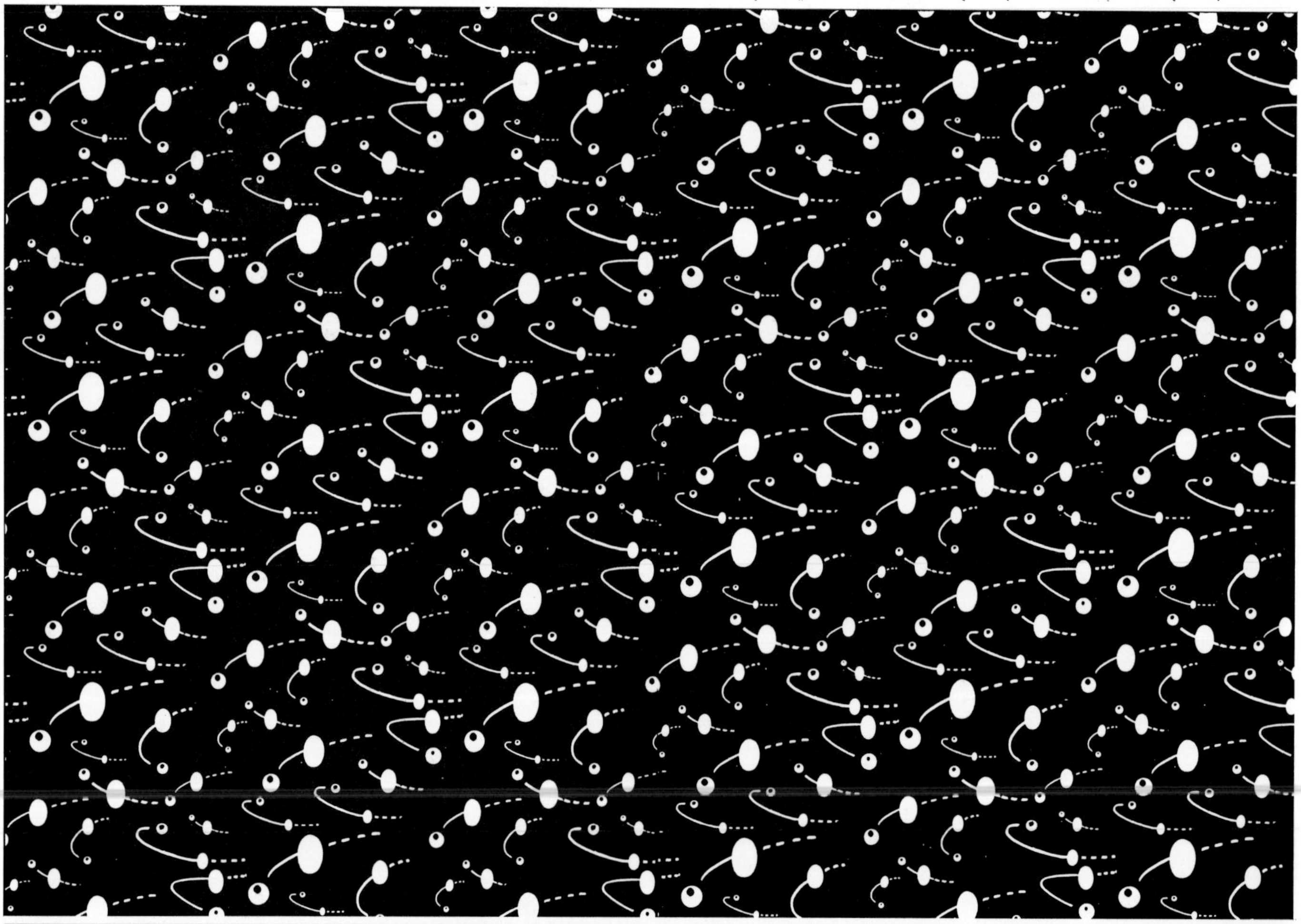

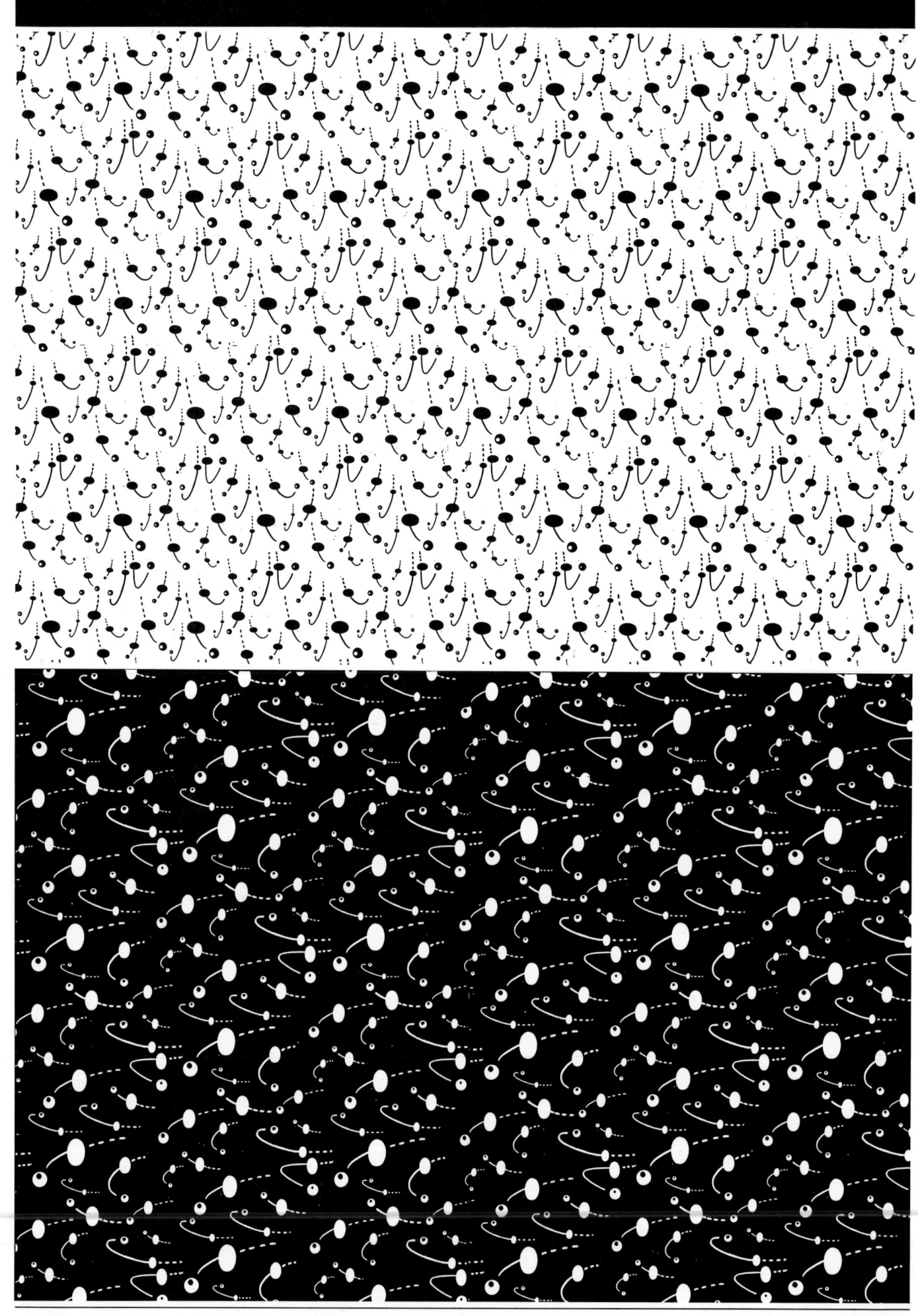

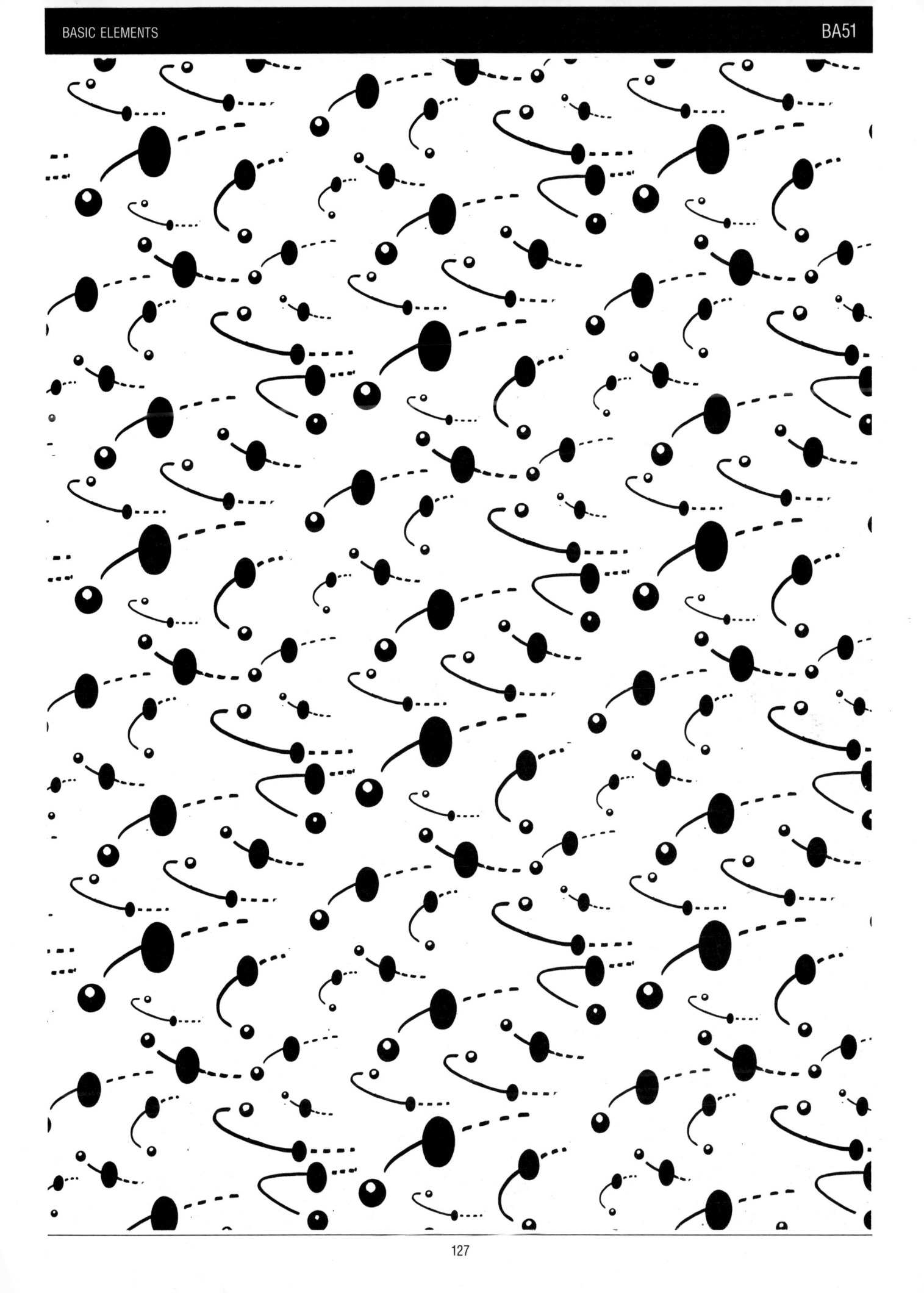

BASIC ELEMENTS BA51

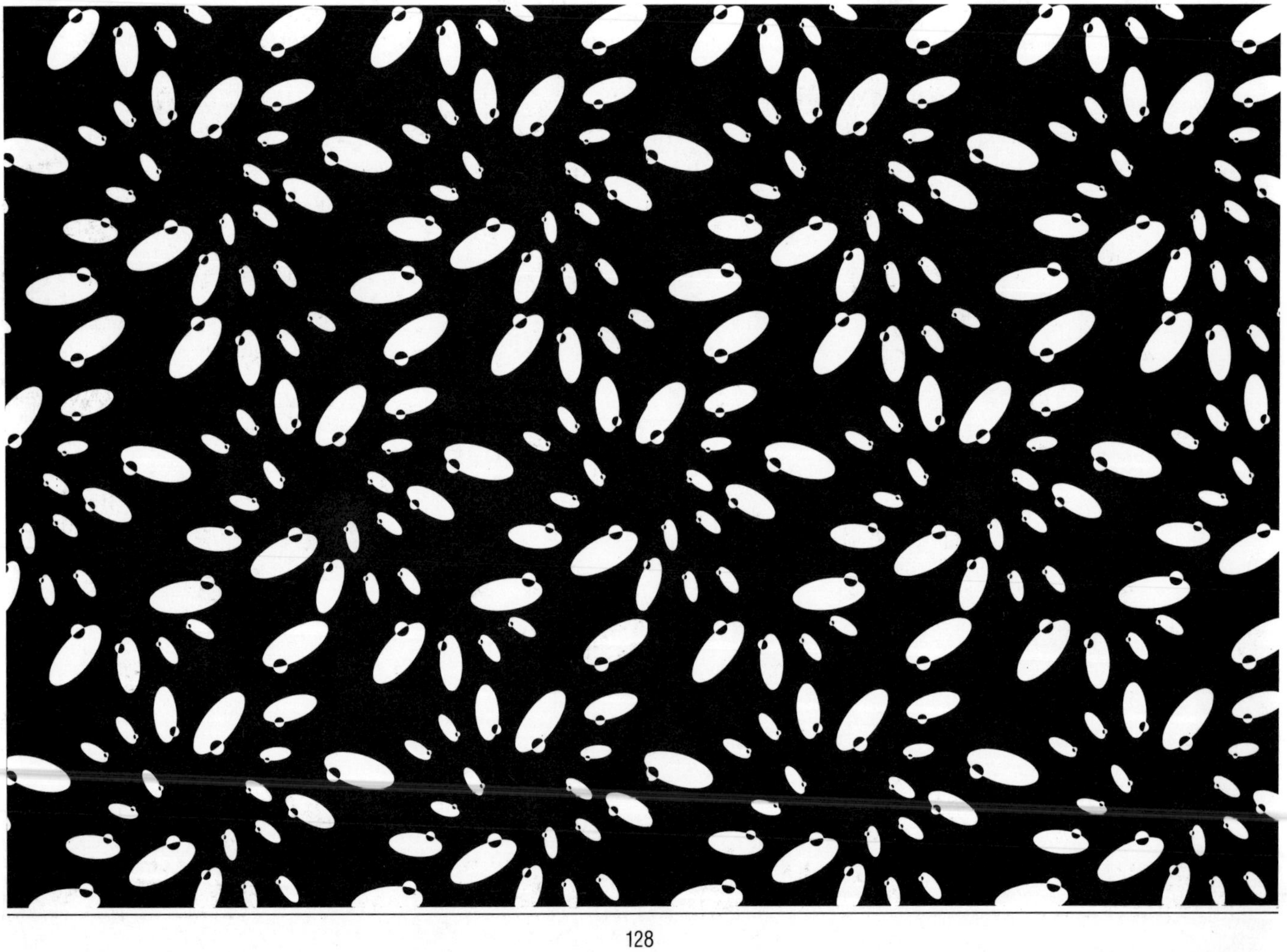

BASIC ELEMENTS BA52

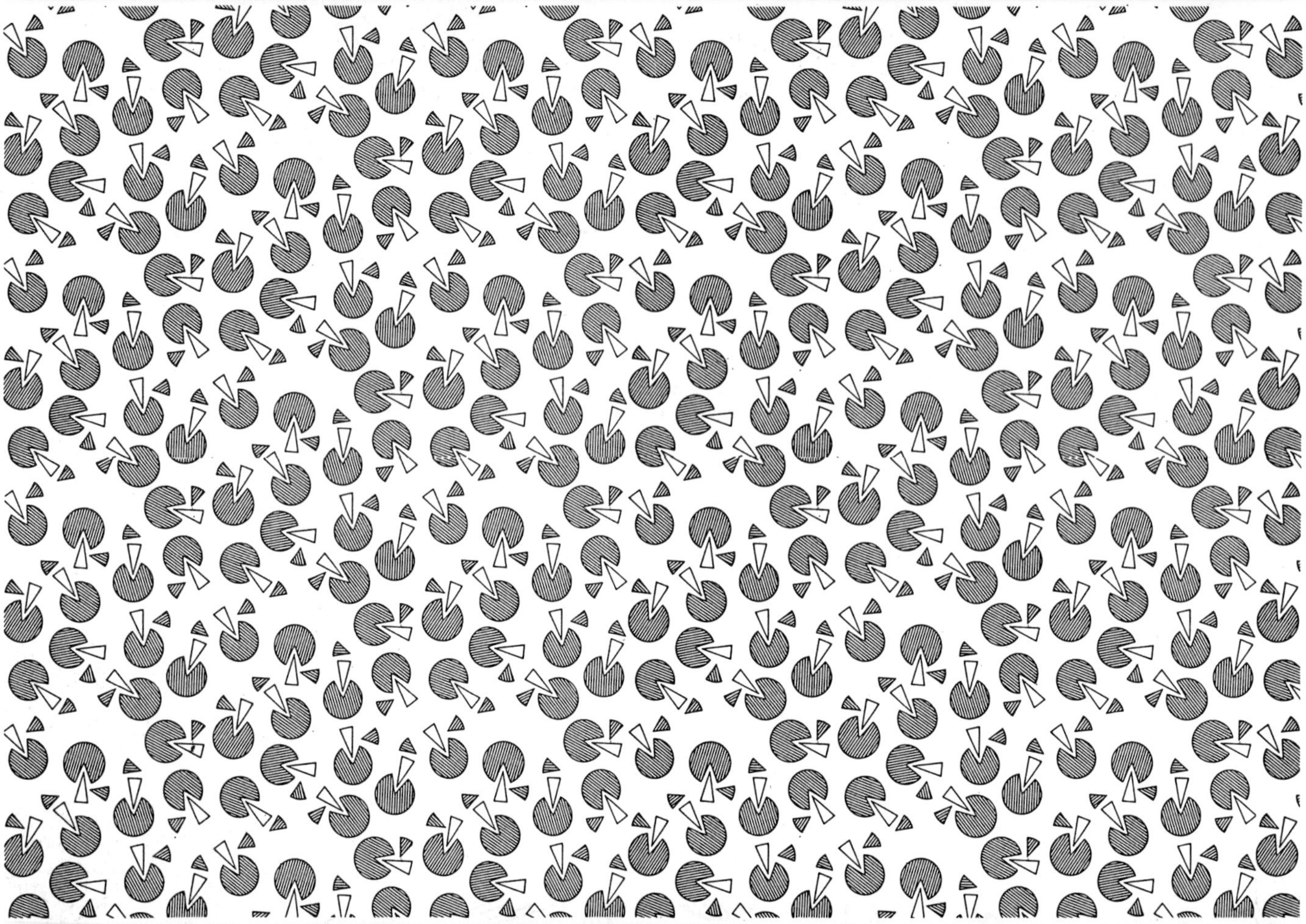

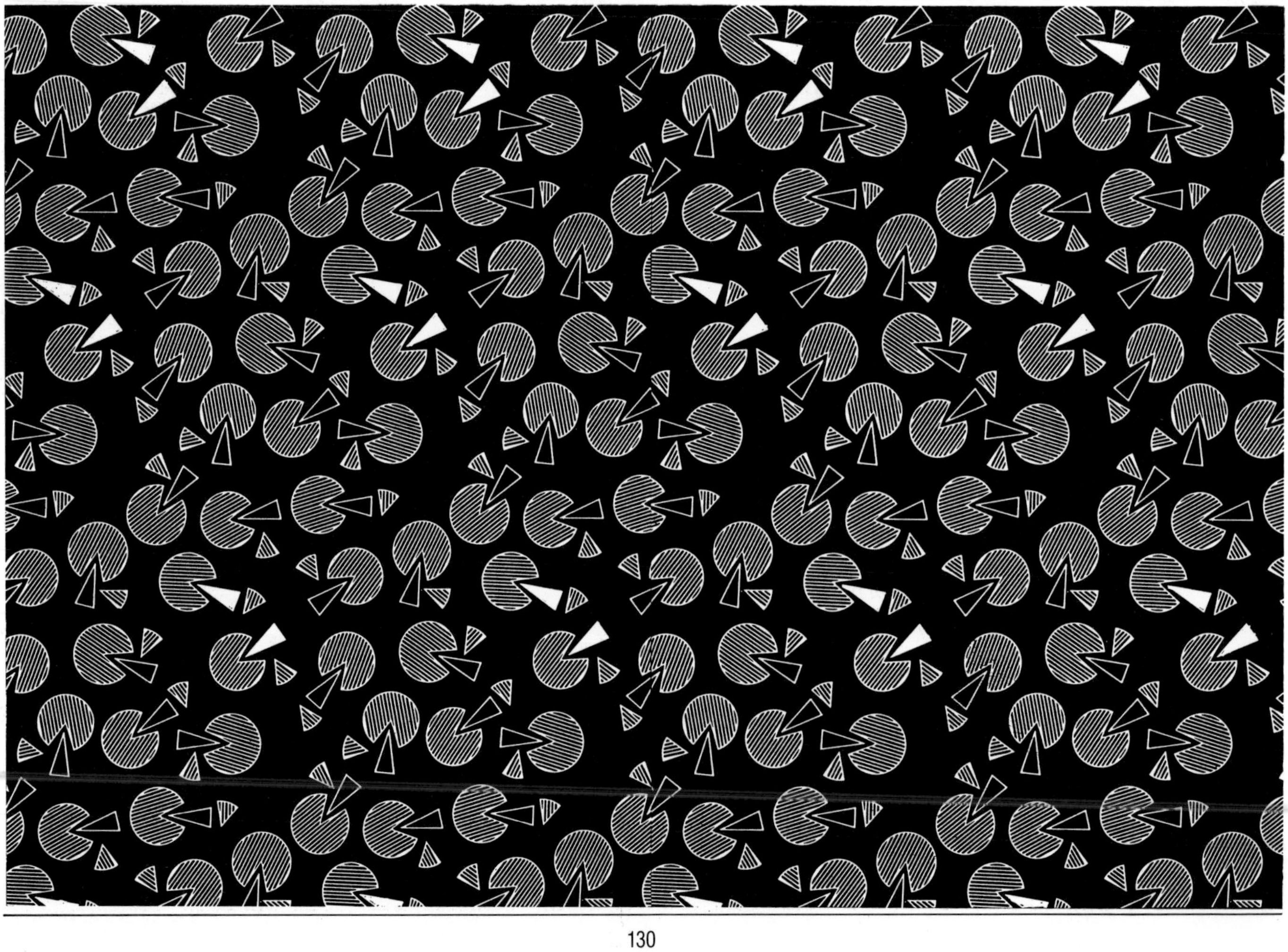

BASIC ELEMENTS · BA53

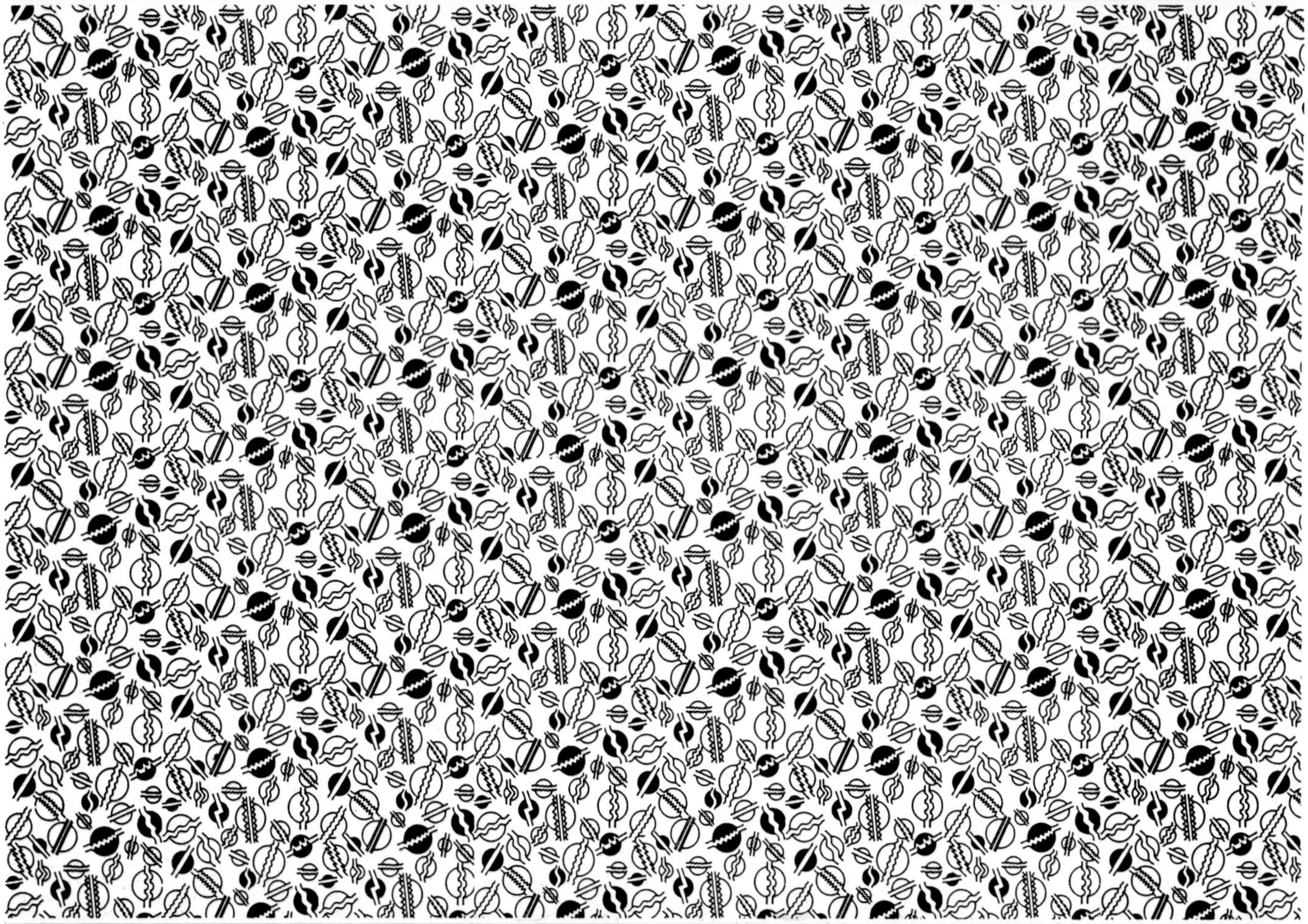
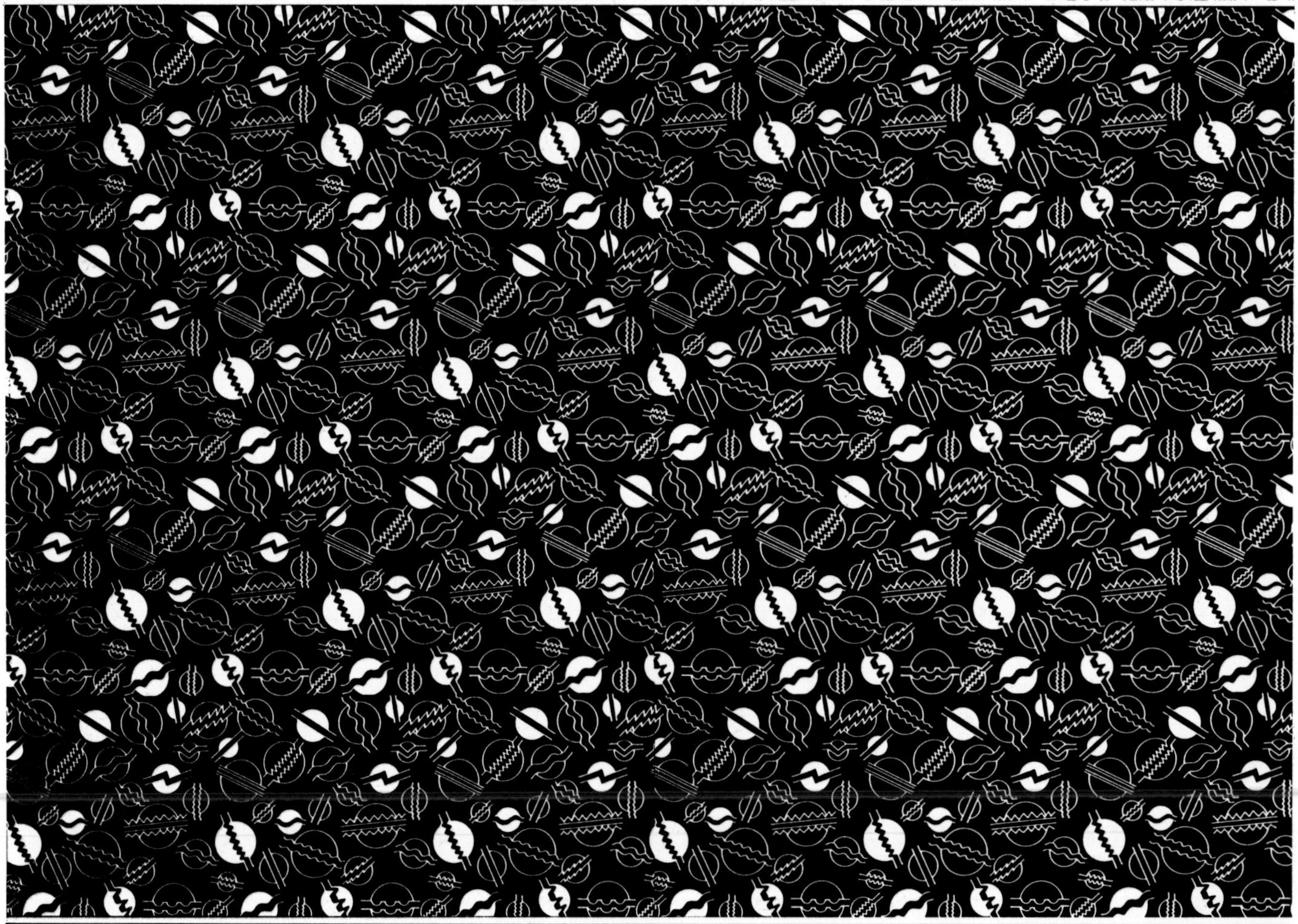

BASIC ELEMENTS BA54

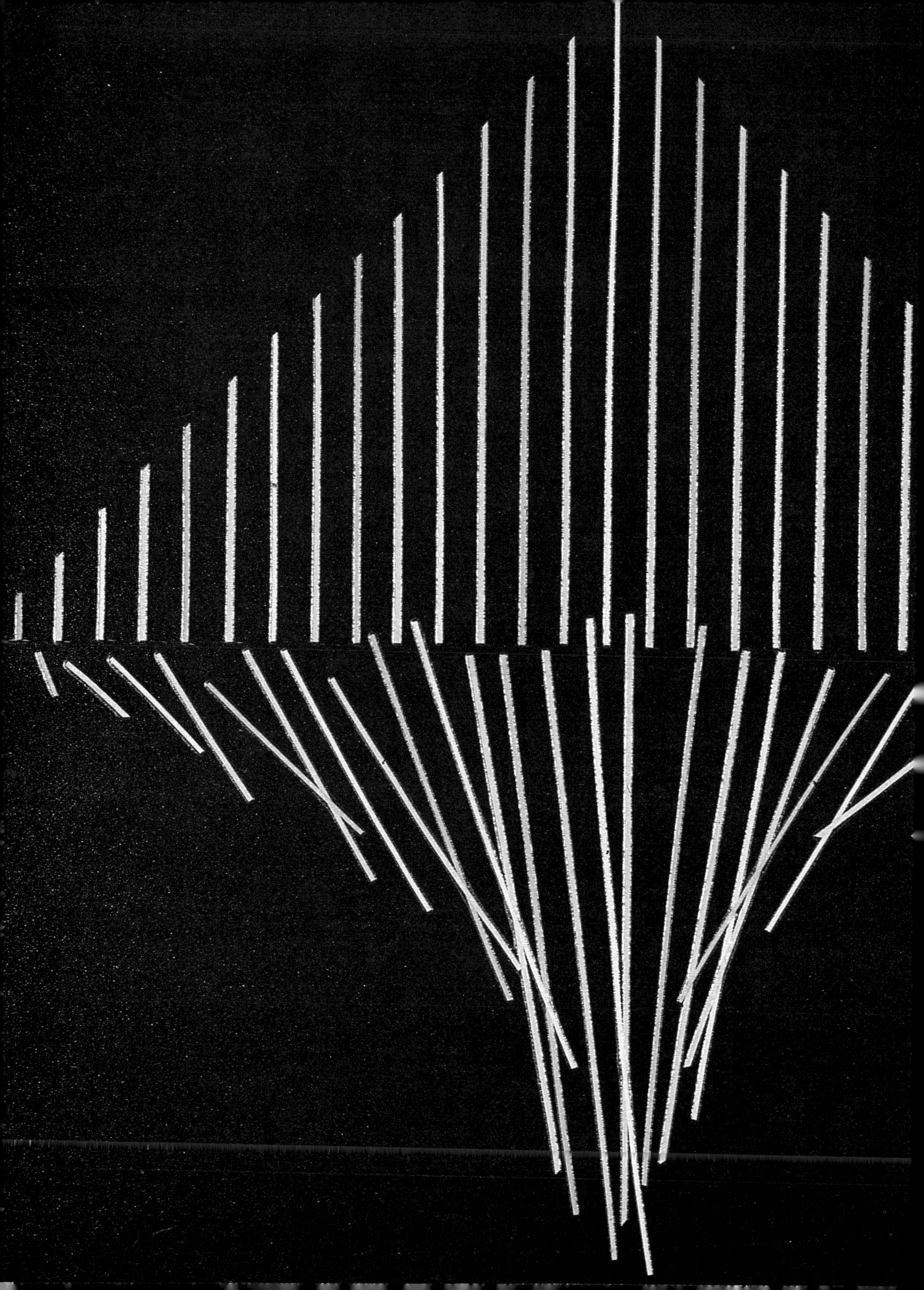

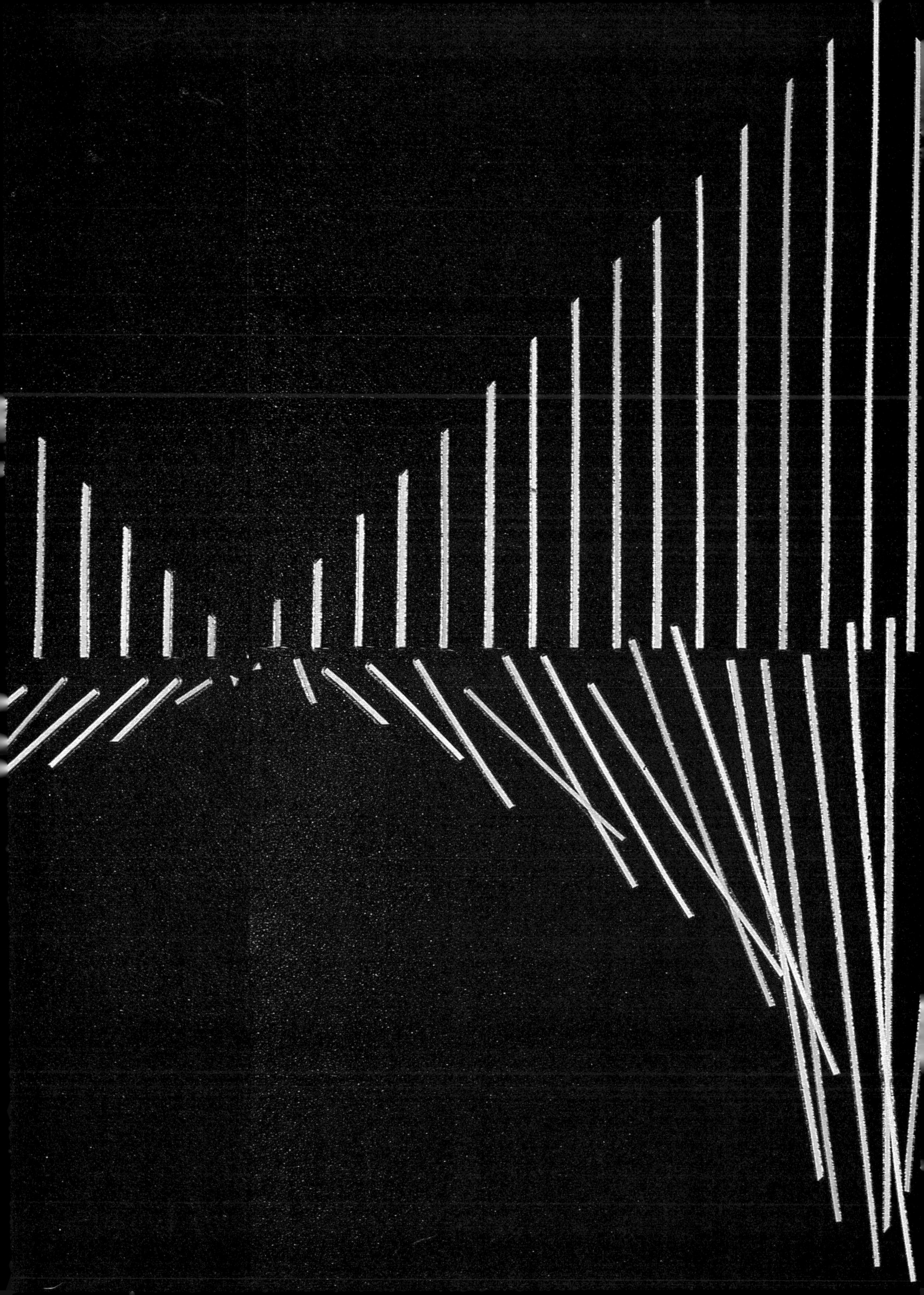

136

BASIC ELEMENTS

BA55

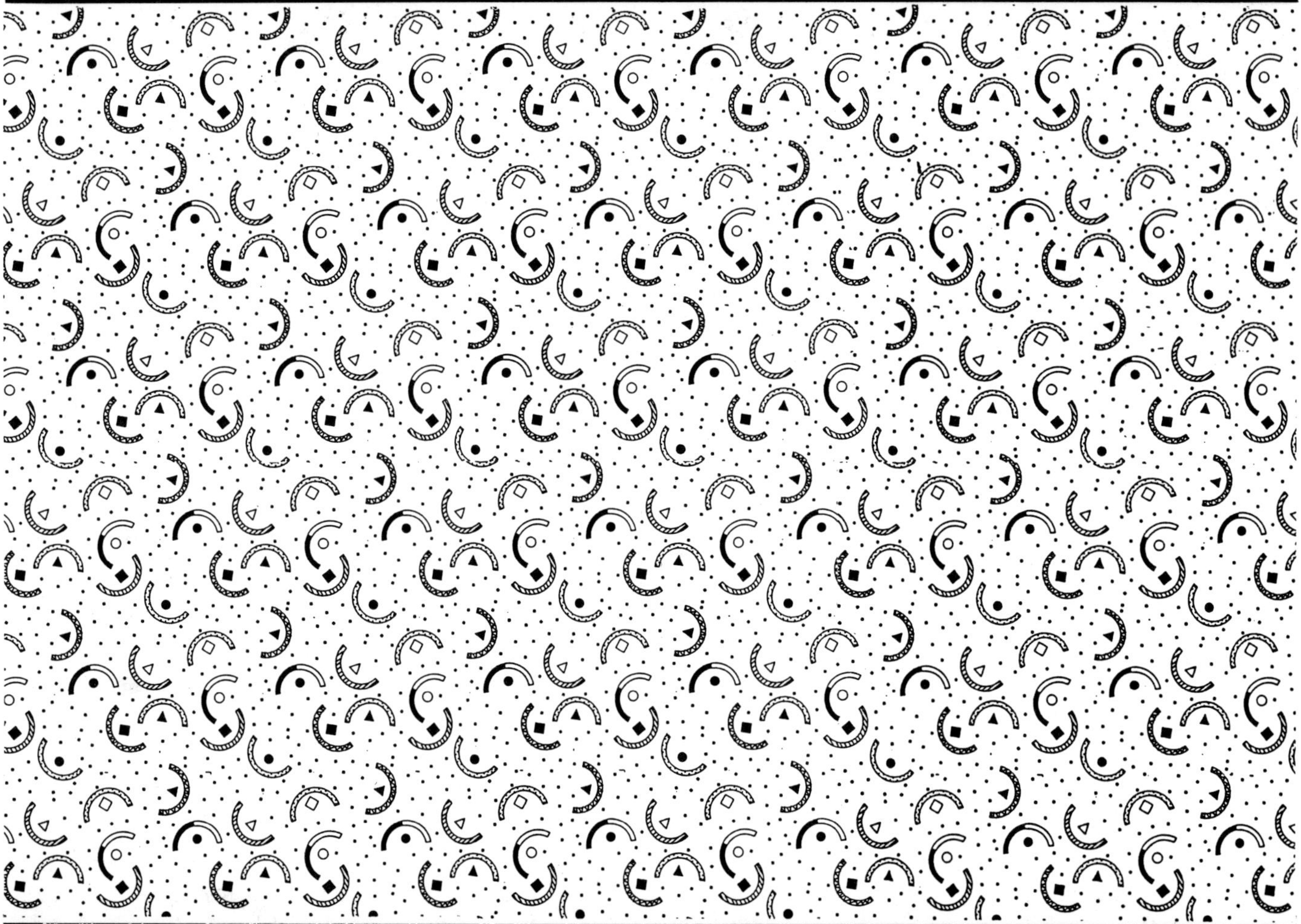

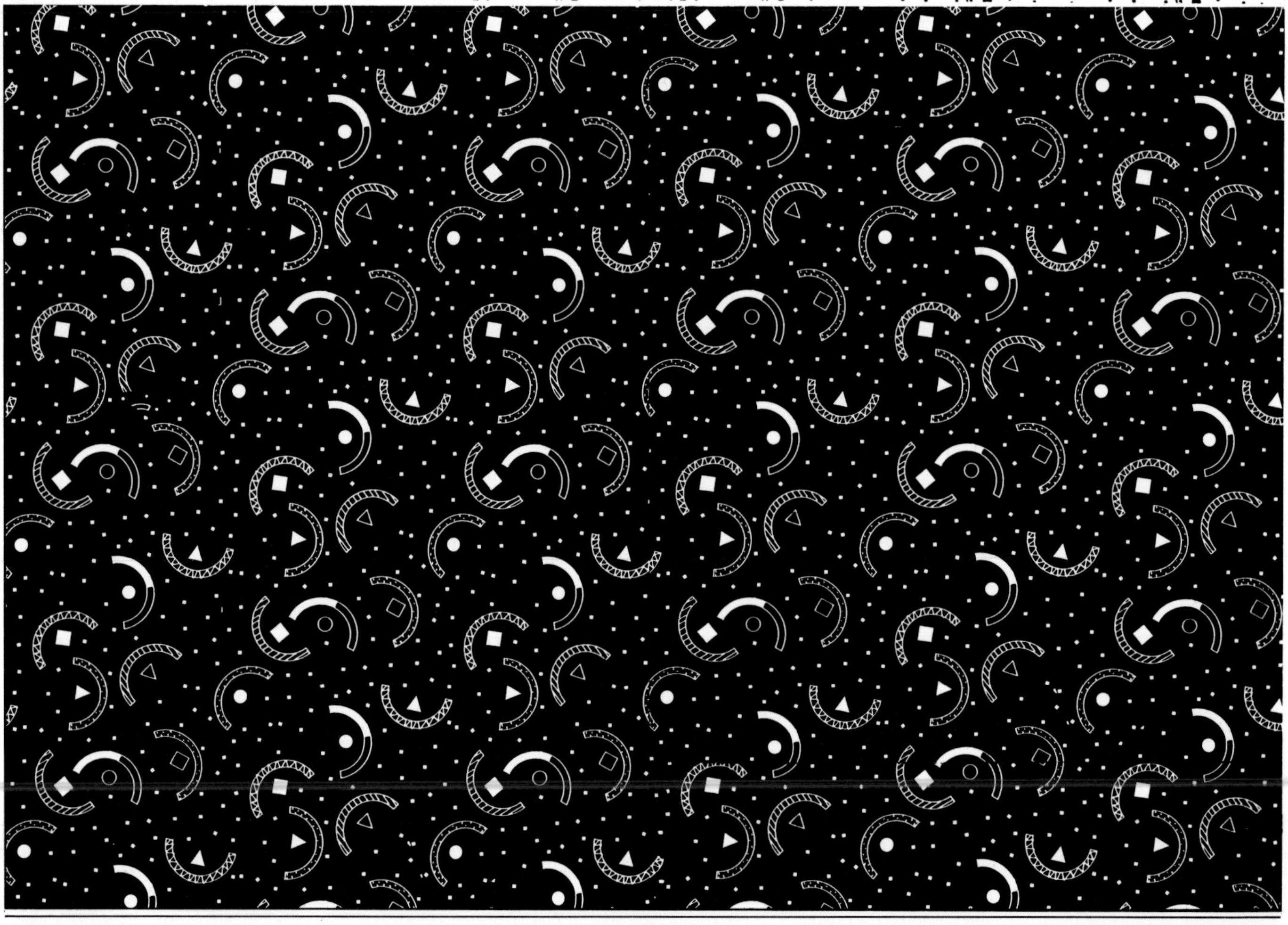

BASIC ELEMENTS   BA56

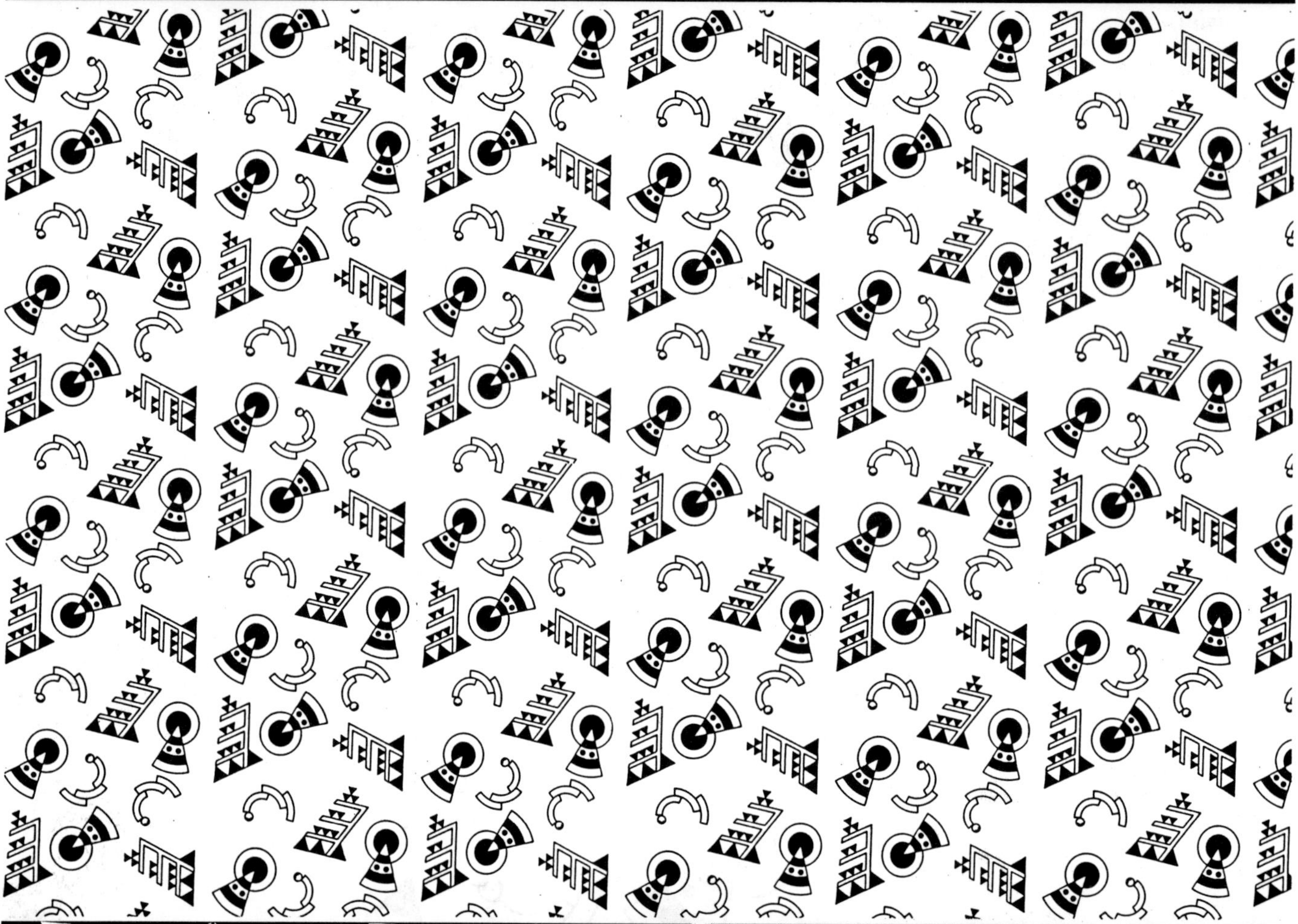

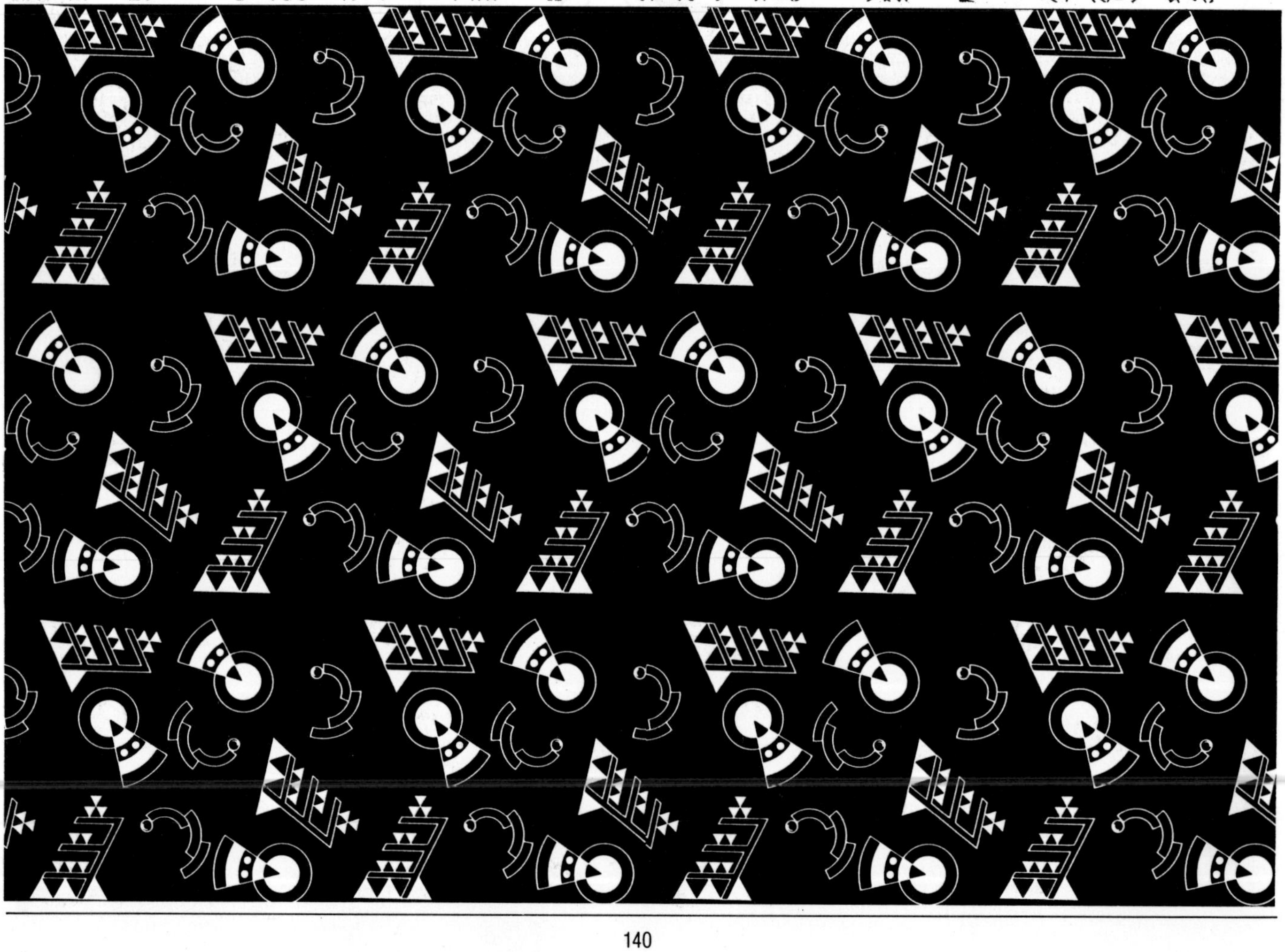

BASIC ELEMENTS

BA57

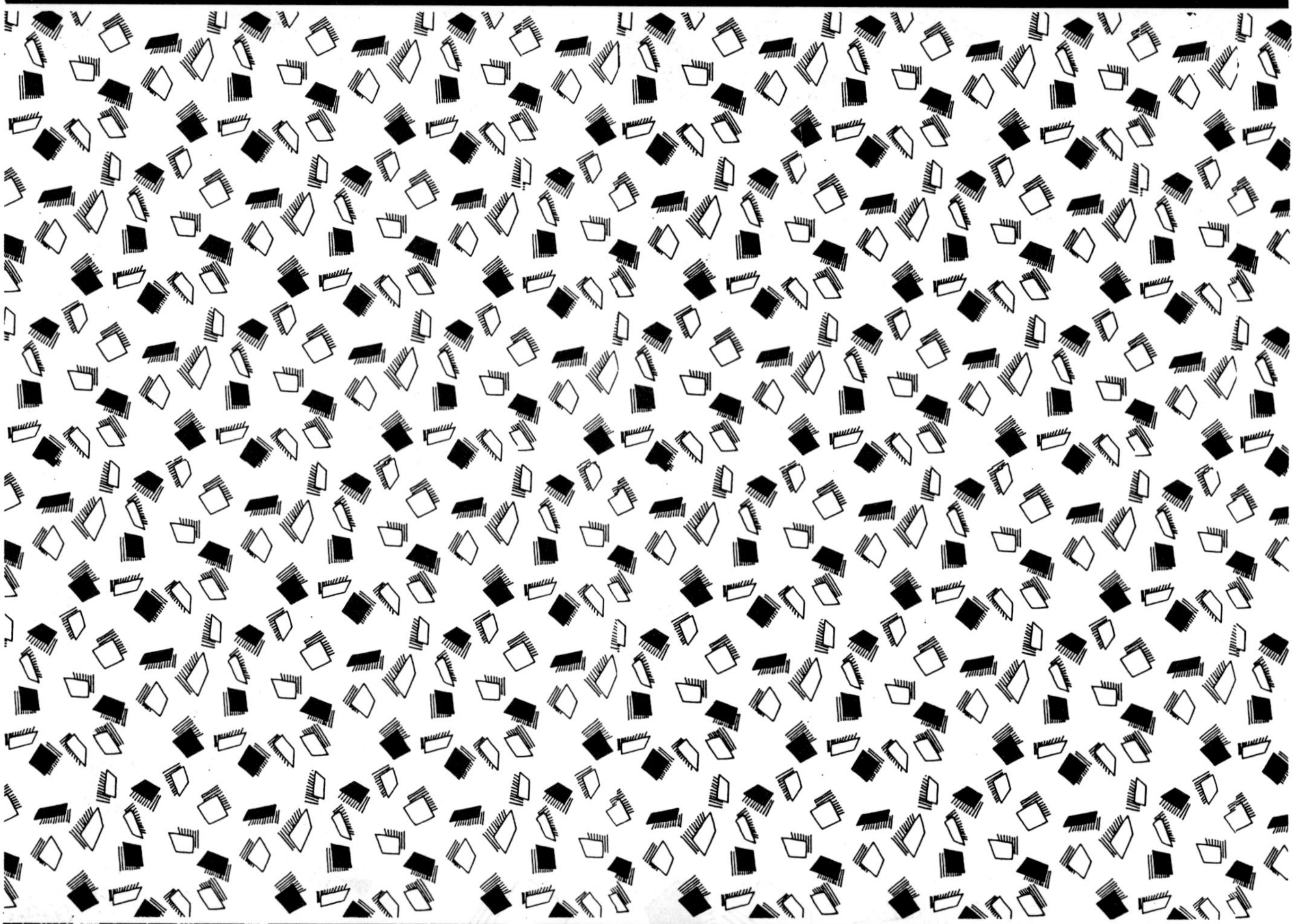

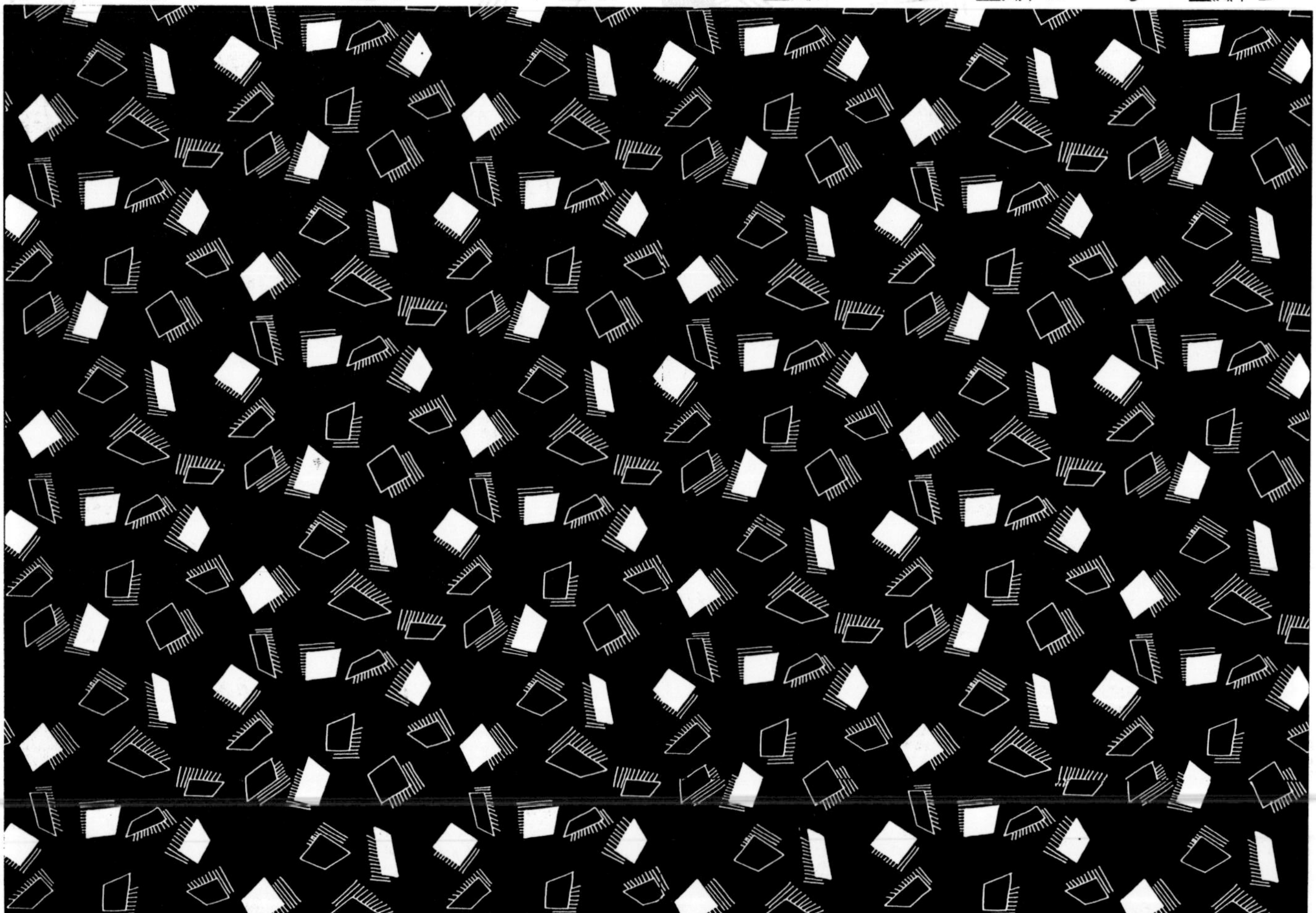

BASIC ELEMENTS   BA58

144

BASIC ELEMENTS

BA59

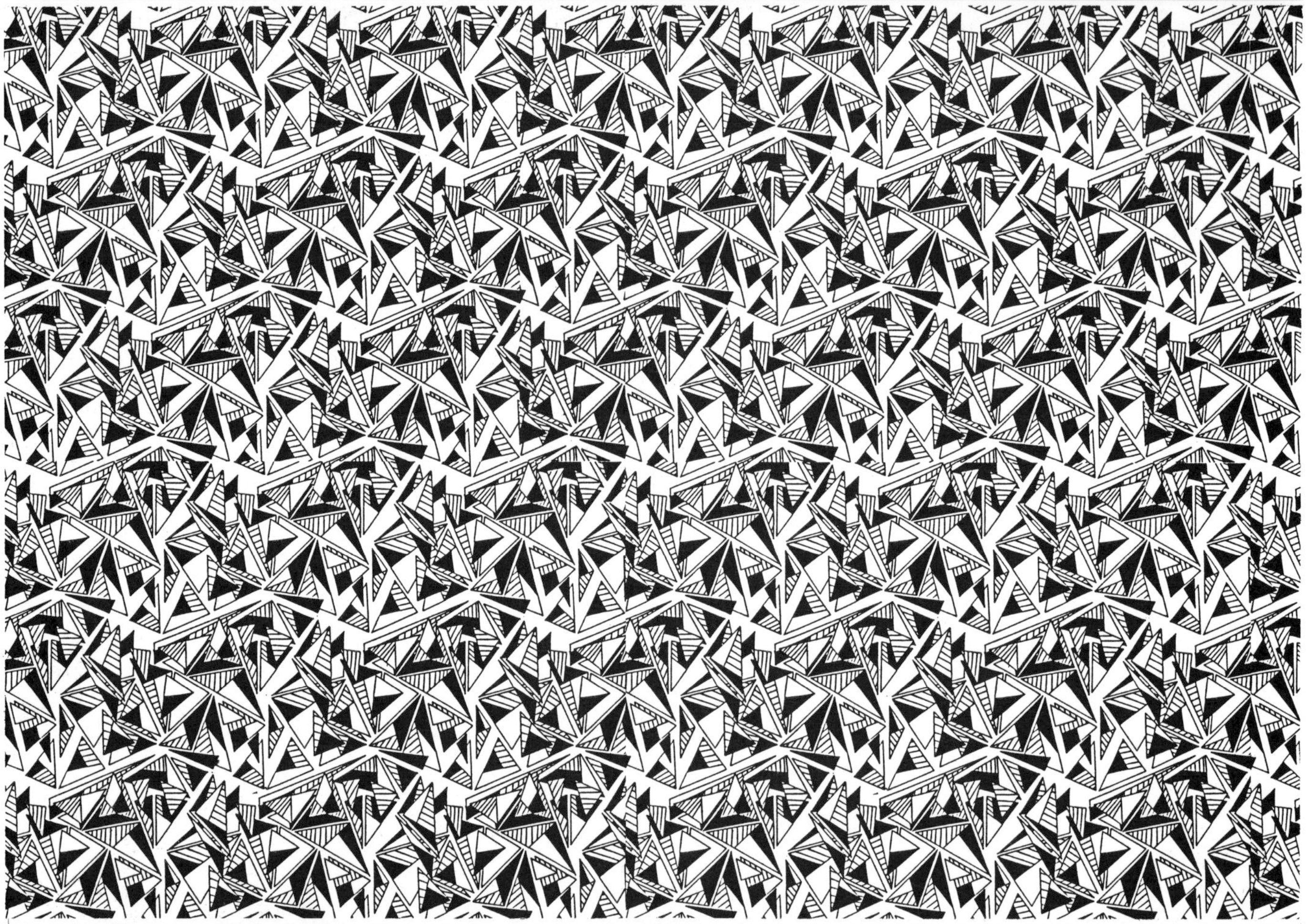

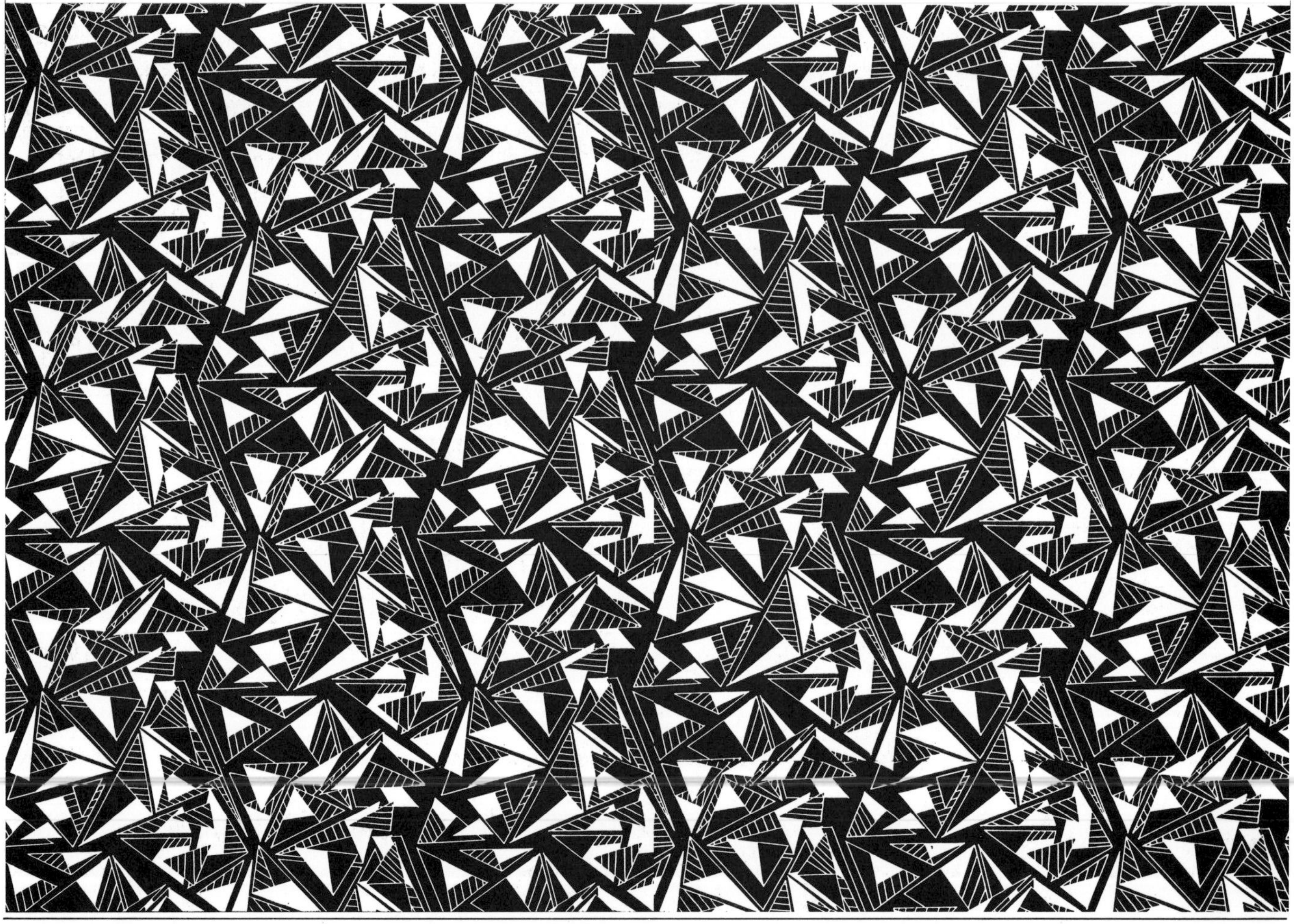

BASIC ELEMENTS — BA60

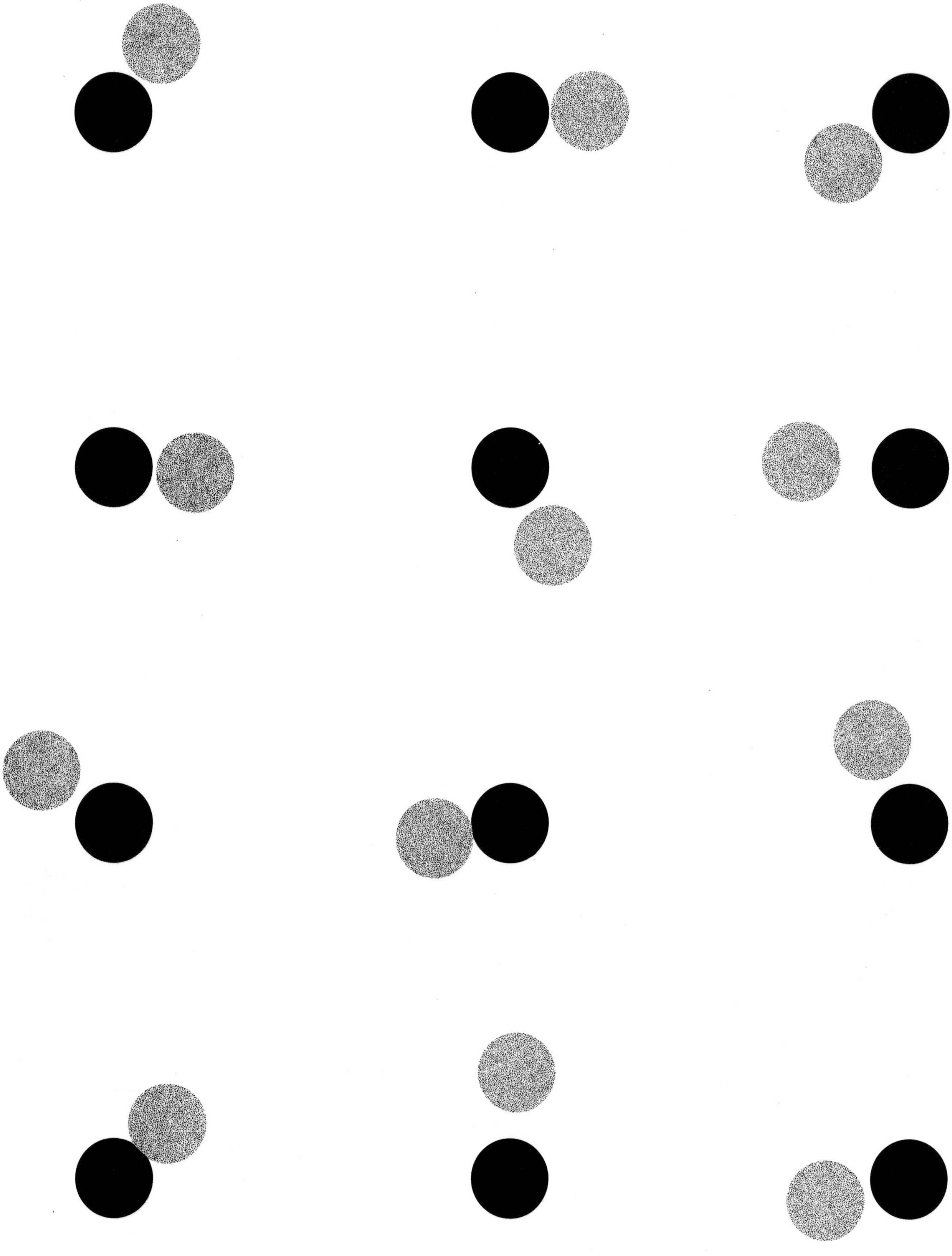

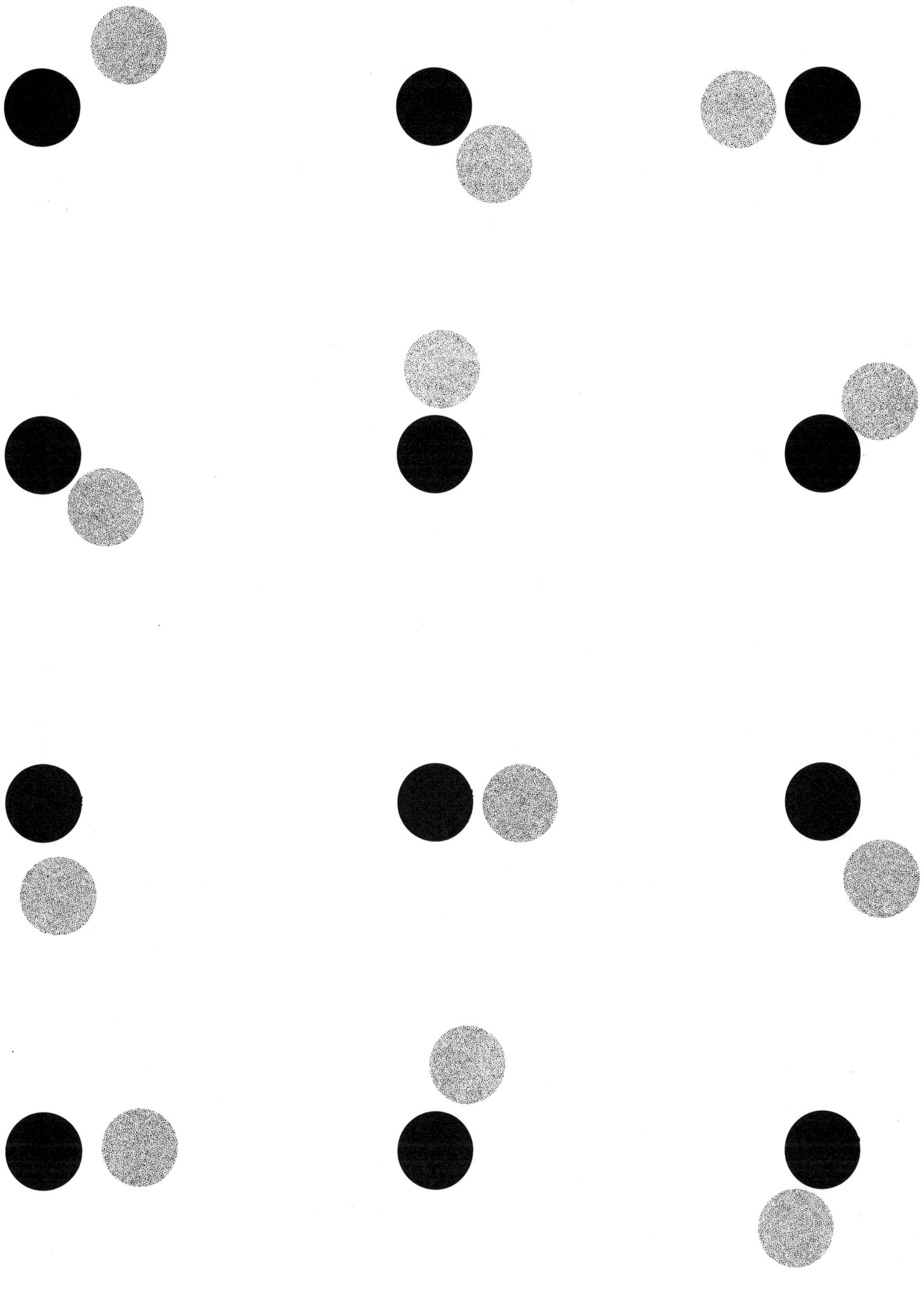

150

BASIC ELEMENTS

BA61

152

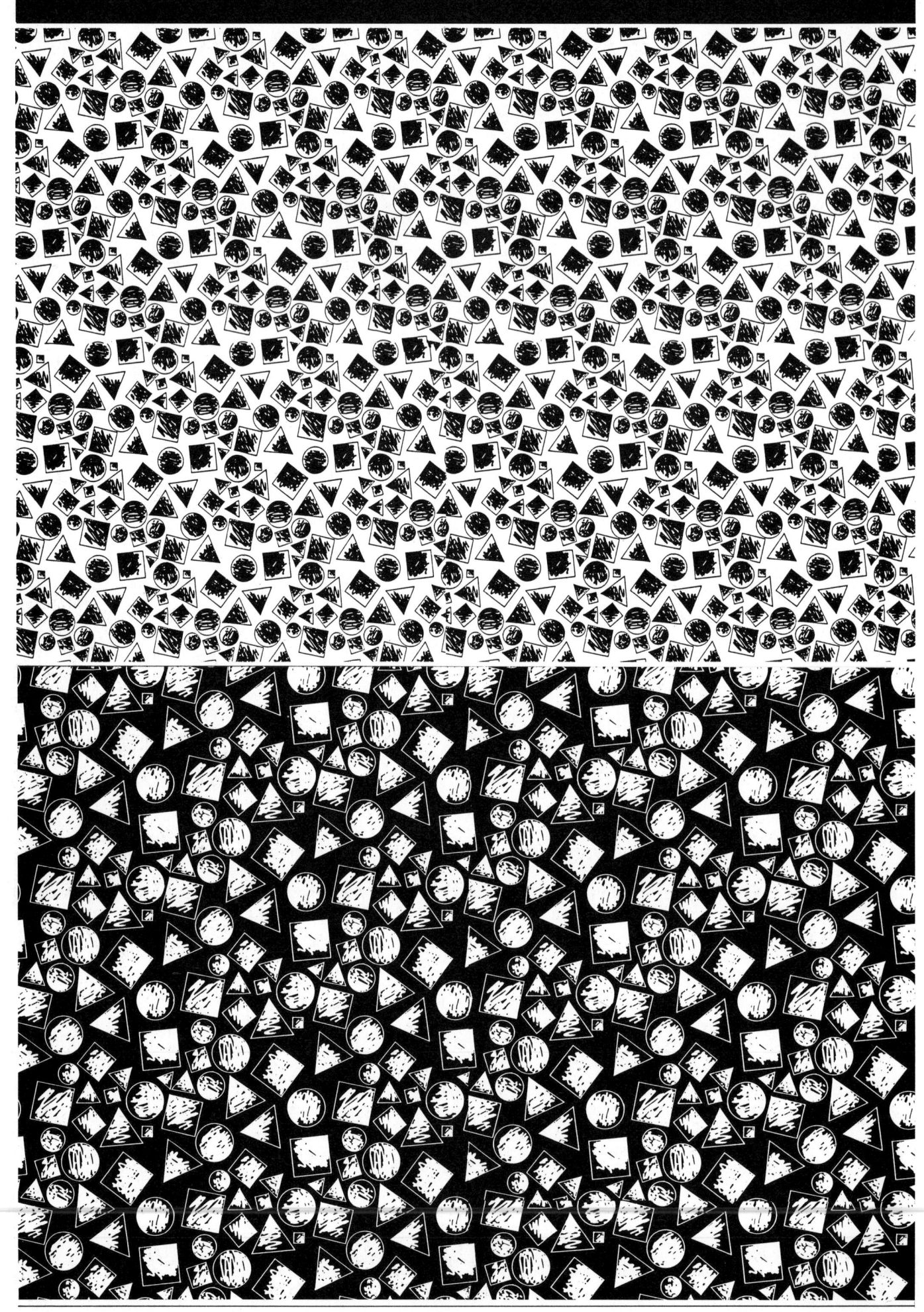

BASIC ELEMENTS BA62

154

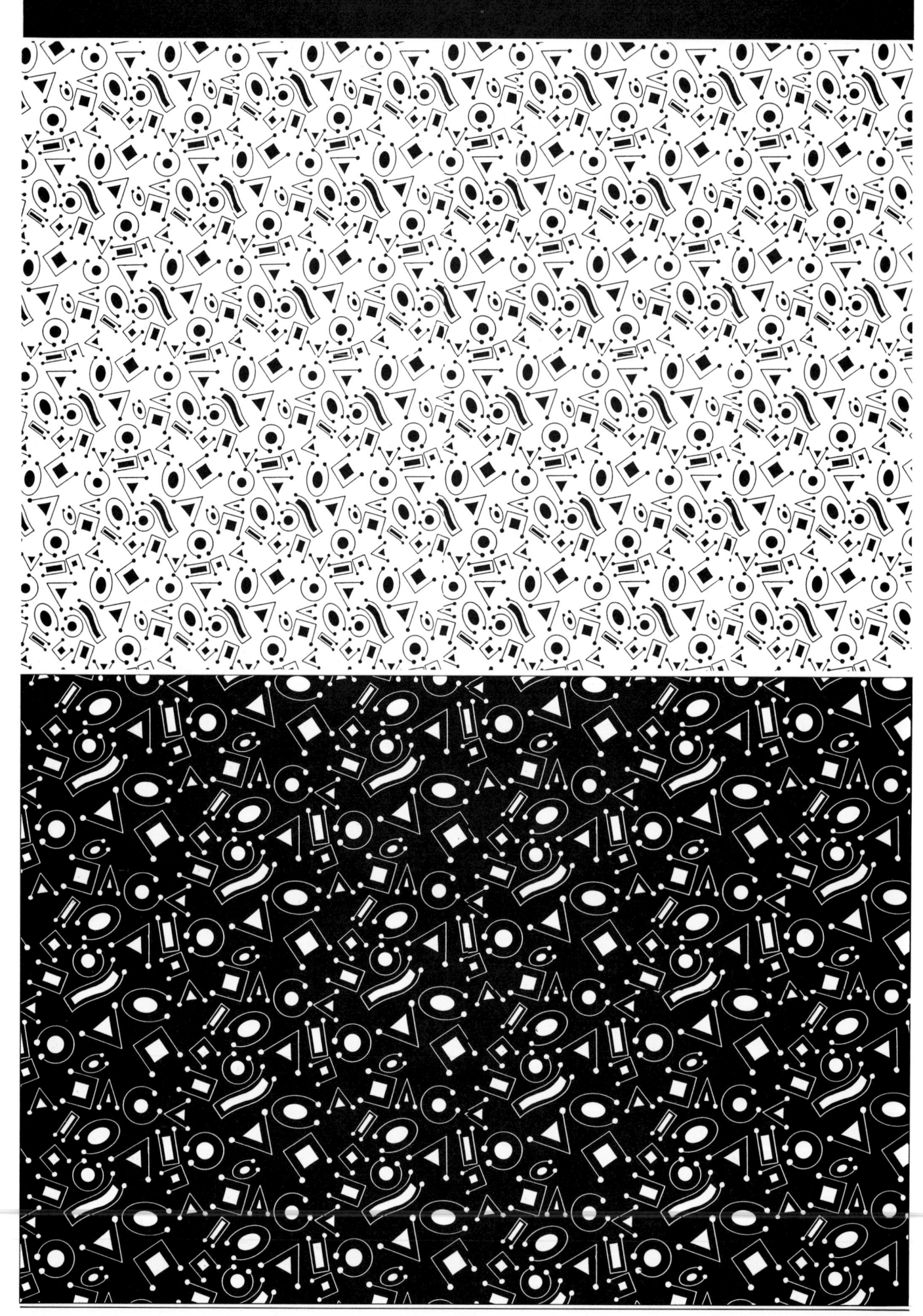

BASIC ELEMENTS BA63

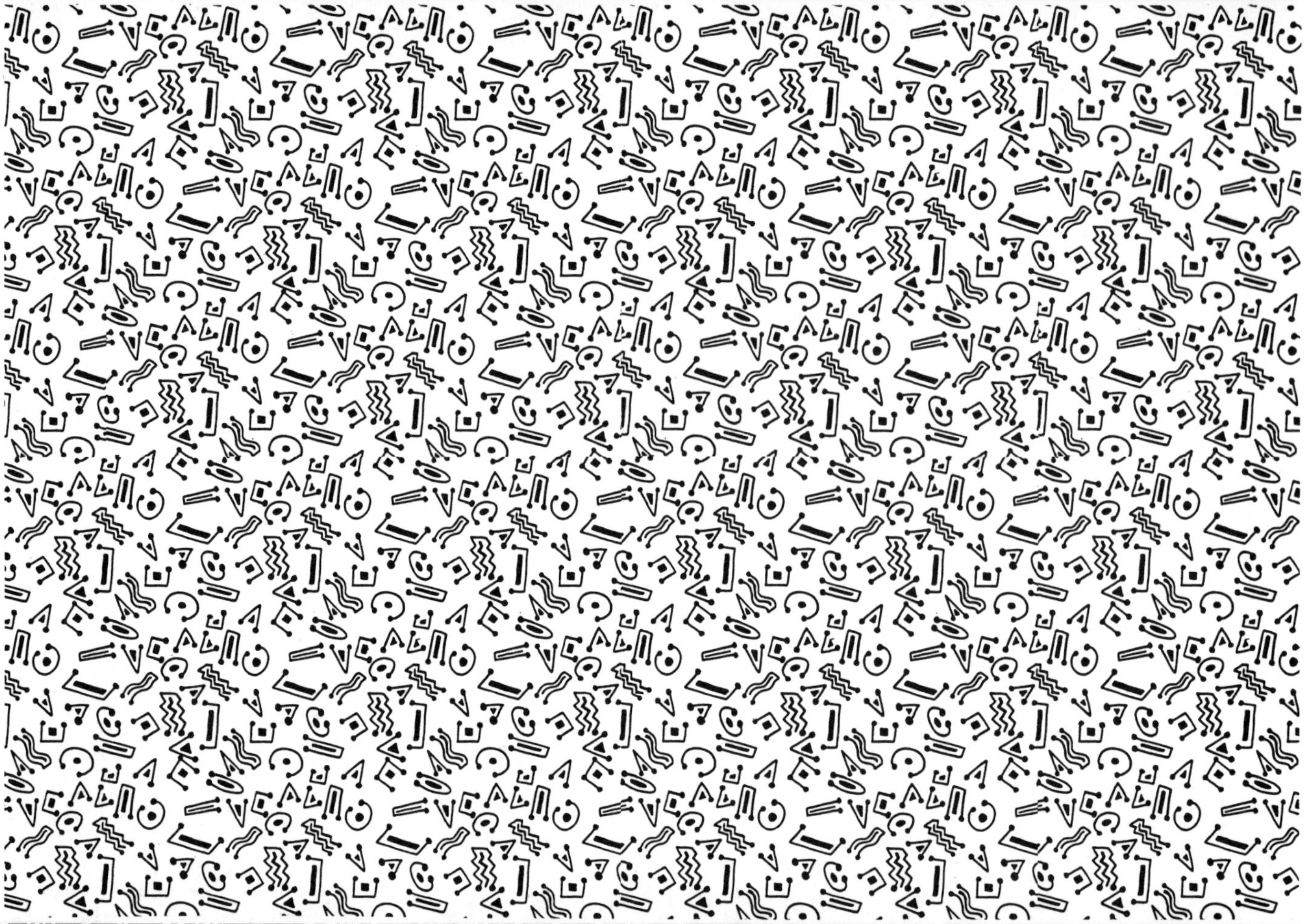

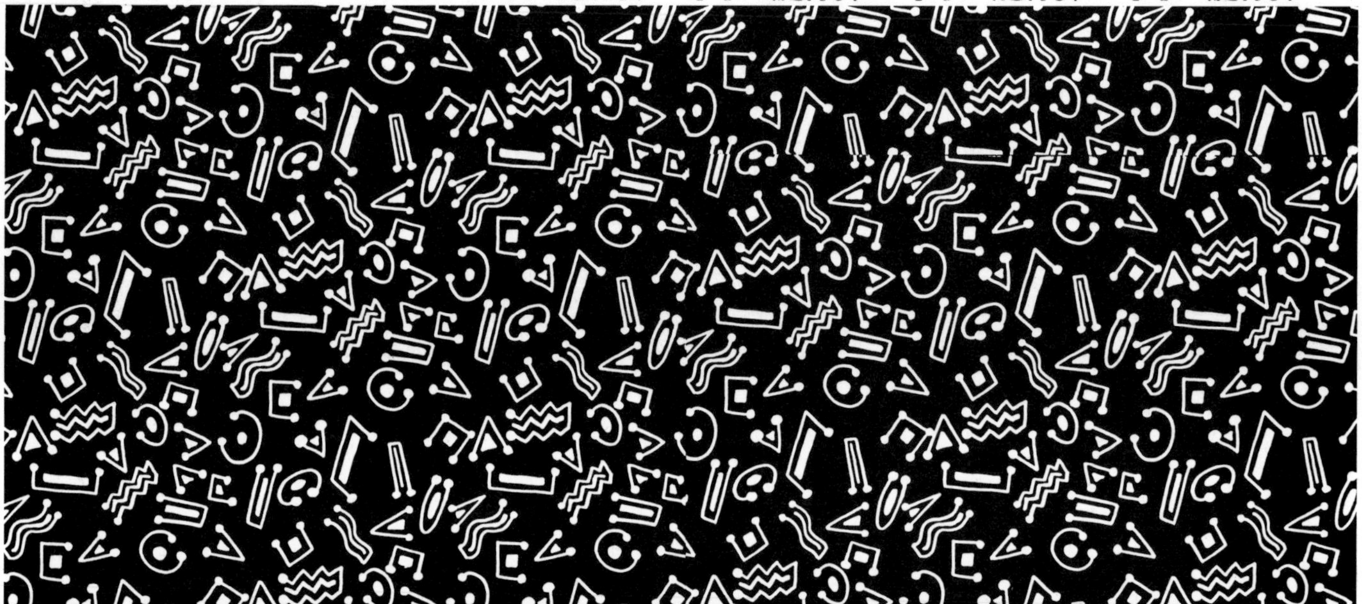

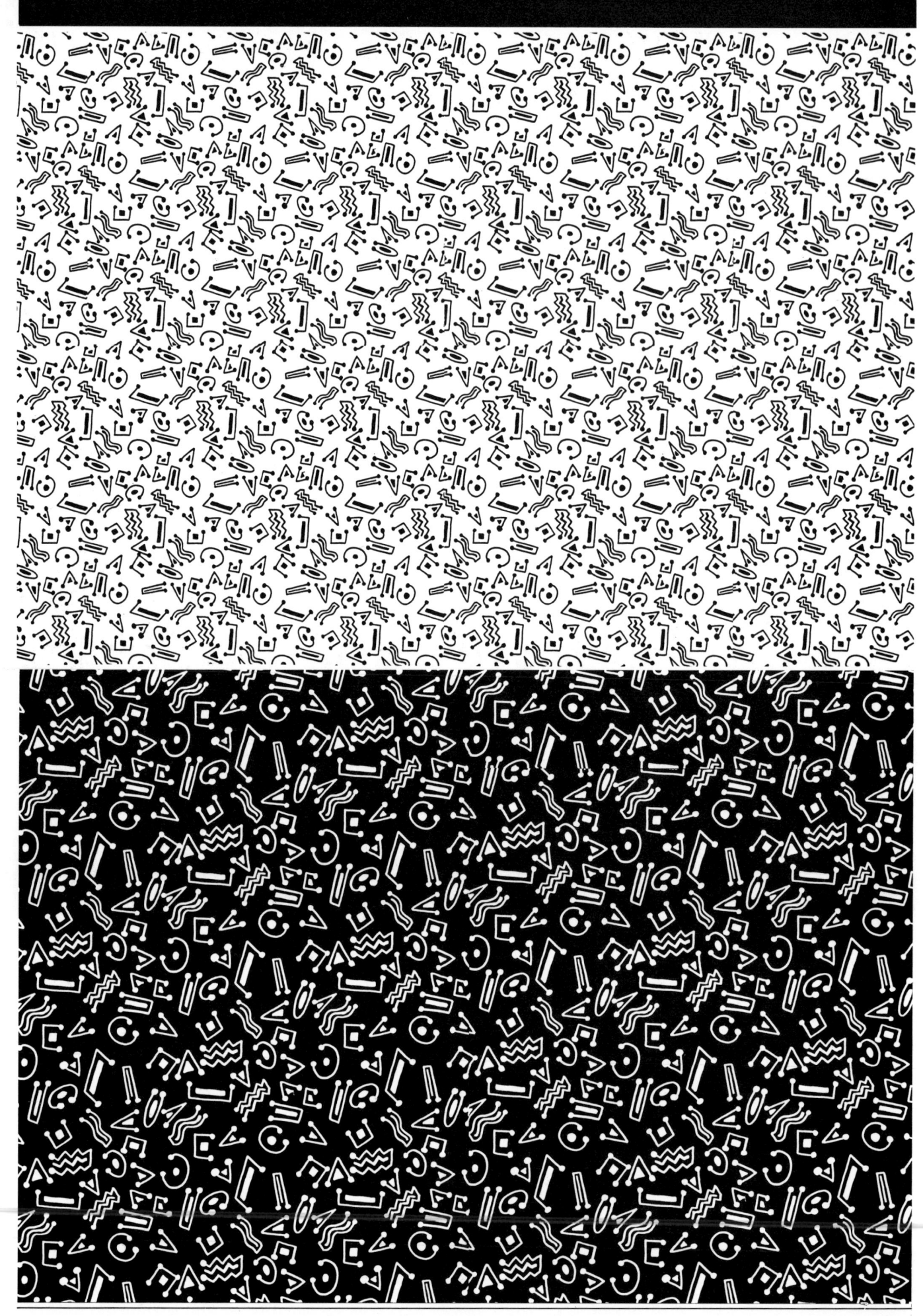

BASIC ELEMENTS BA64

158

BASIC ELEMENTS BA65

160

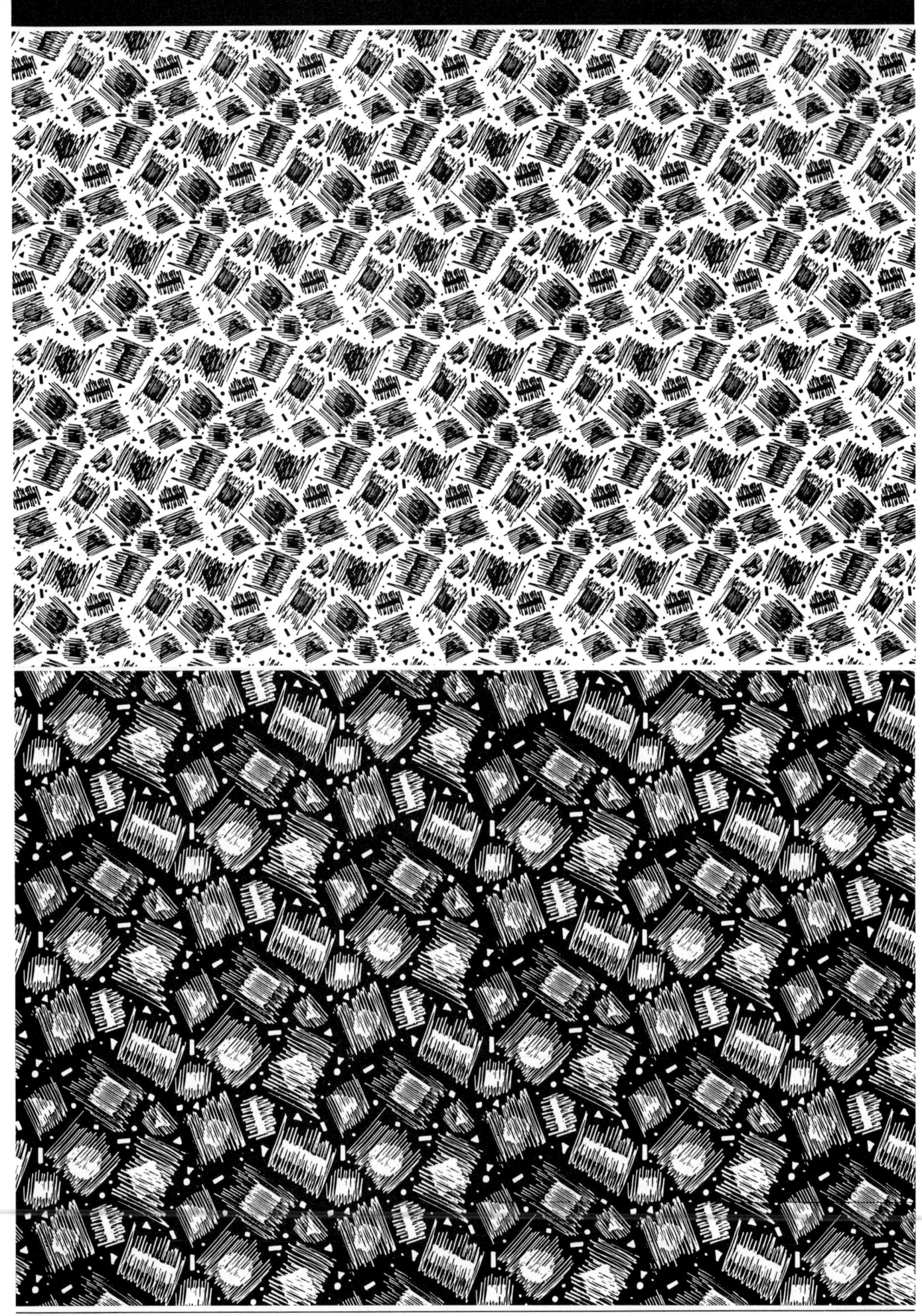

BASIC ELEMENTS BA66

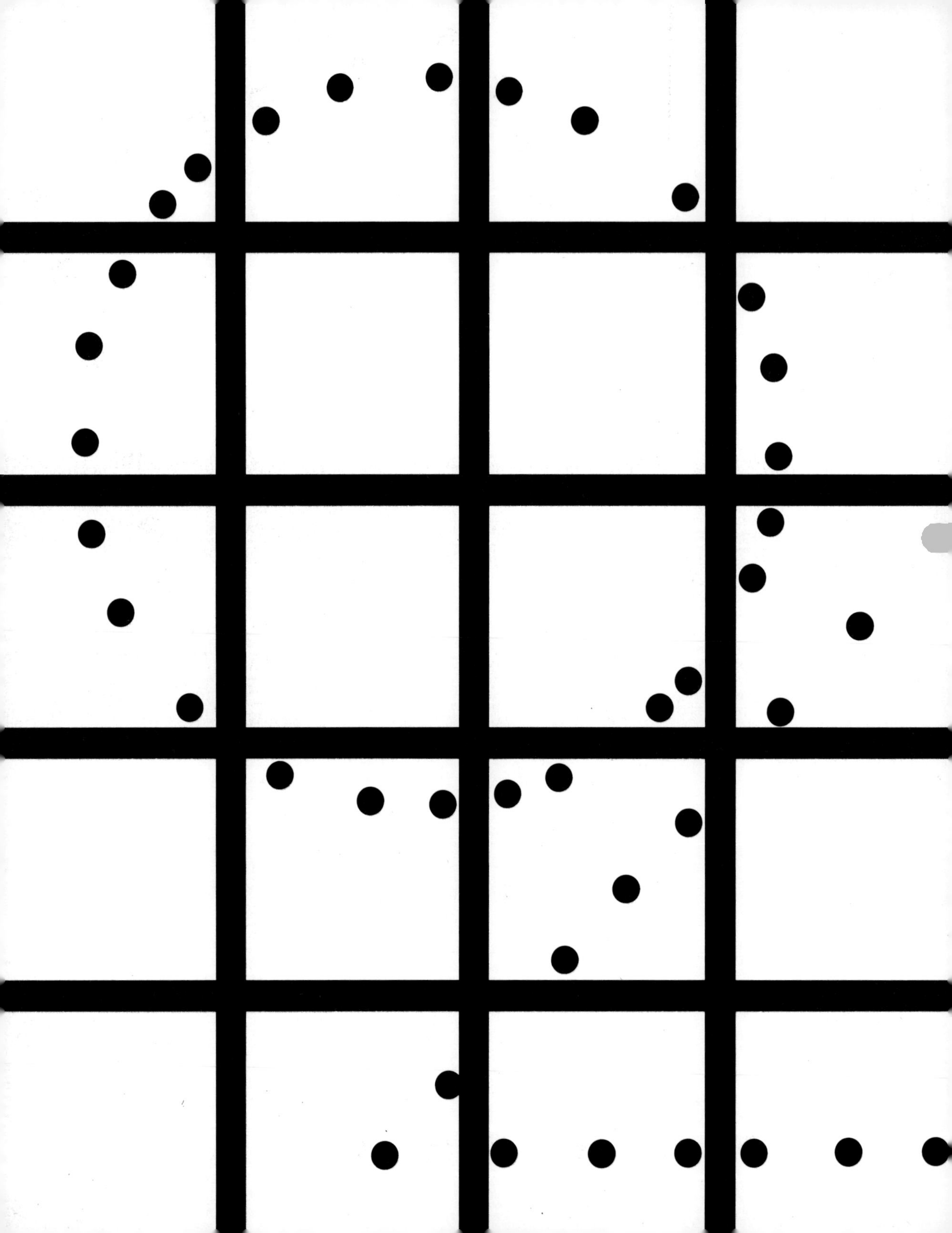

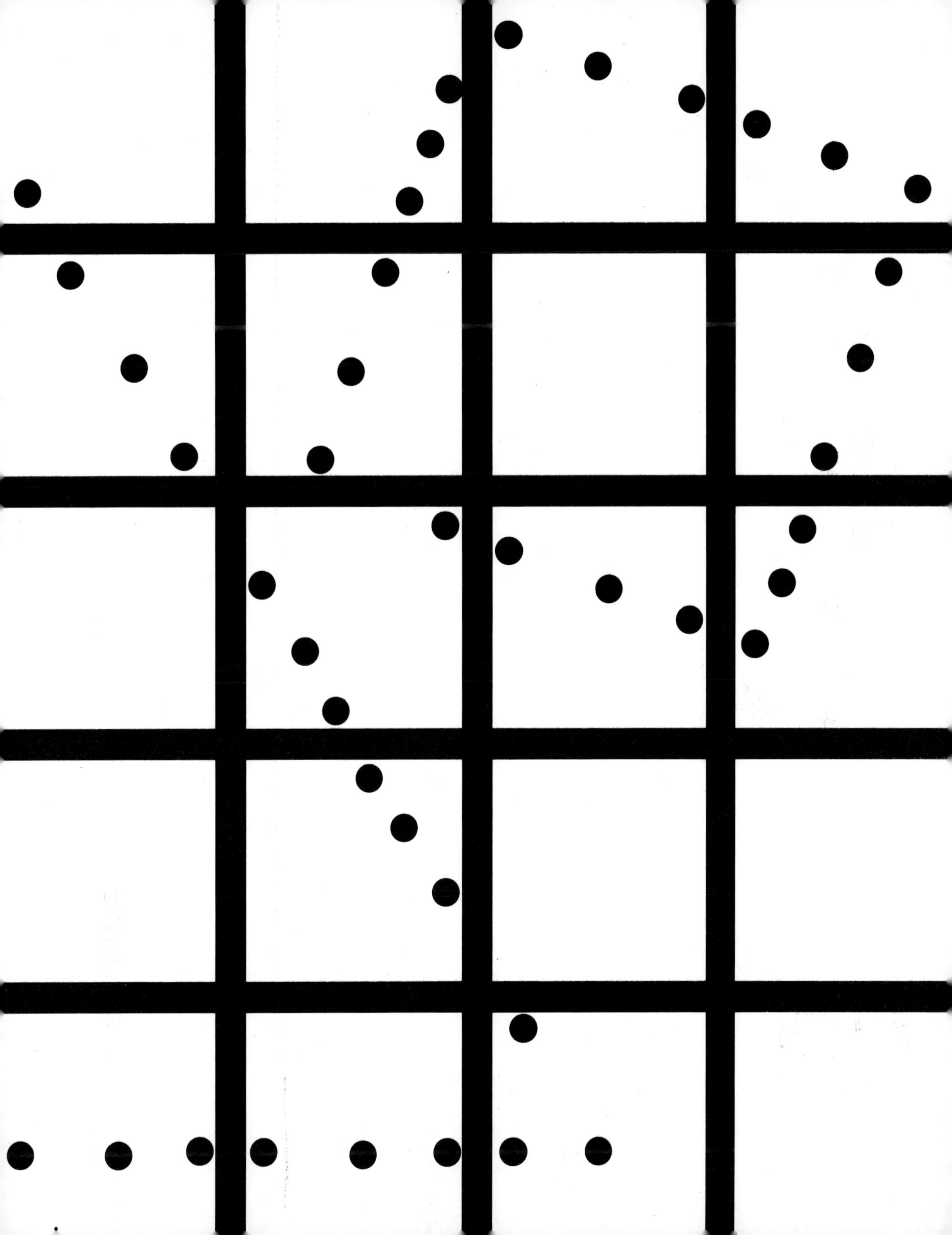

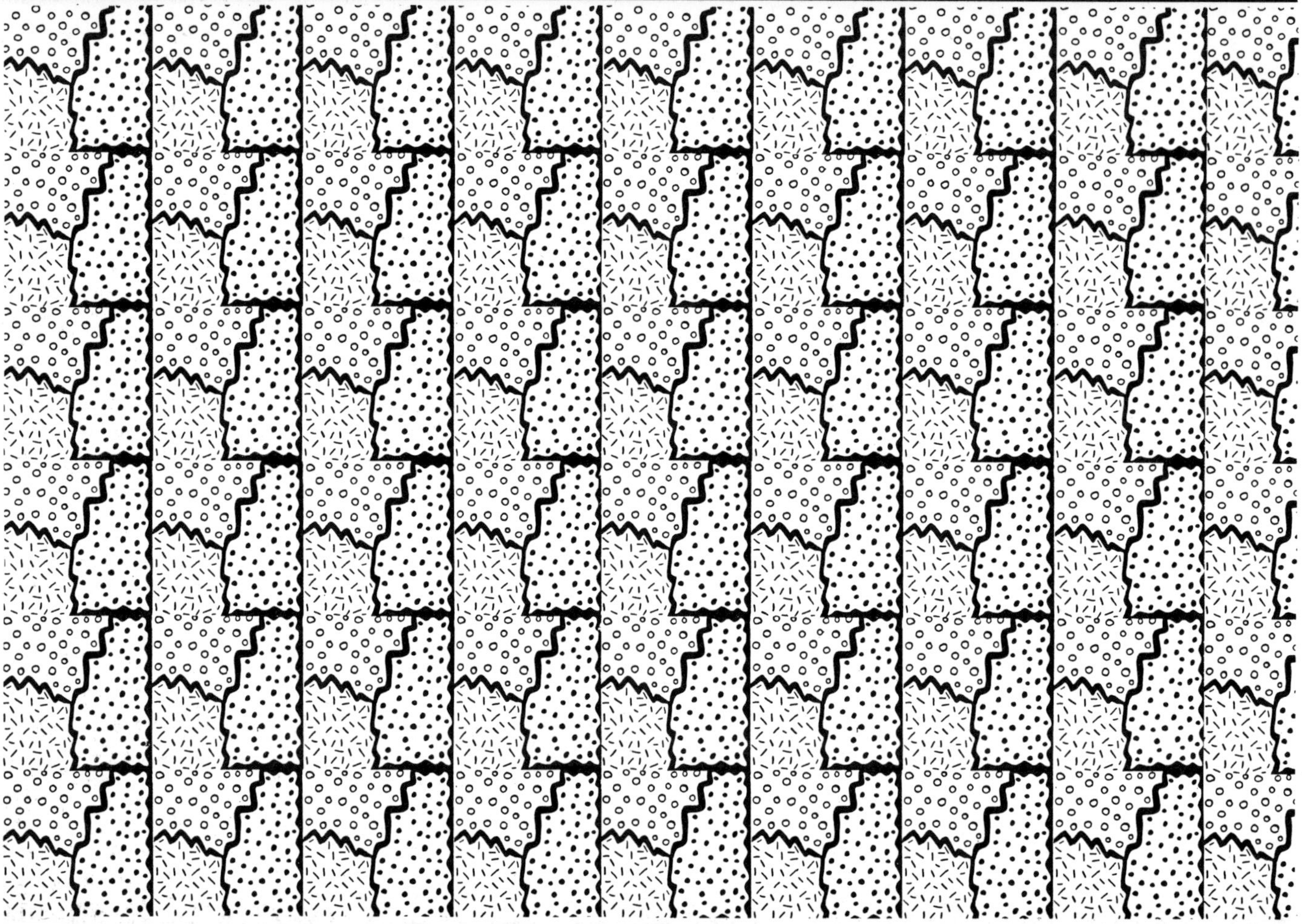

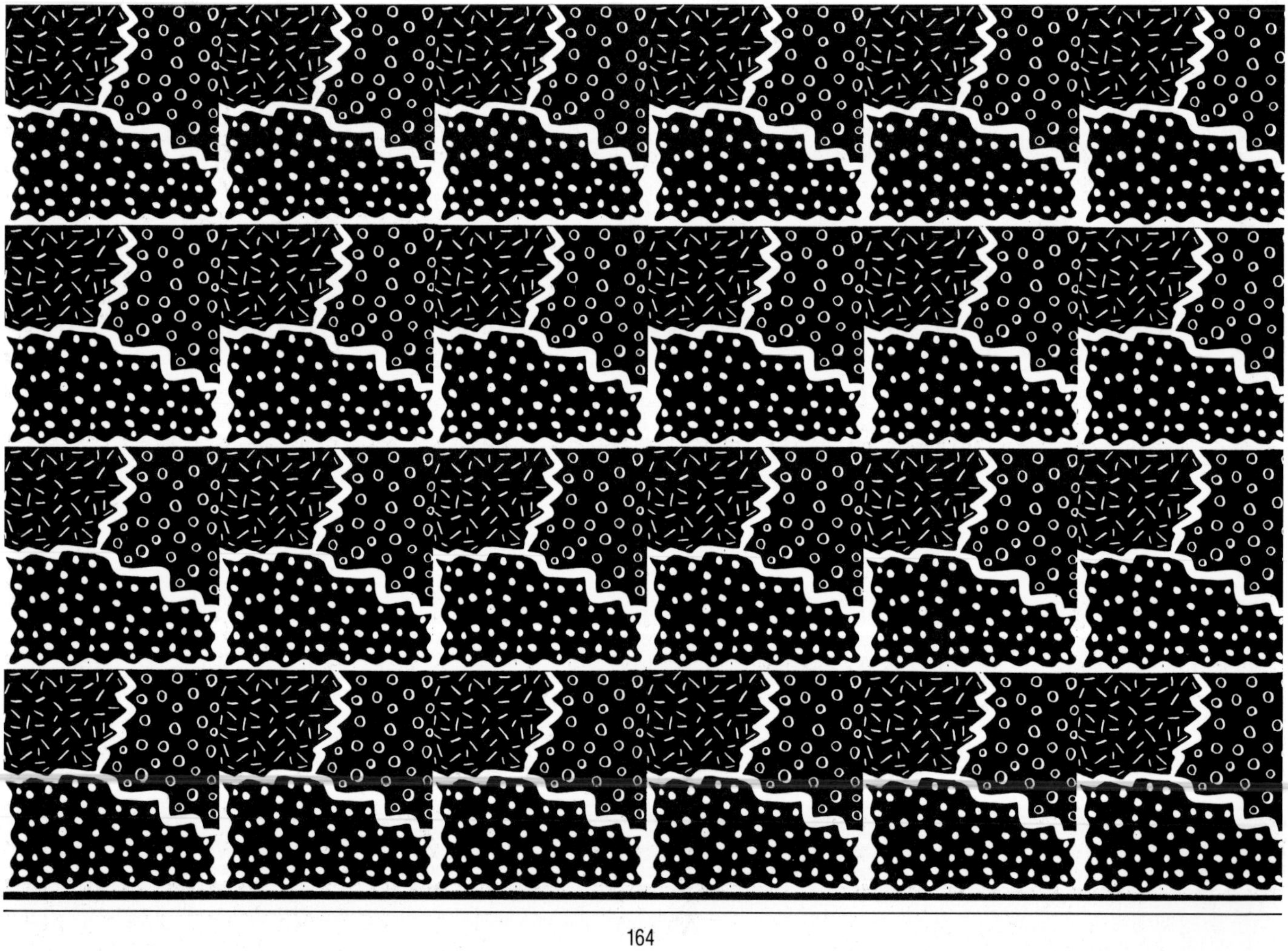

BASIC ELEMENTS   BA67

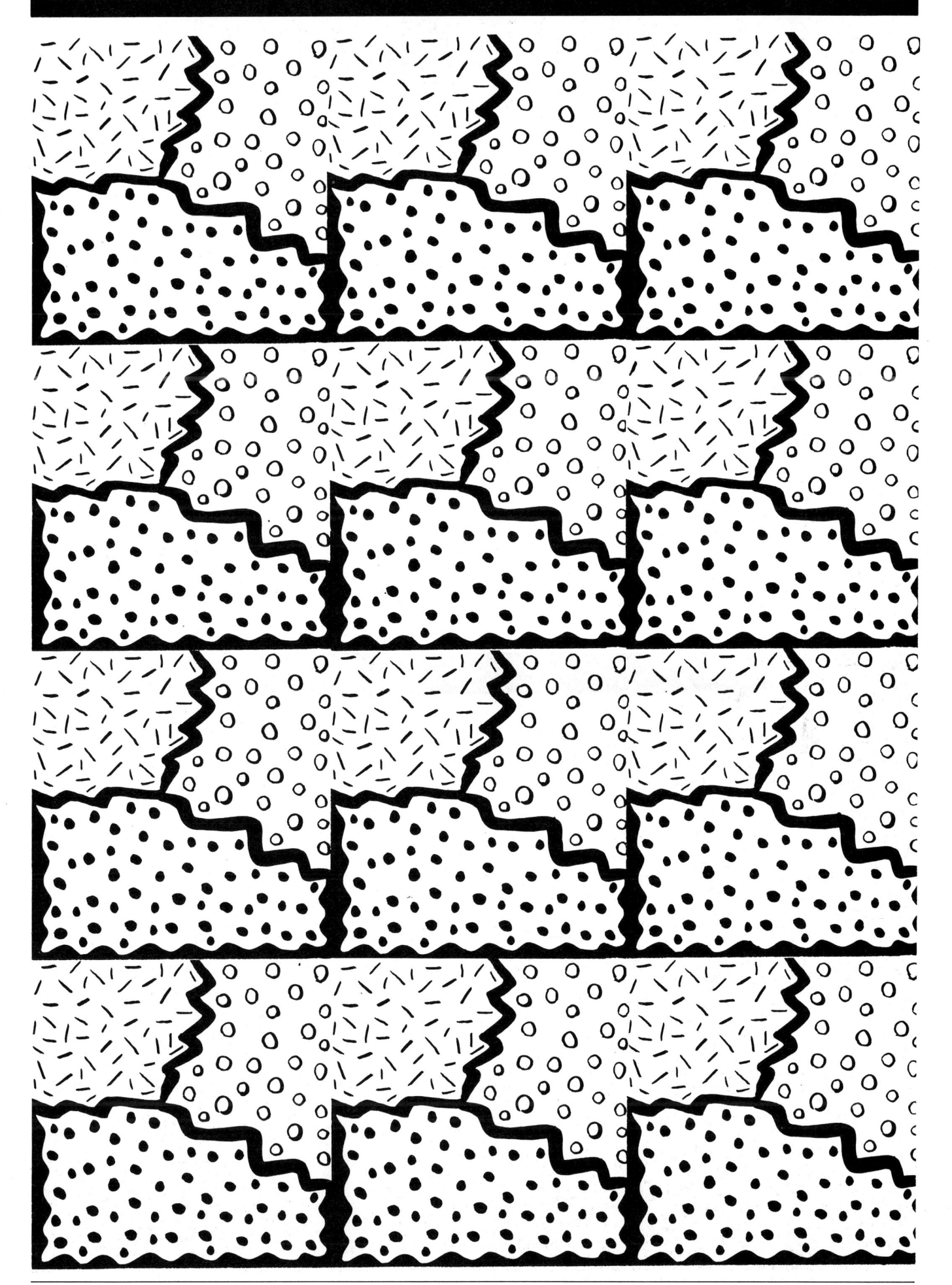

166

BASIC ELEMENTS

BA68

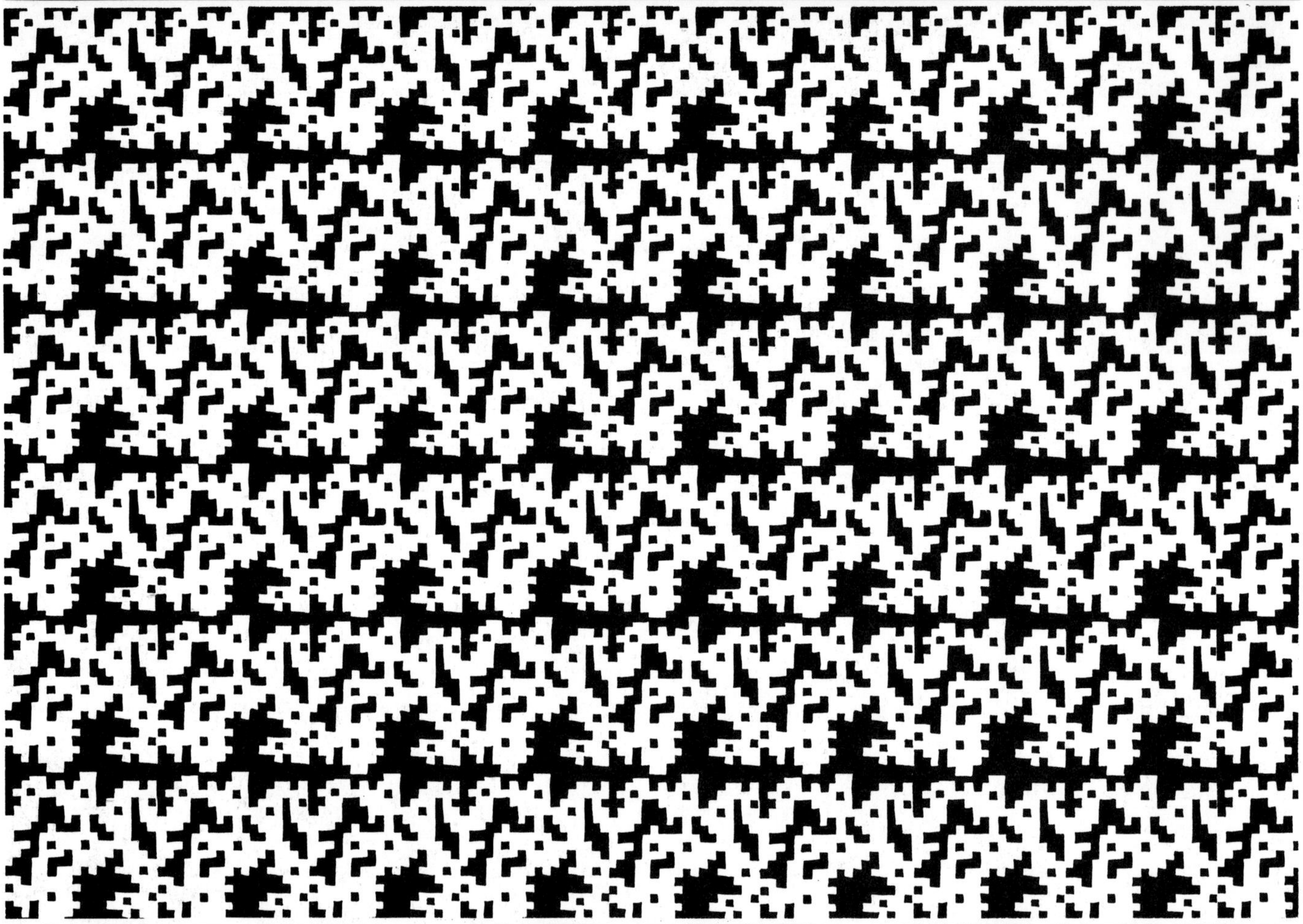

BASIC ELEMENTS BA69

170

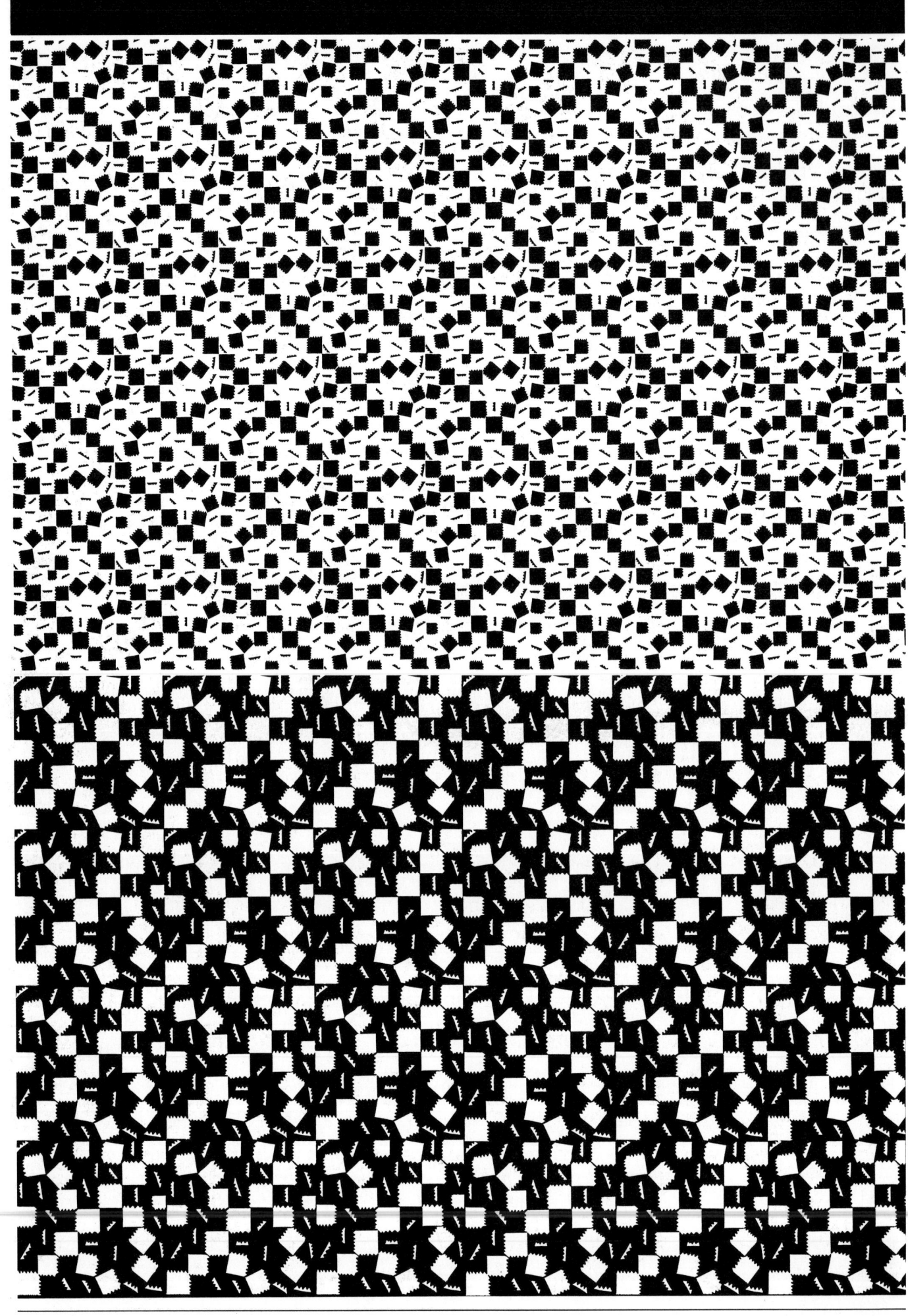

BASIC ELEMENTS BA70

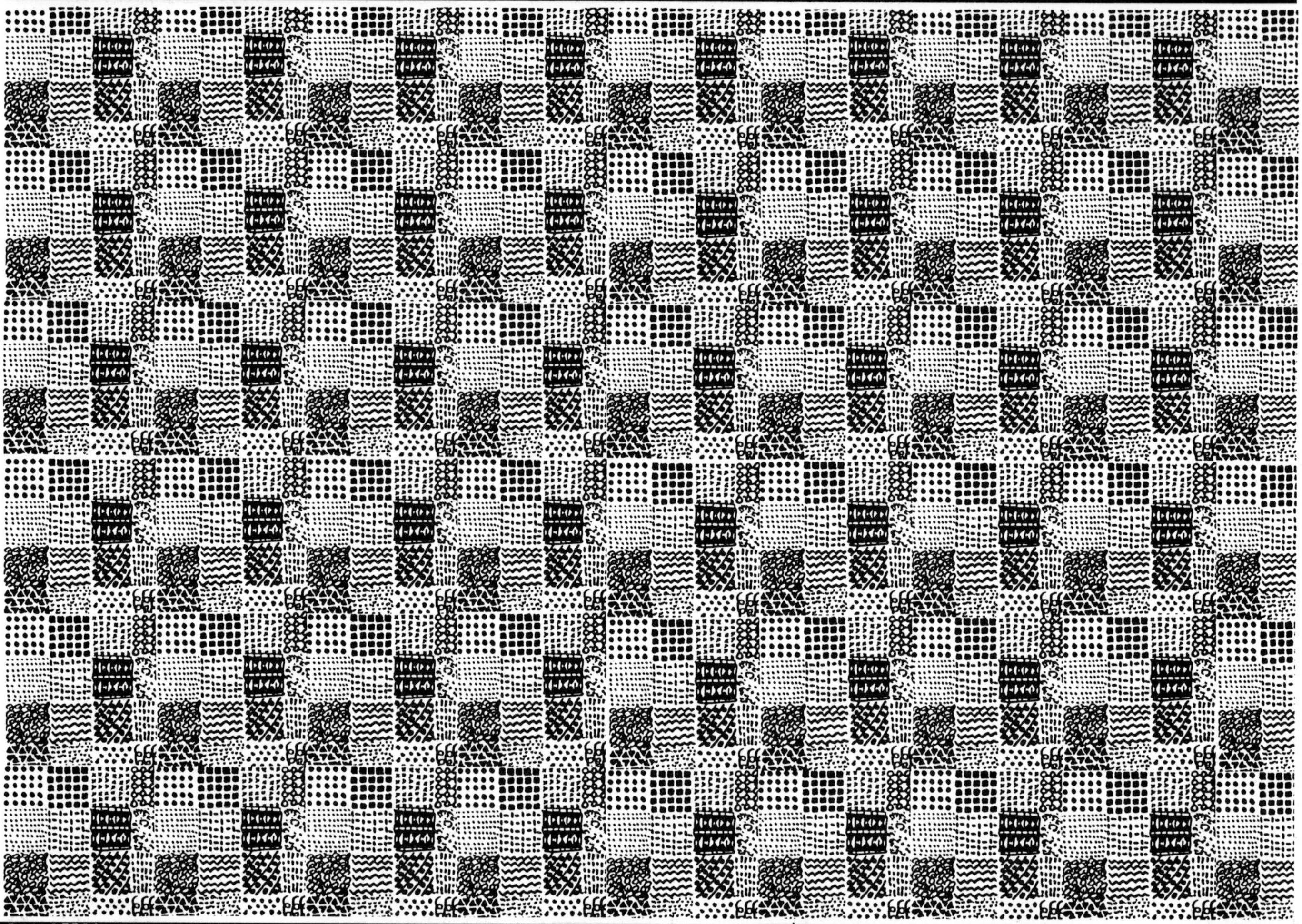

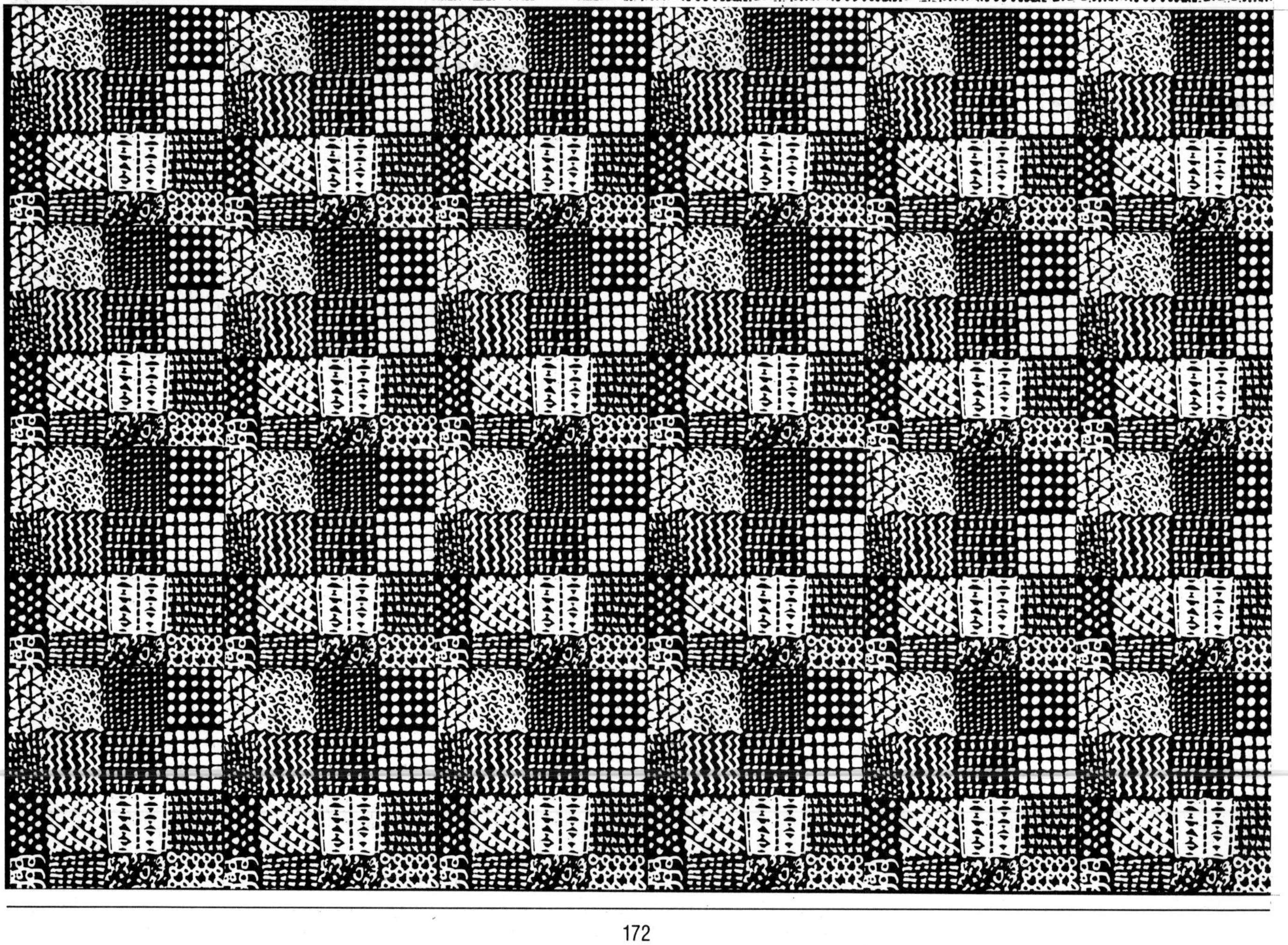

BASIC ELEMENTS BA71

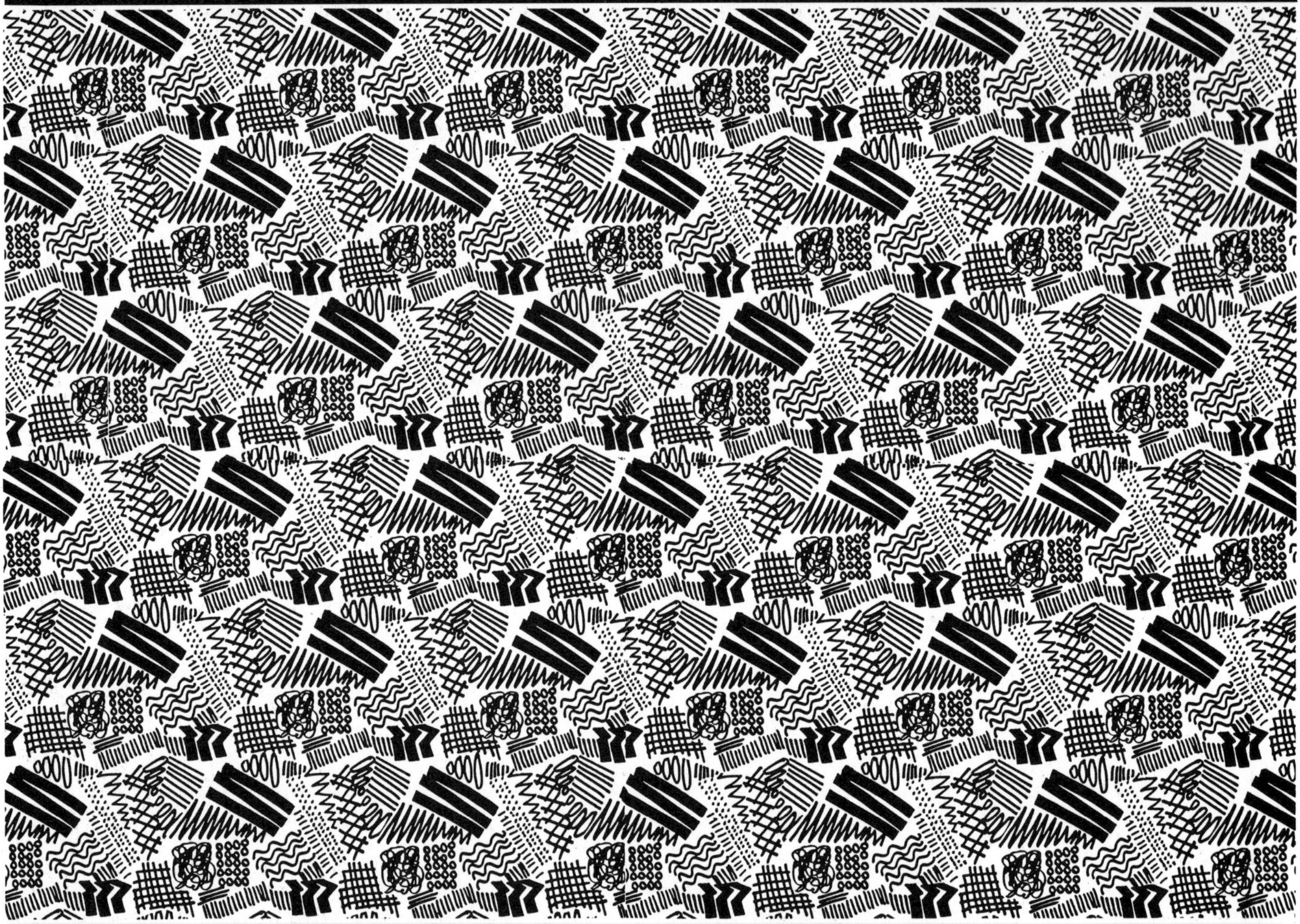

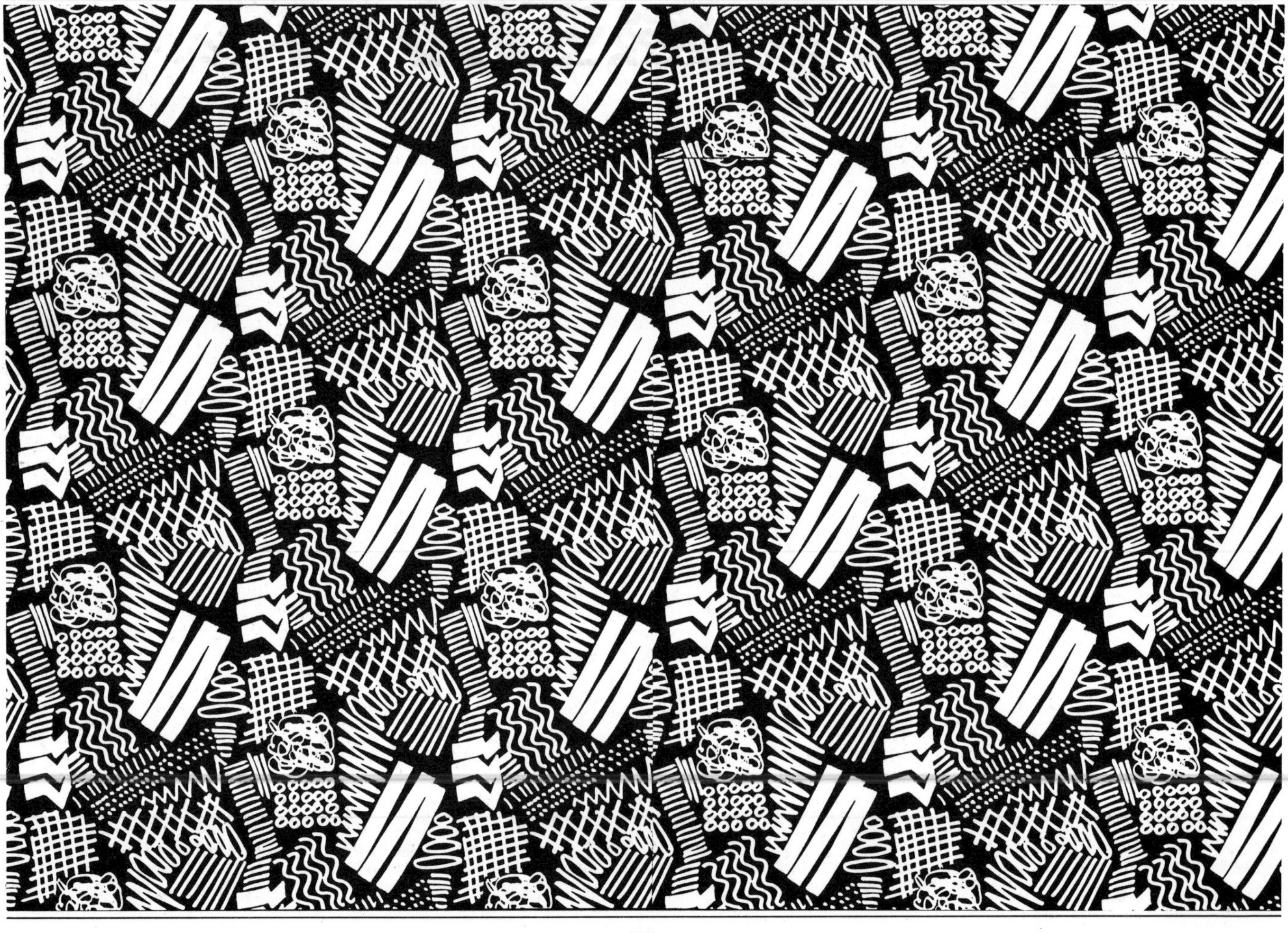

BASIC ELEMENTS

BA72

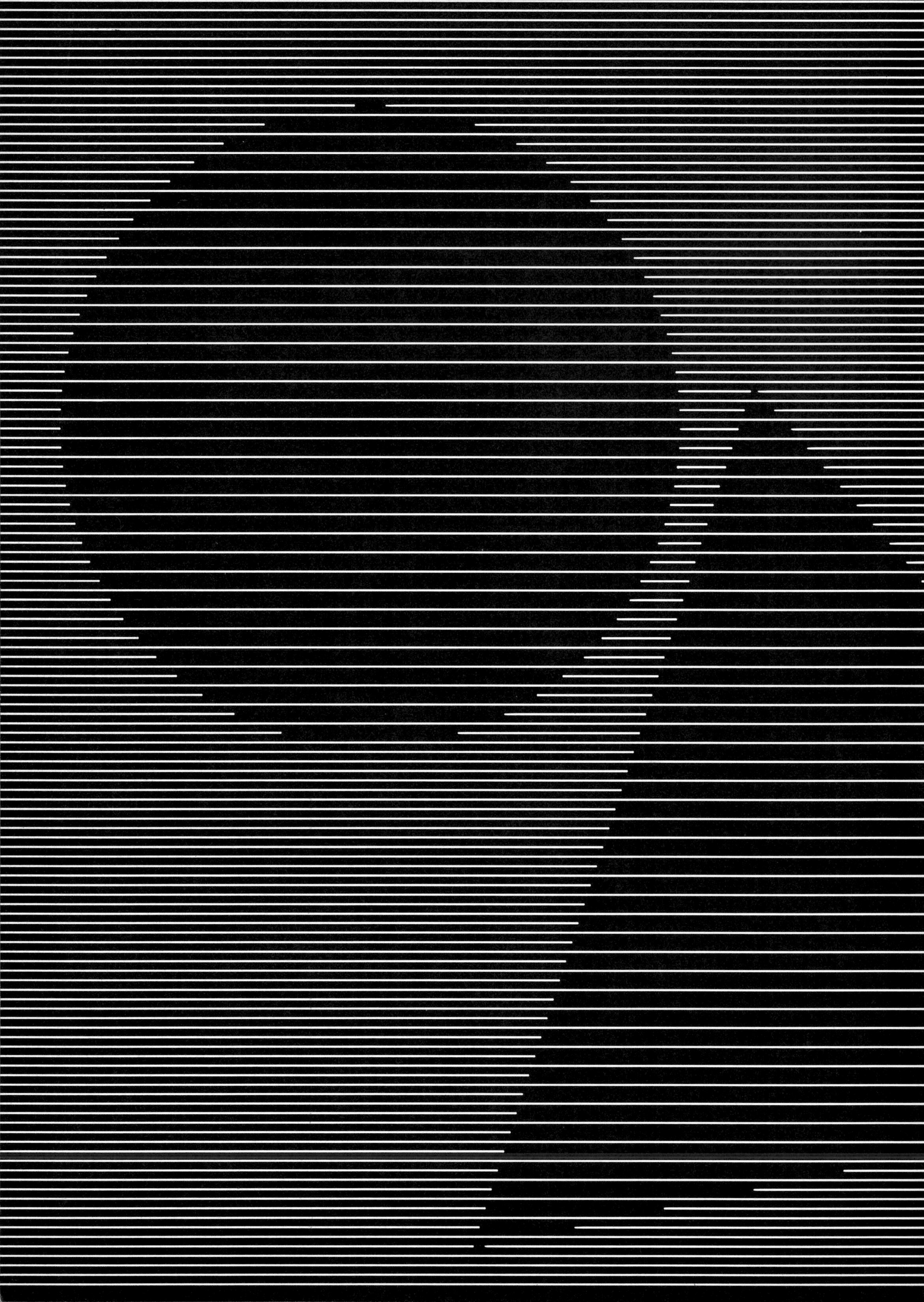

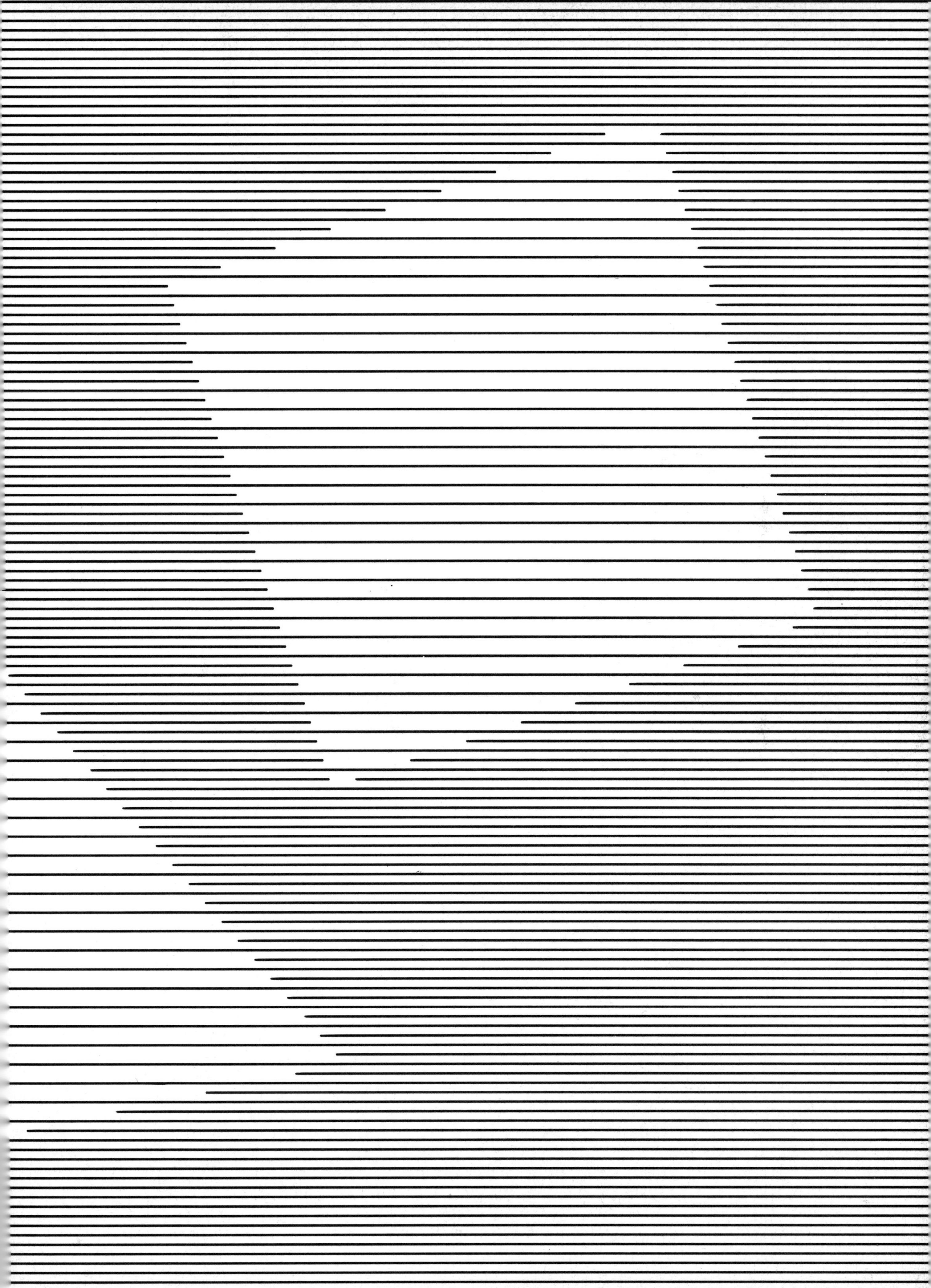

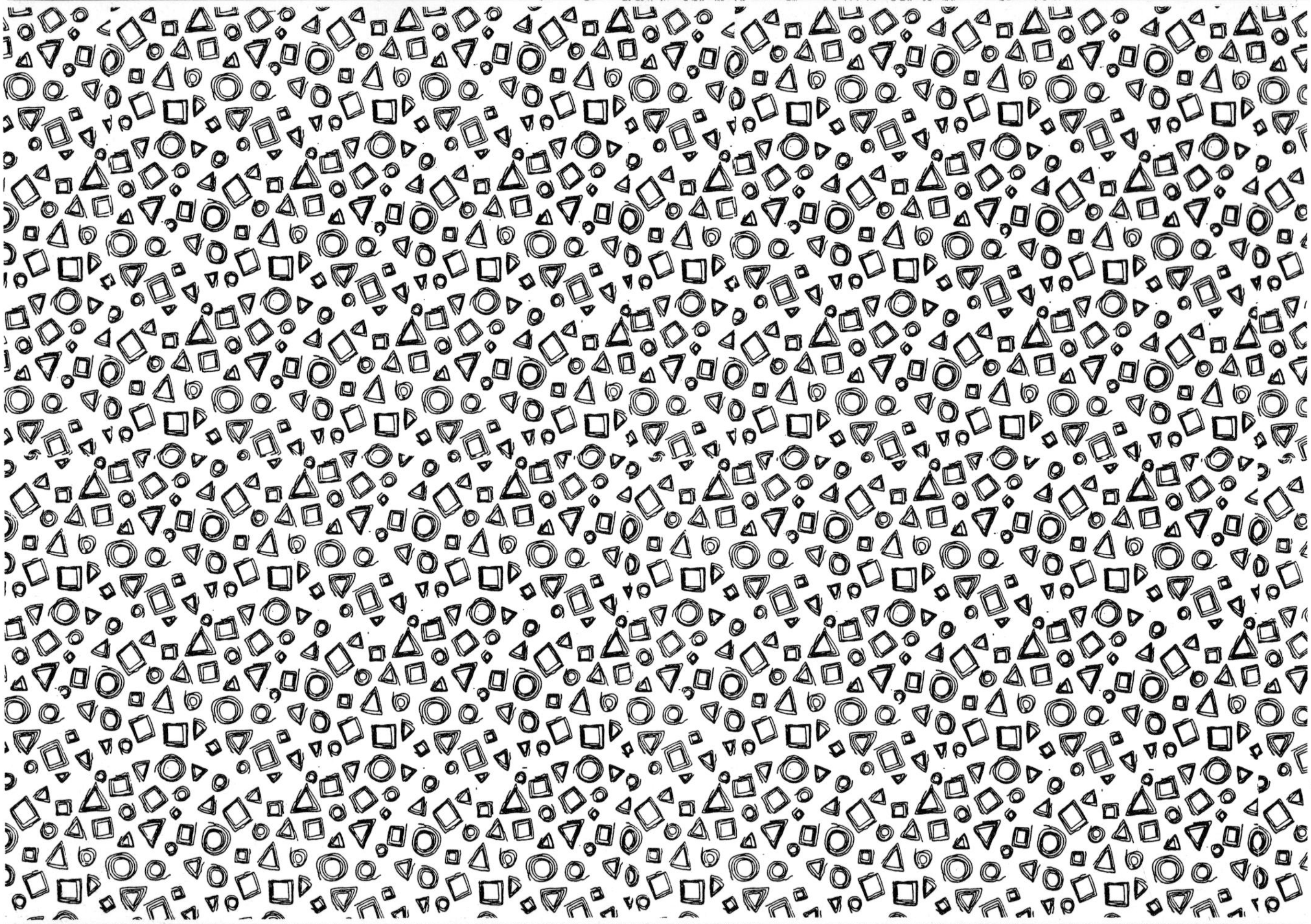

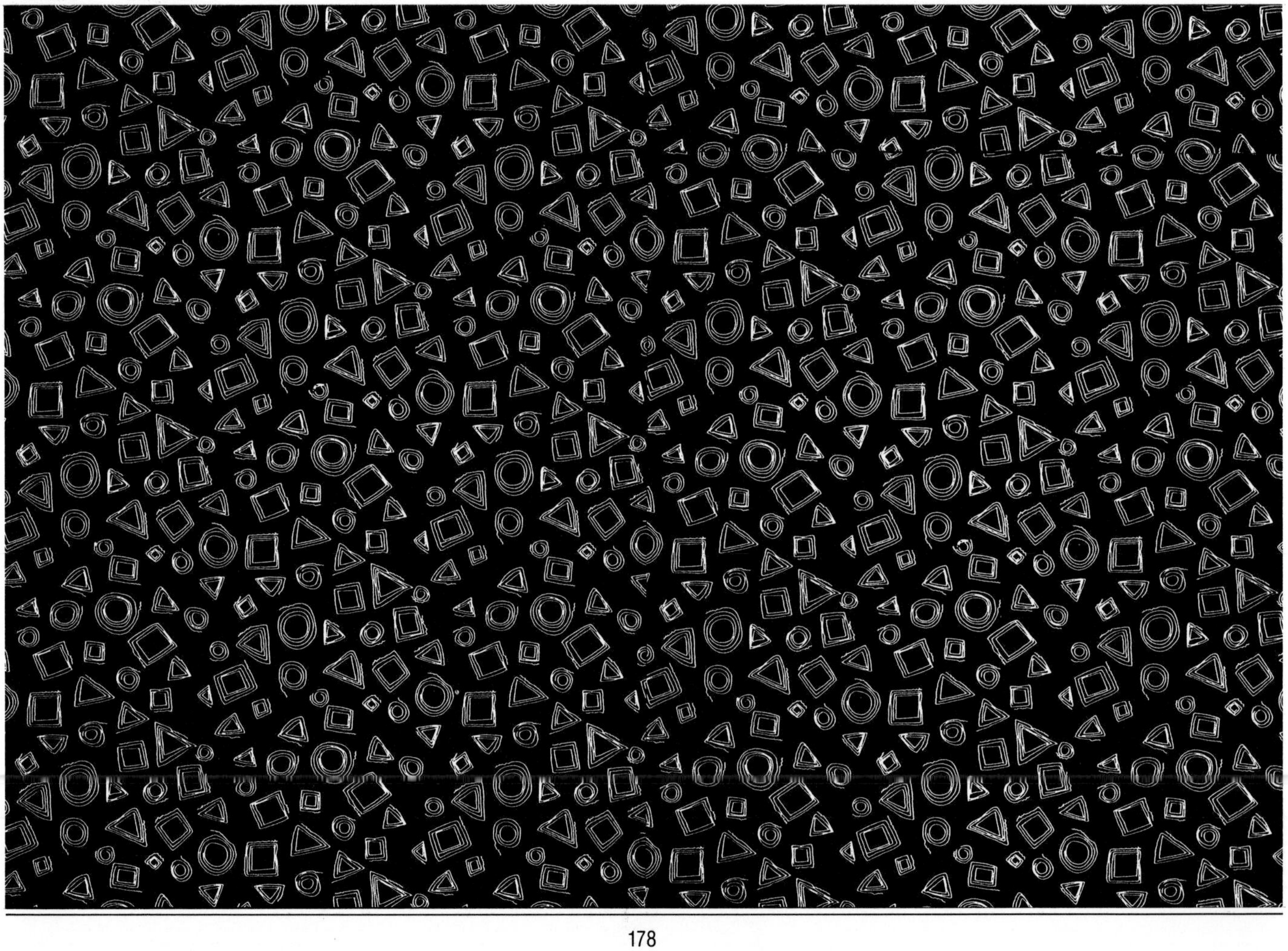

BASIC ELEMENTS BA73

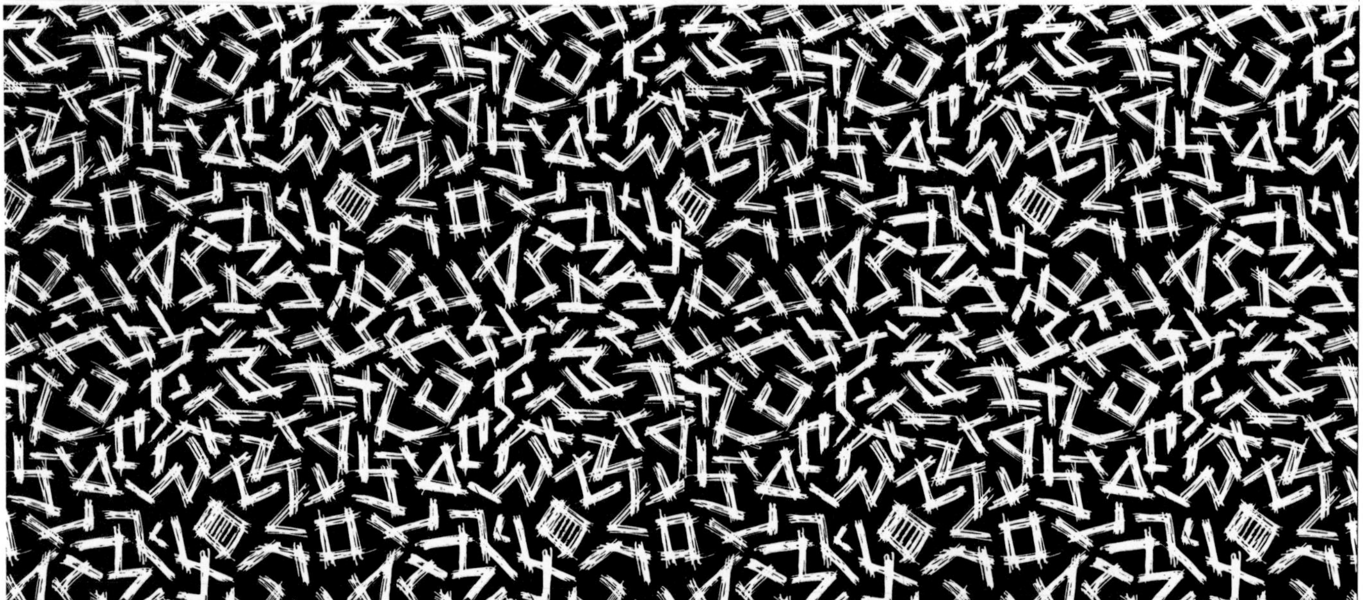

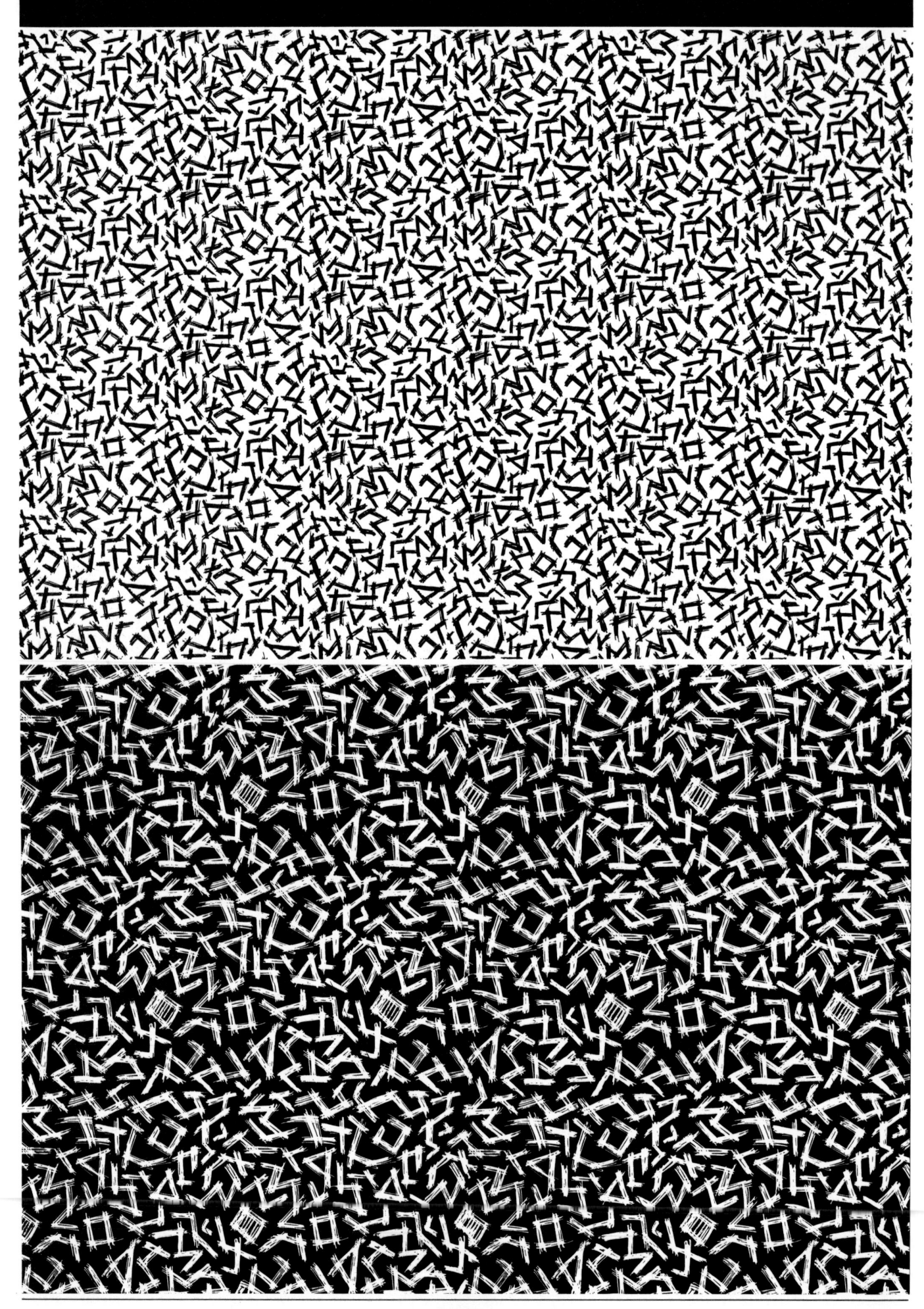

BASIC ELEMENTS

BA74

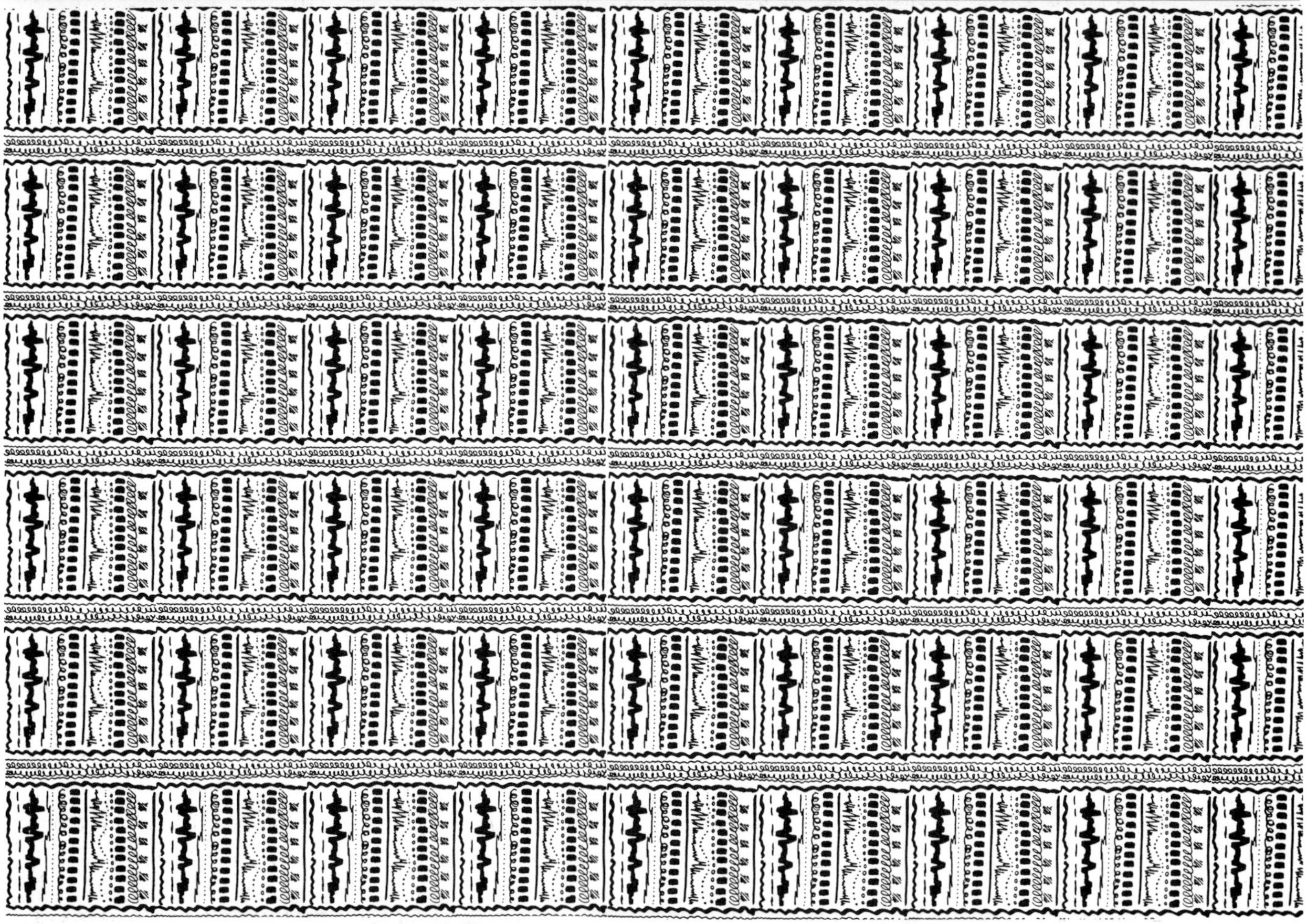

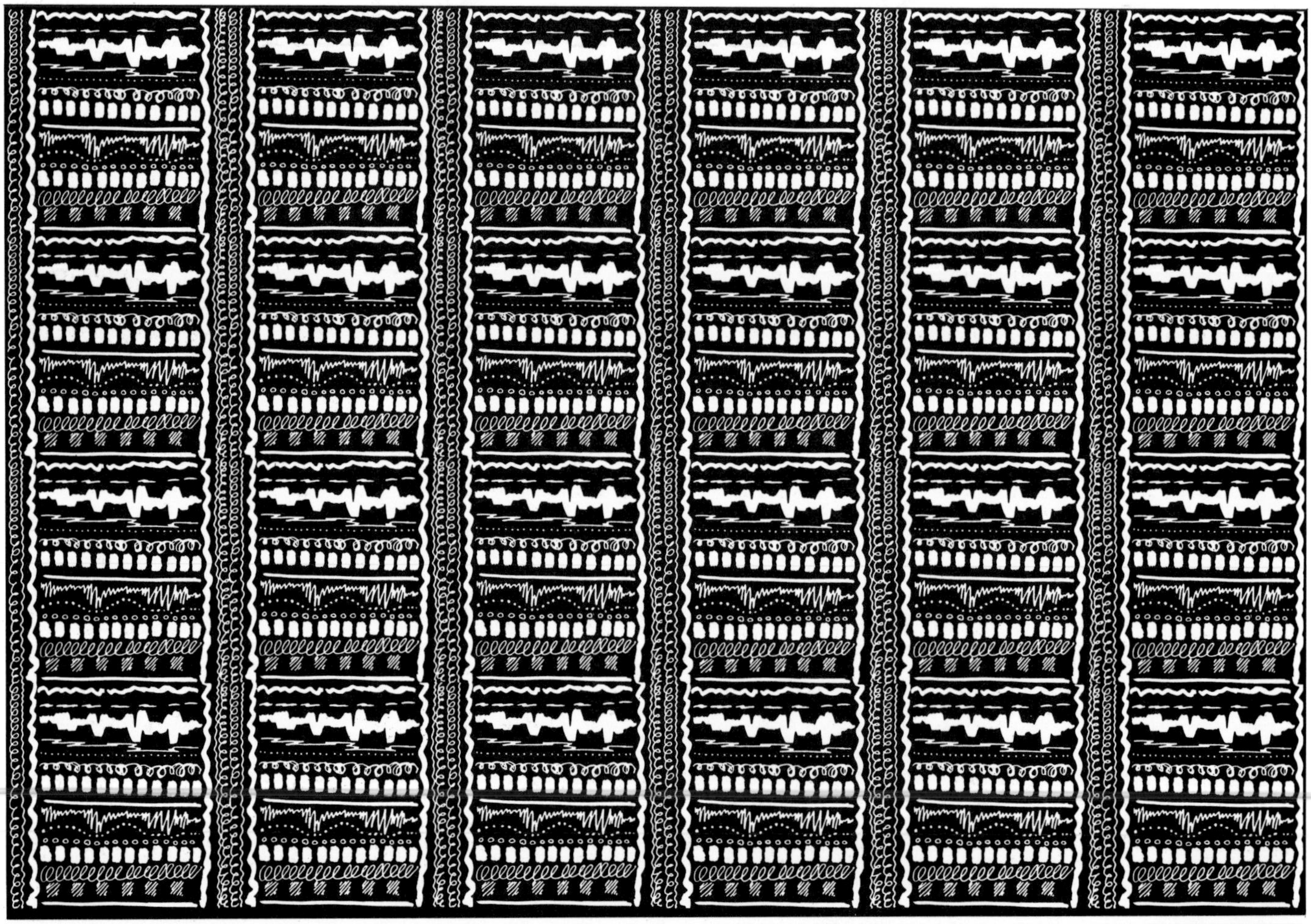

BASIC ELEMENTS BA75

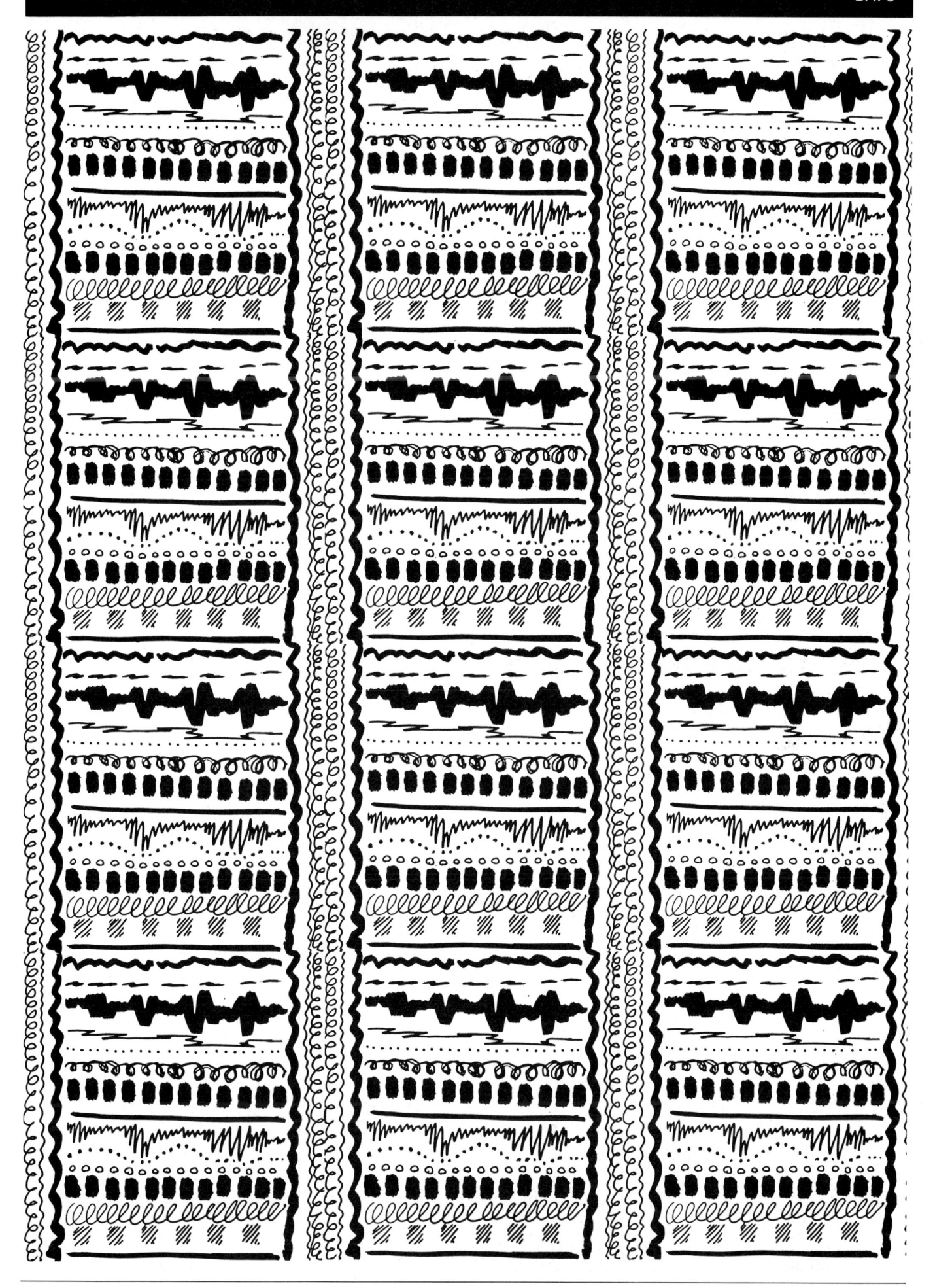

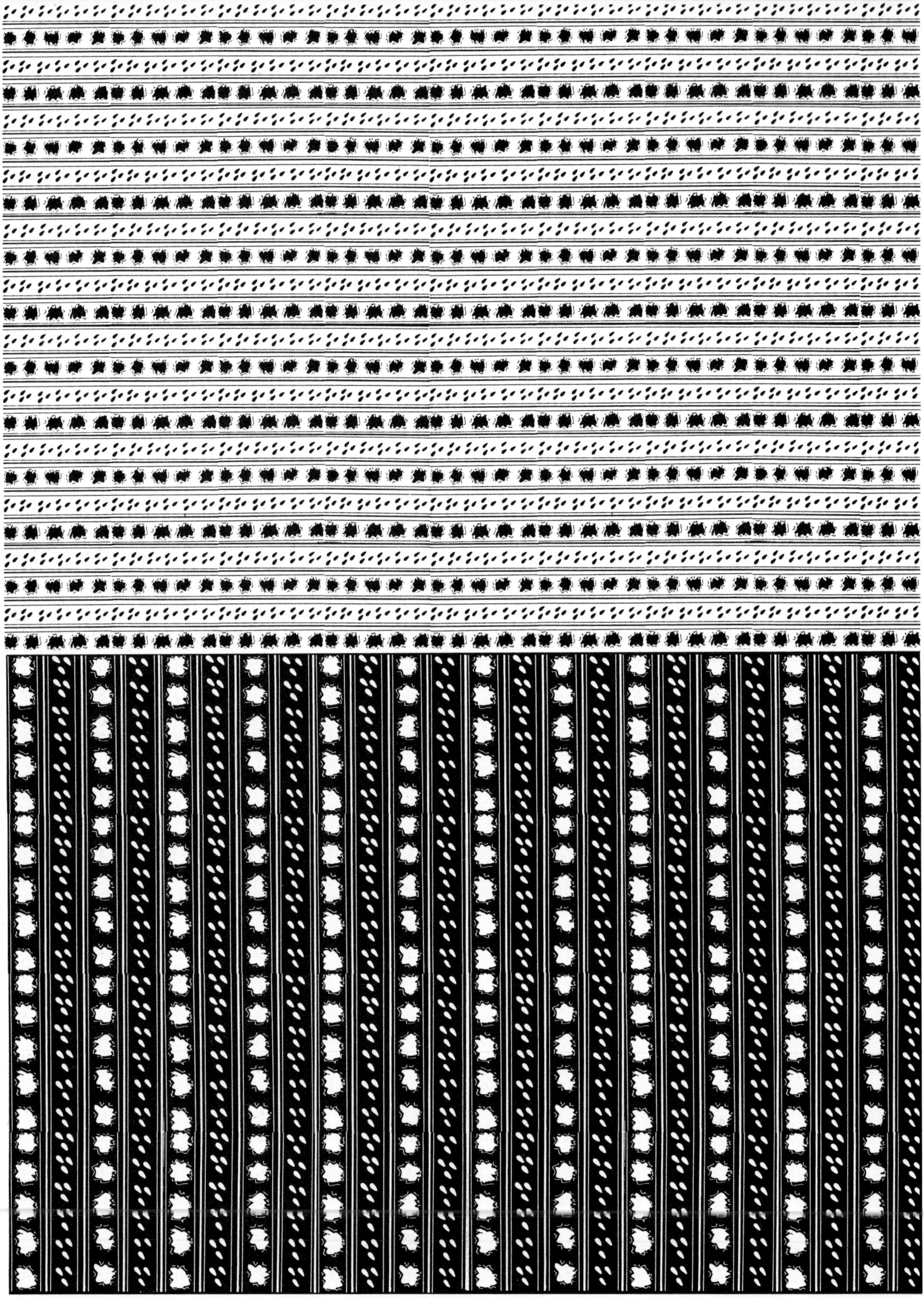

BASIC ELEMENTS

BA76

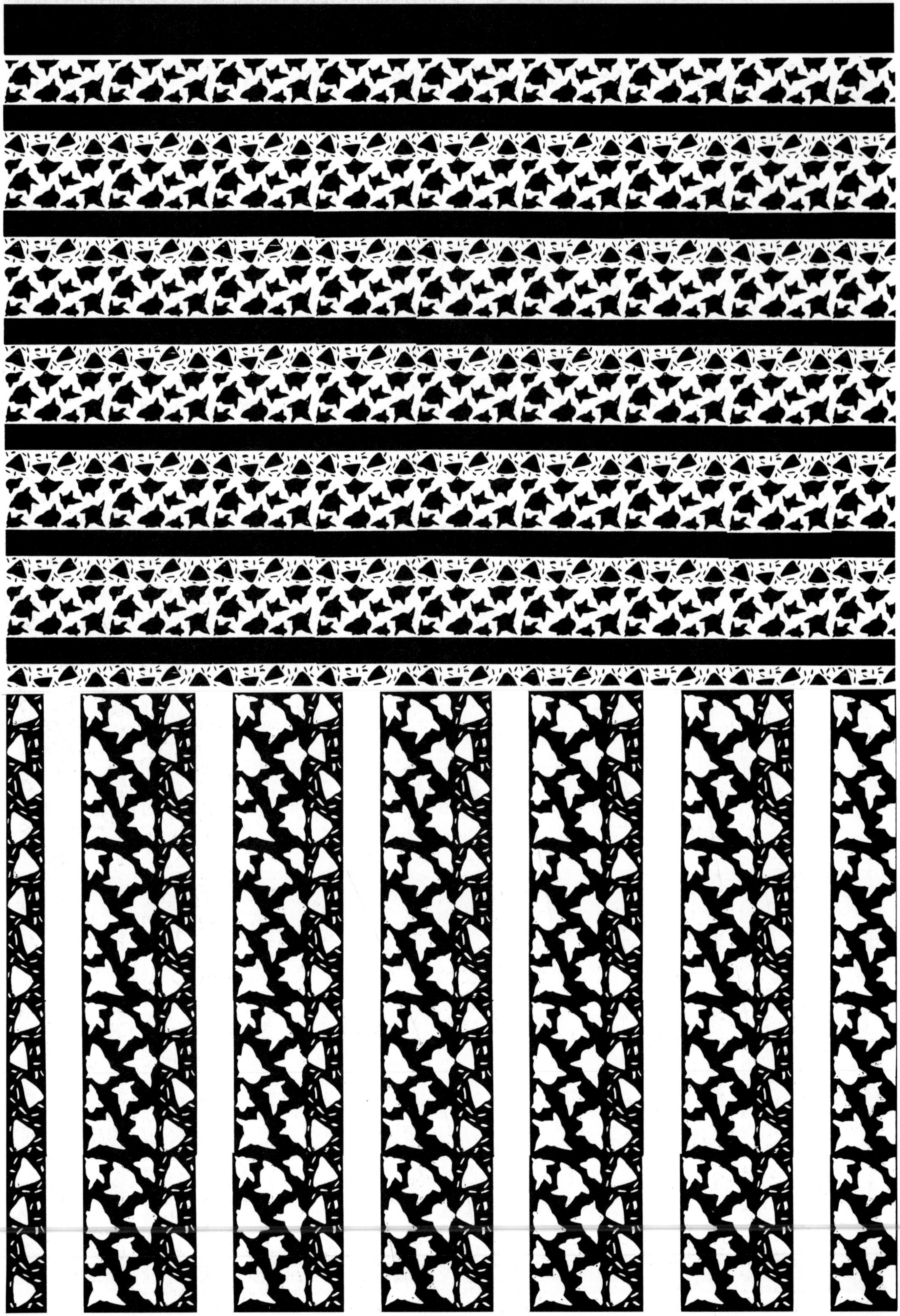

BASIC ELEMENTS

BA77

188

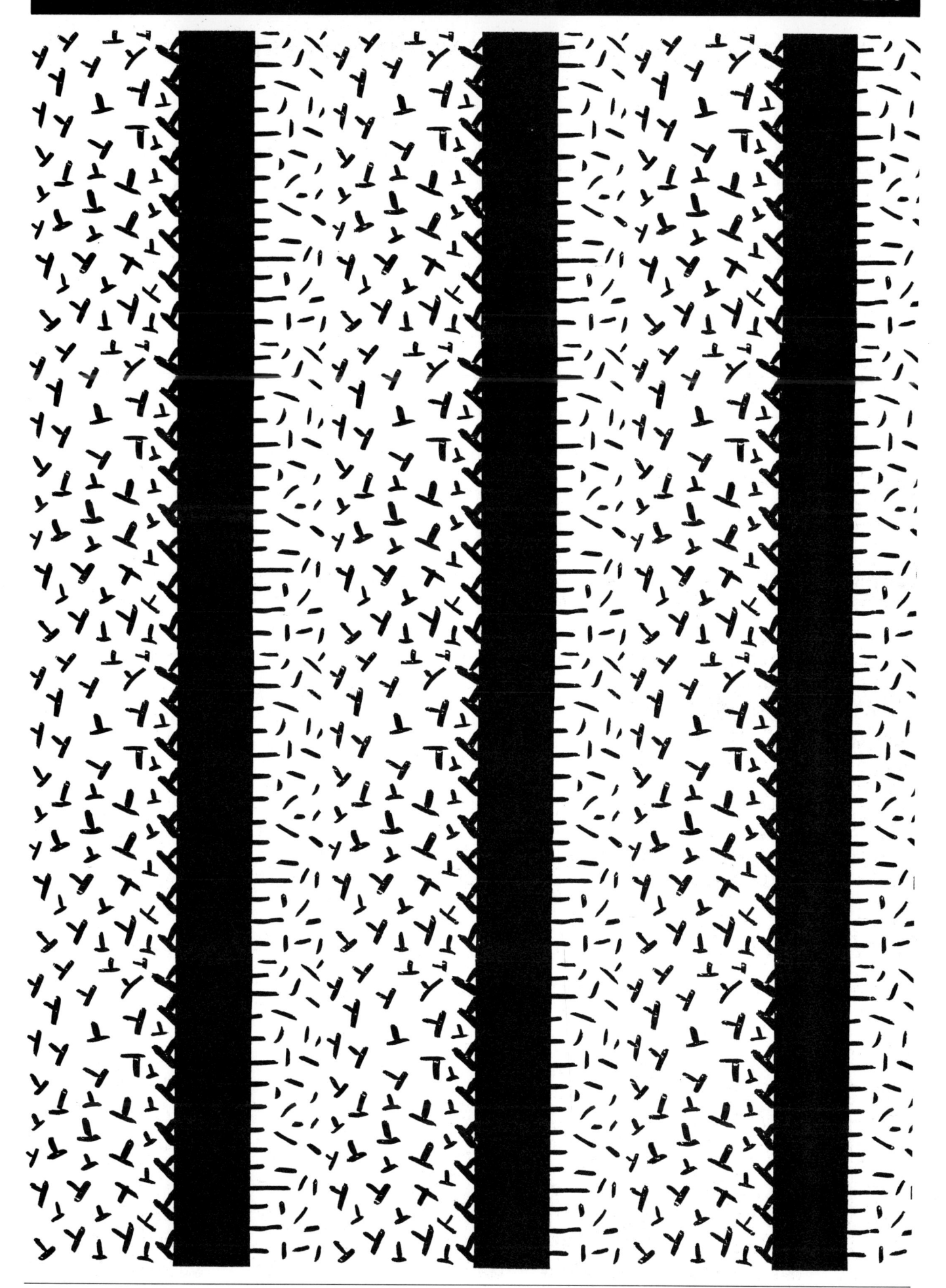

BASIC ELEMENTS — BA78

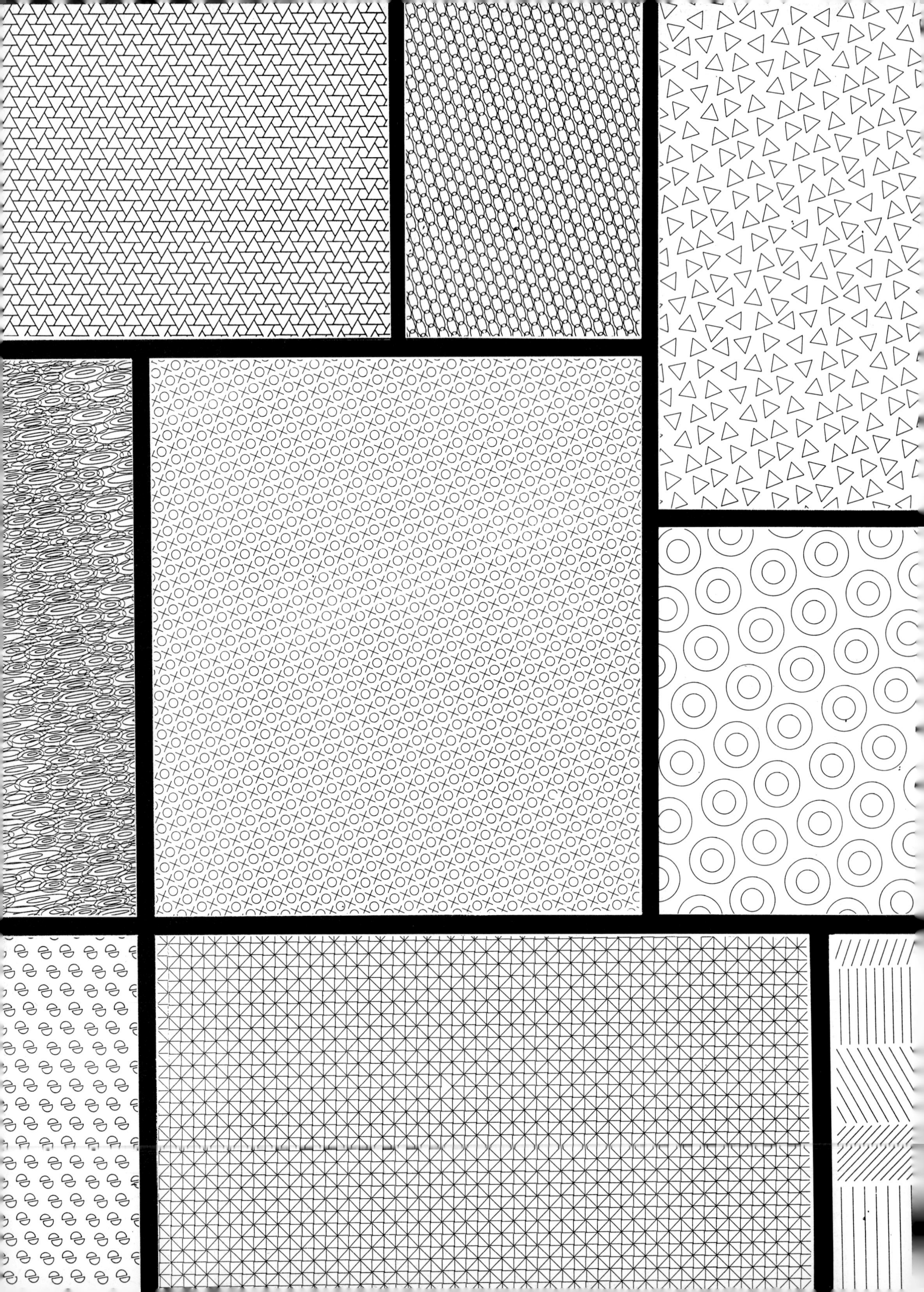

192

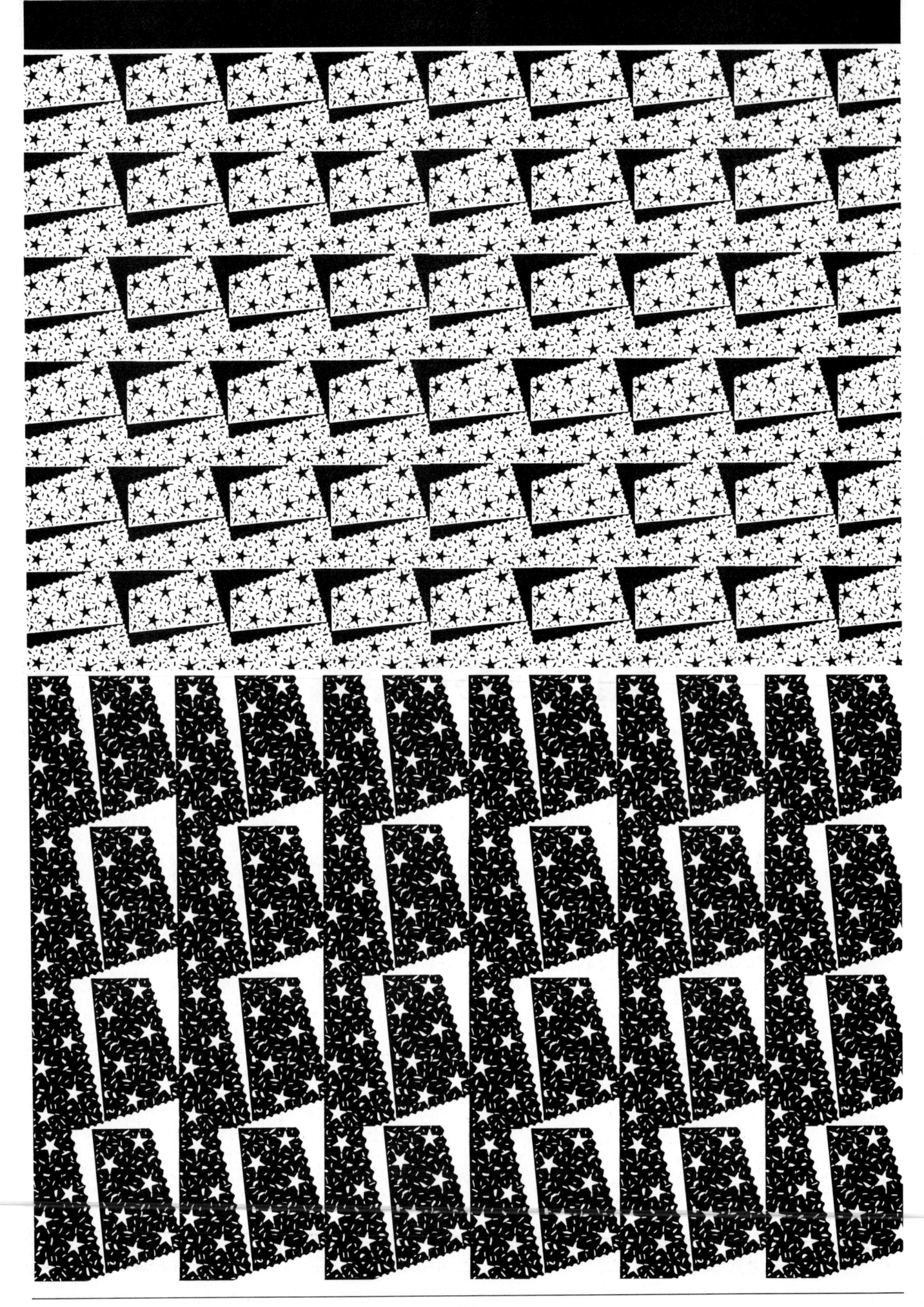

BASIC ELEMENTS BA79

194

BASIC ELEMENTS

BA80

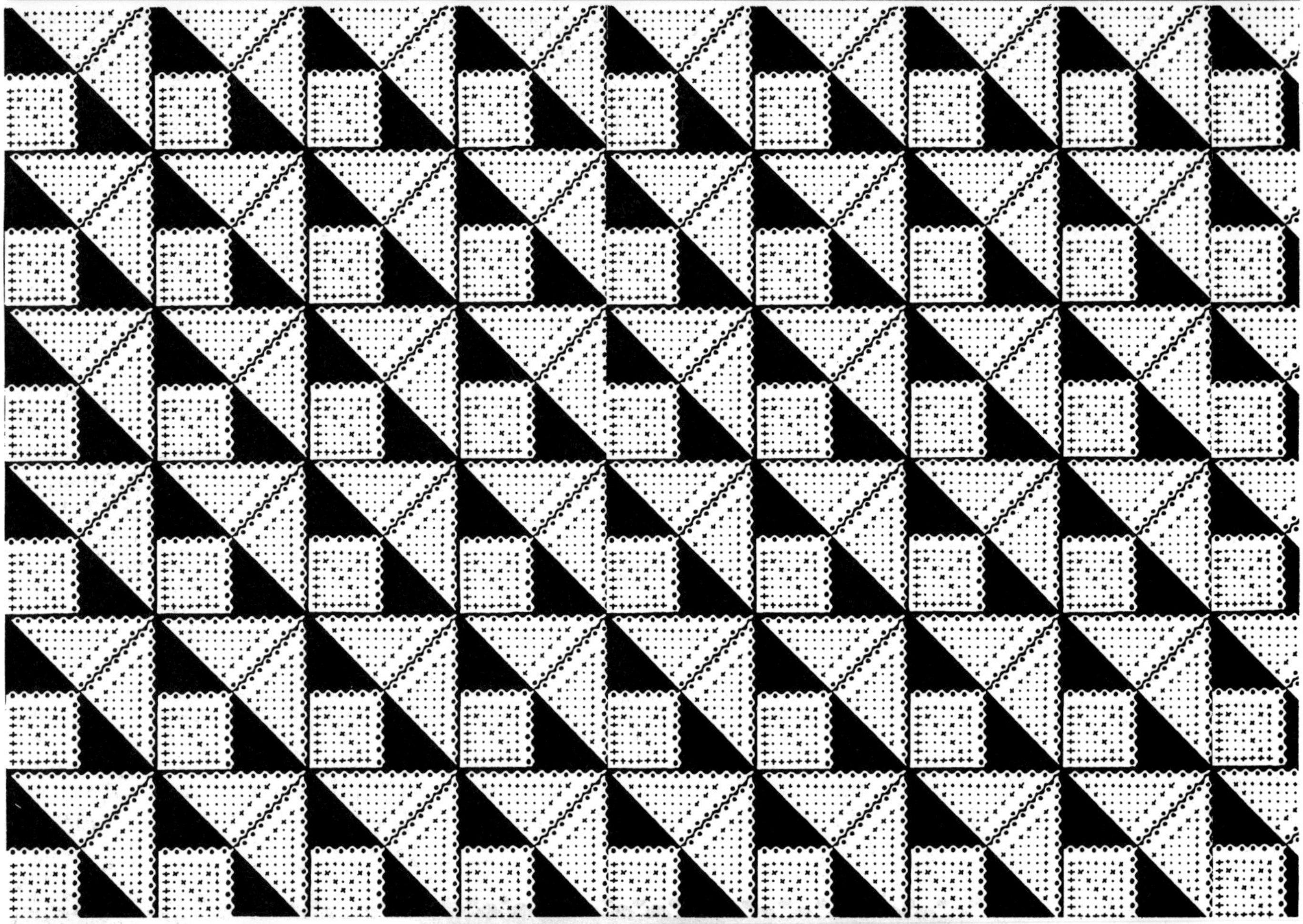

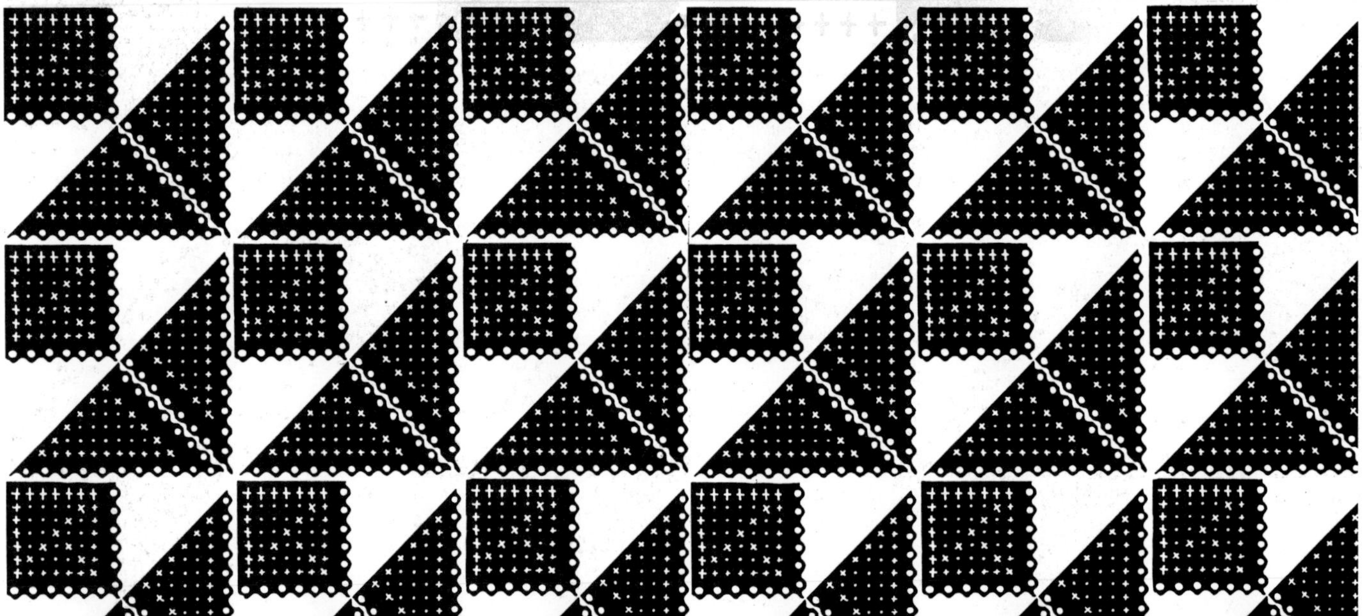

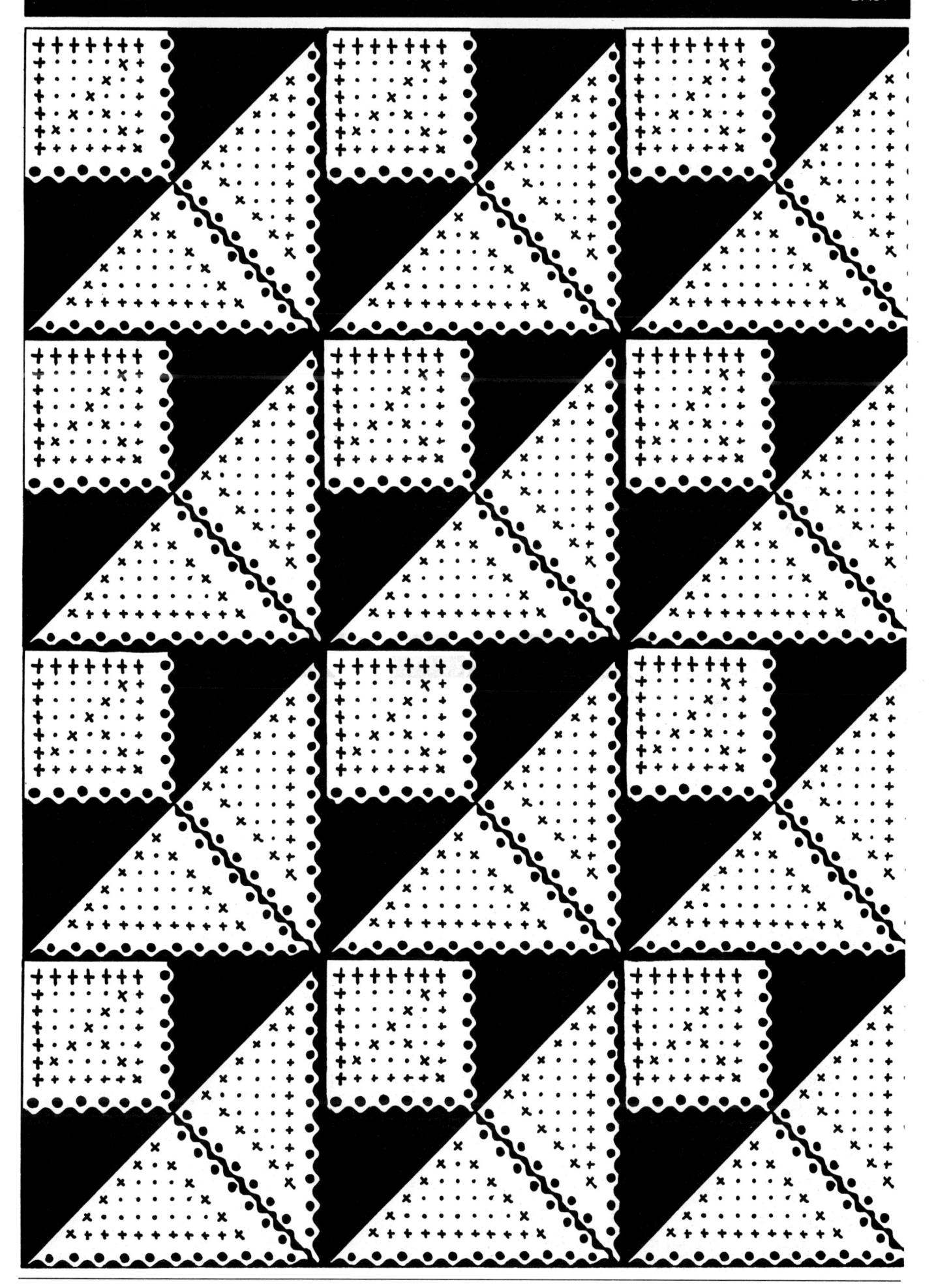

BASIC ELEMENTS

BA81

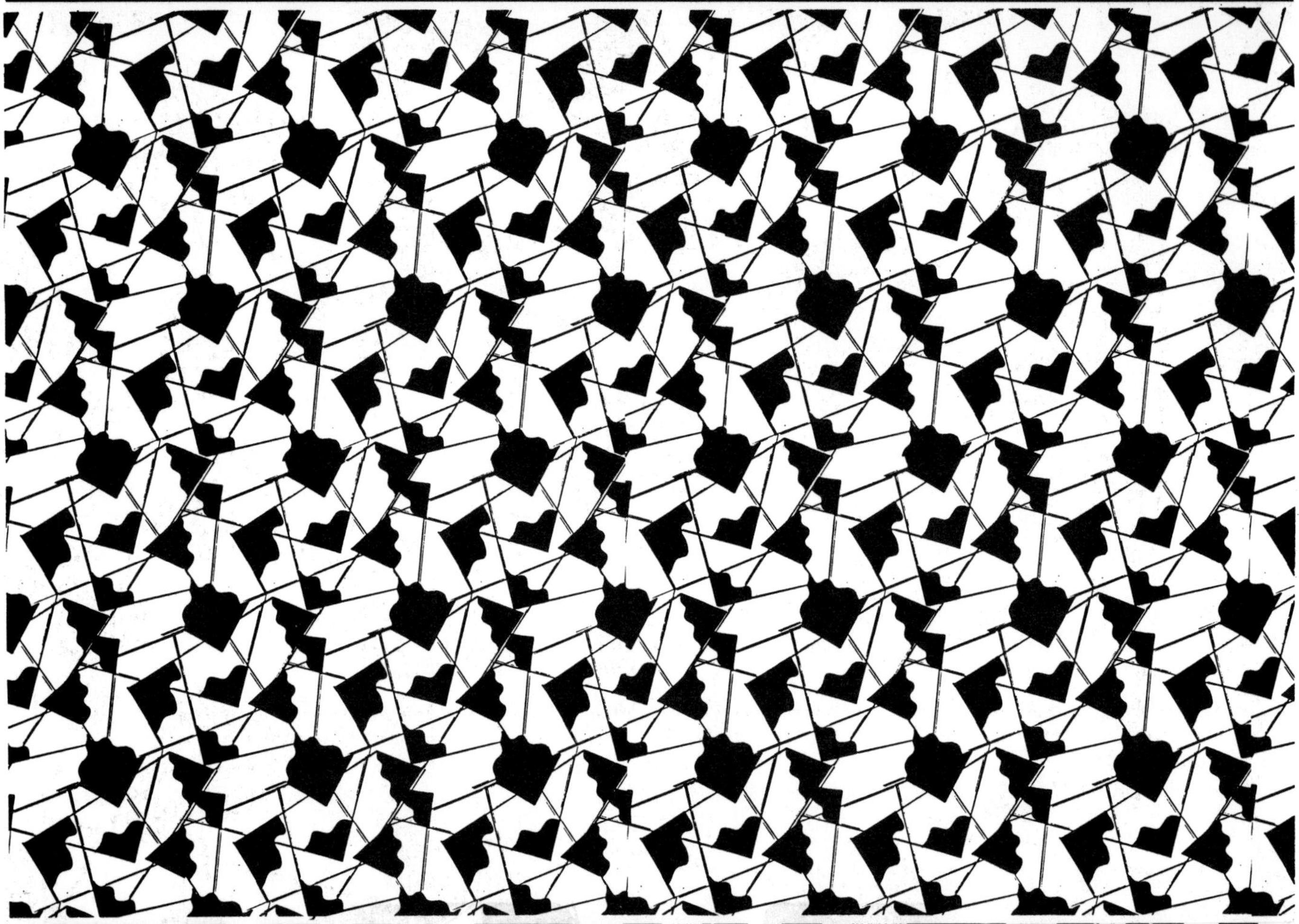

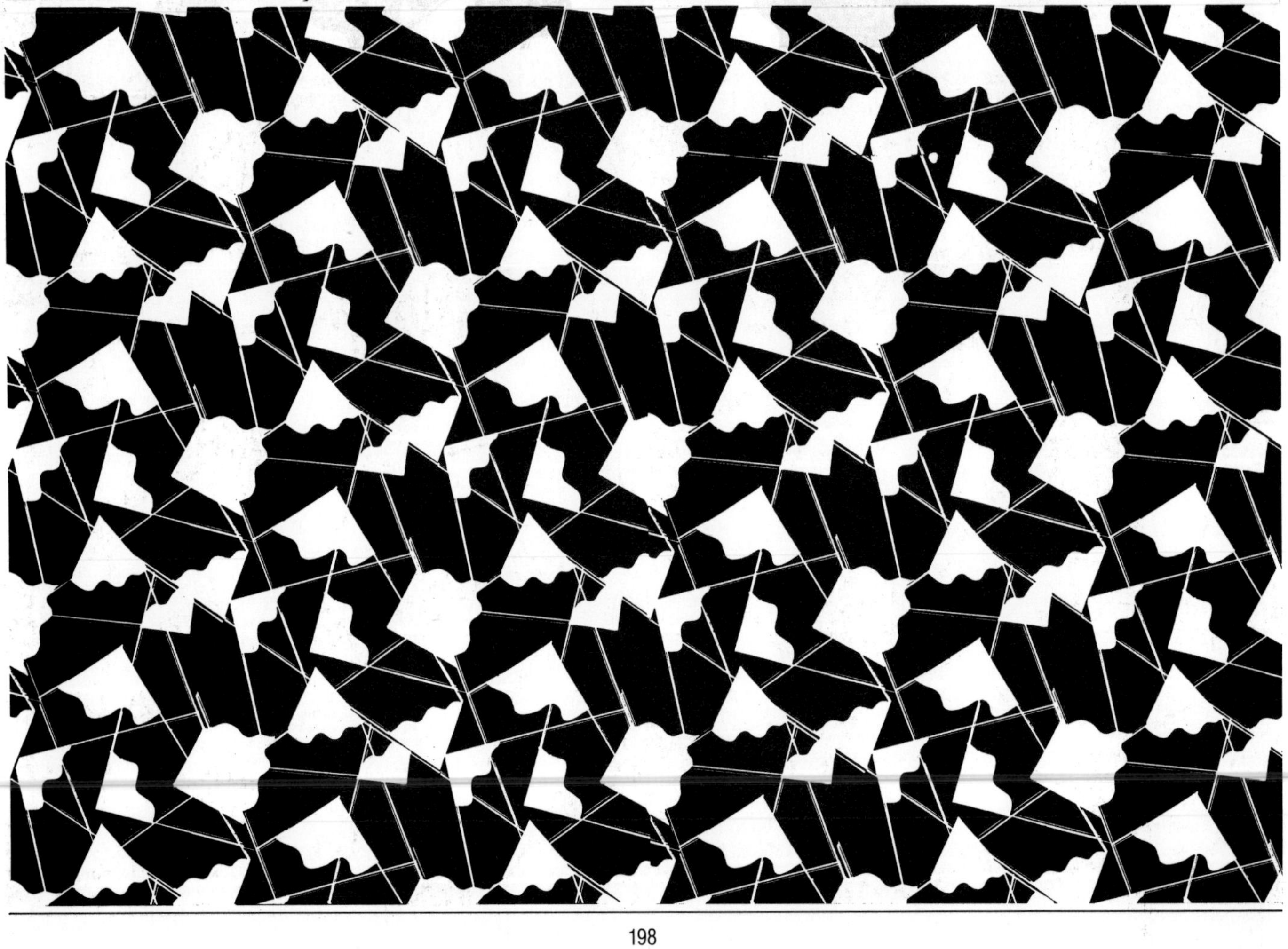

BASIC ELEMENTS BA82

200

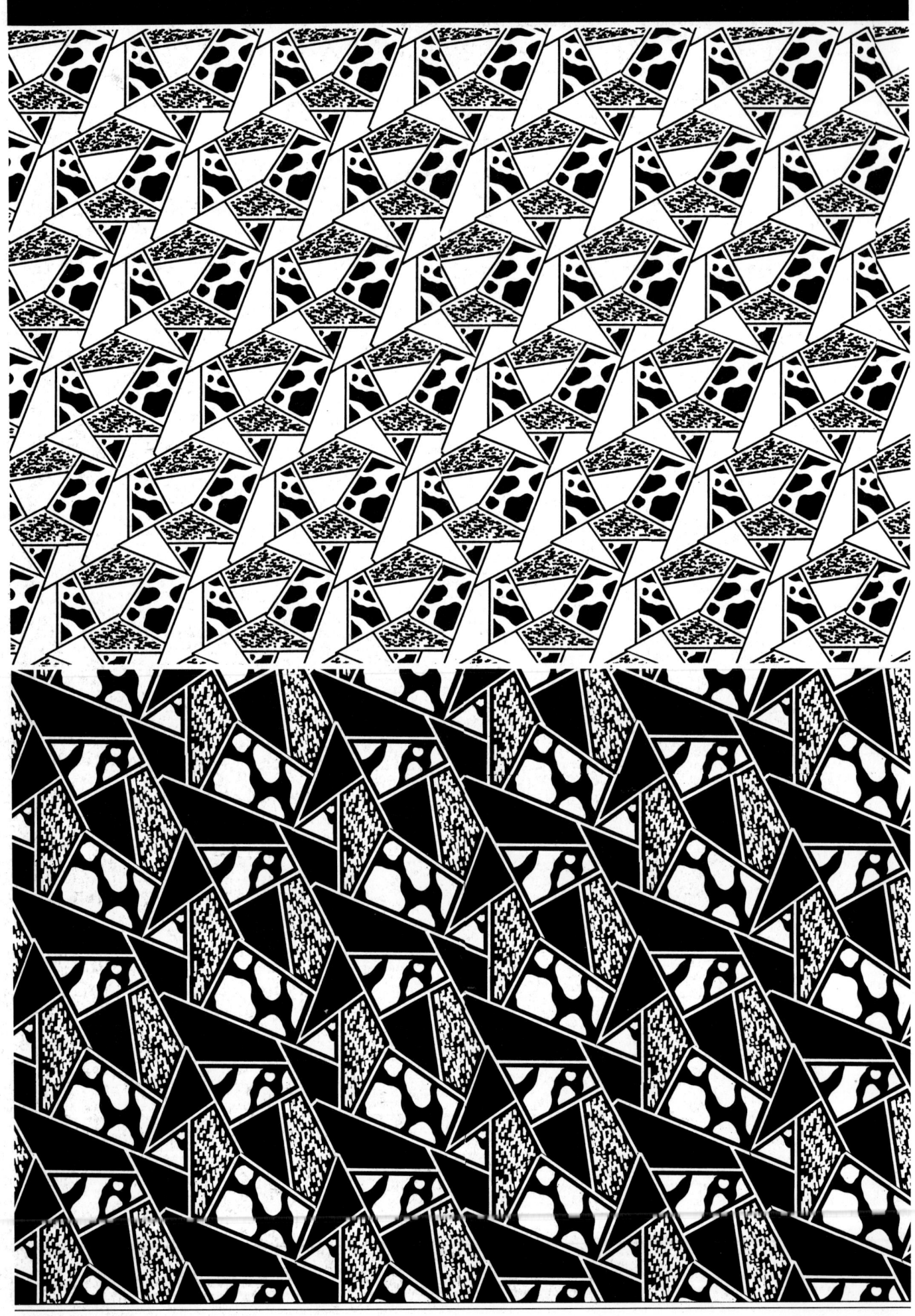

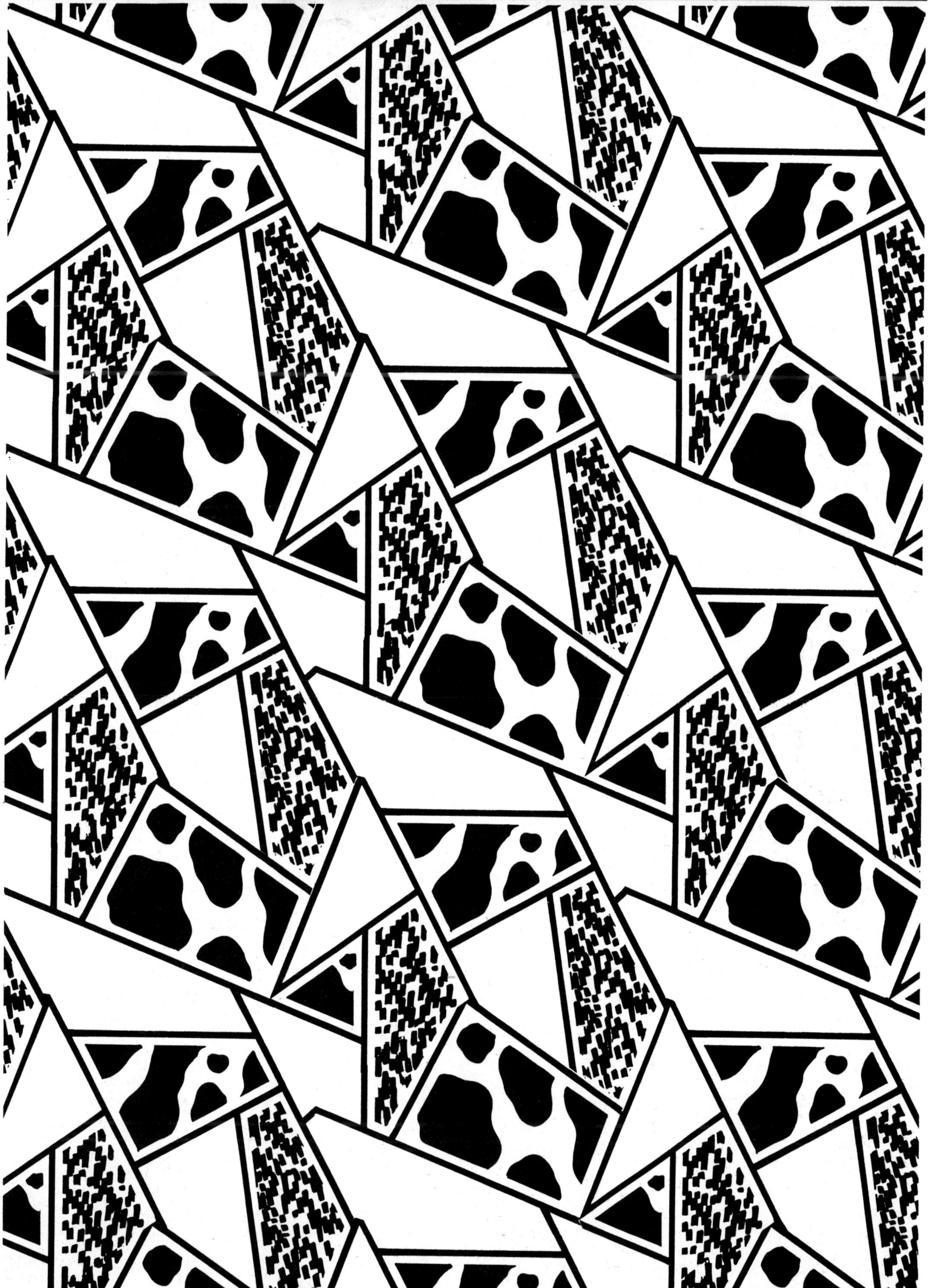

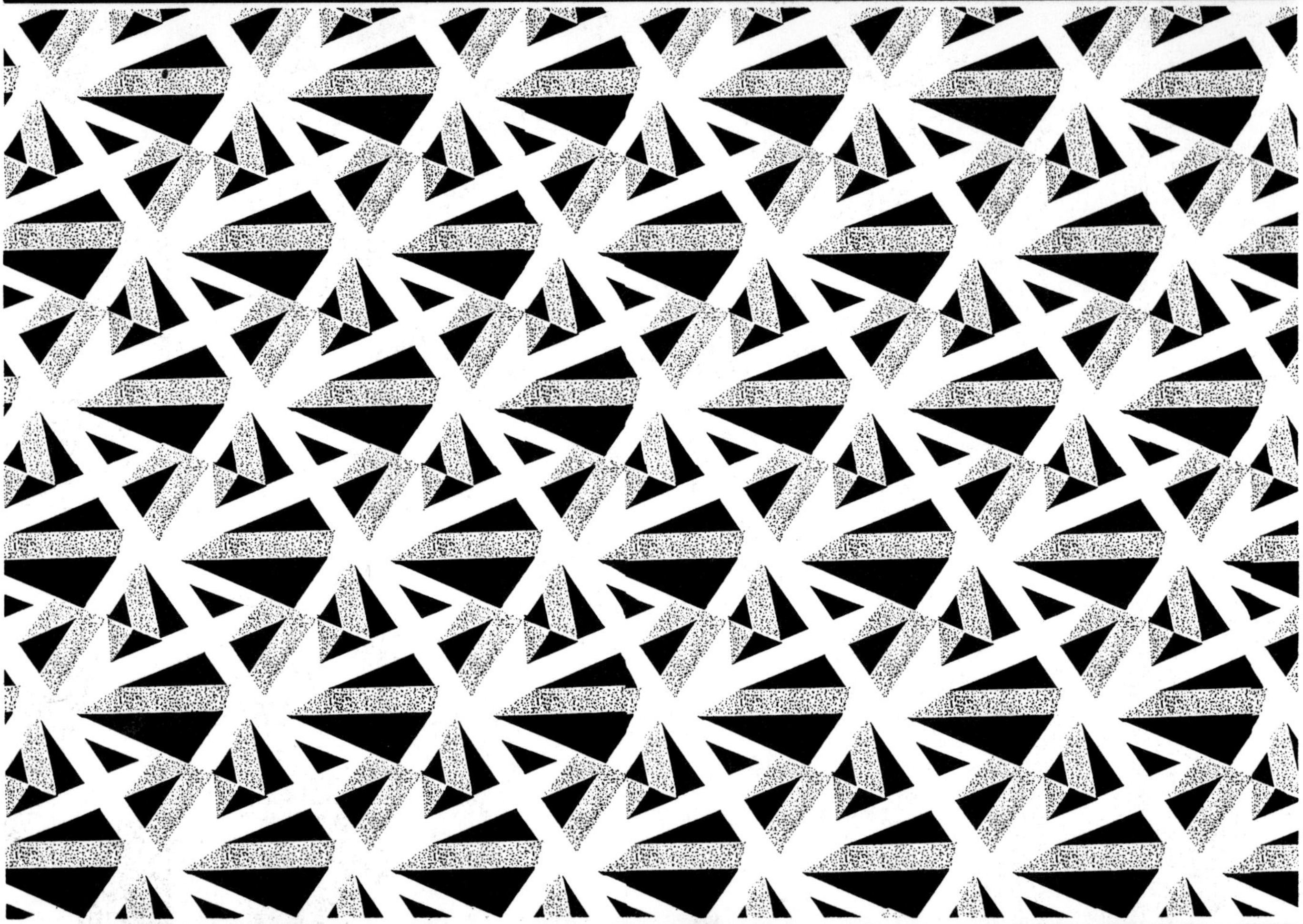

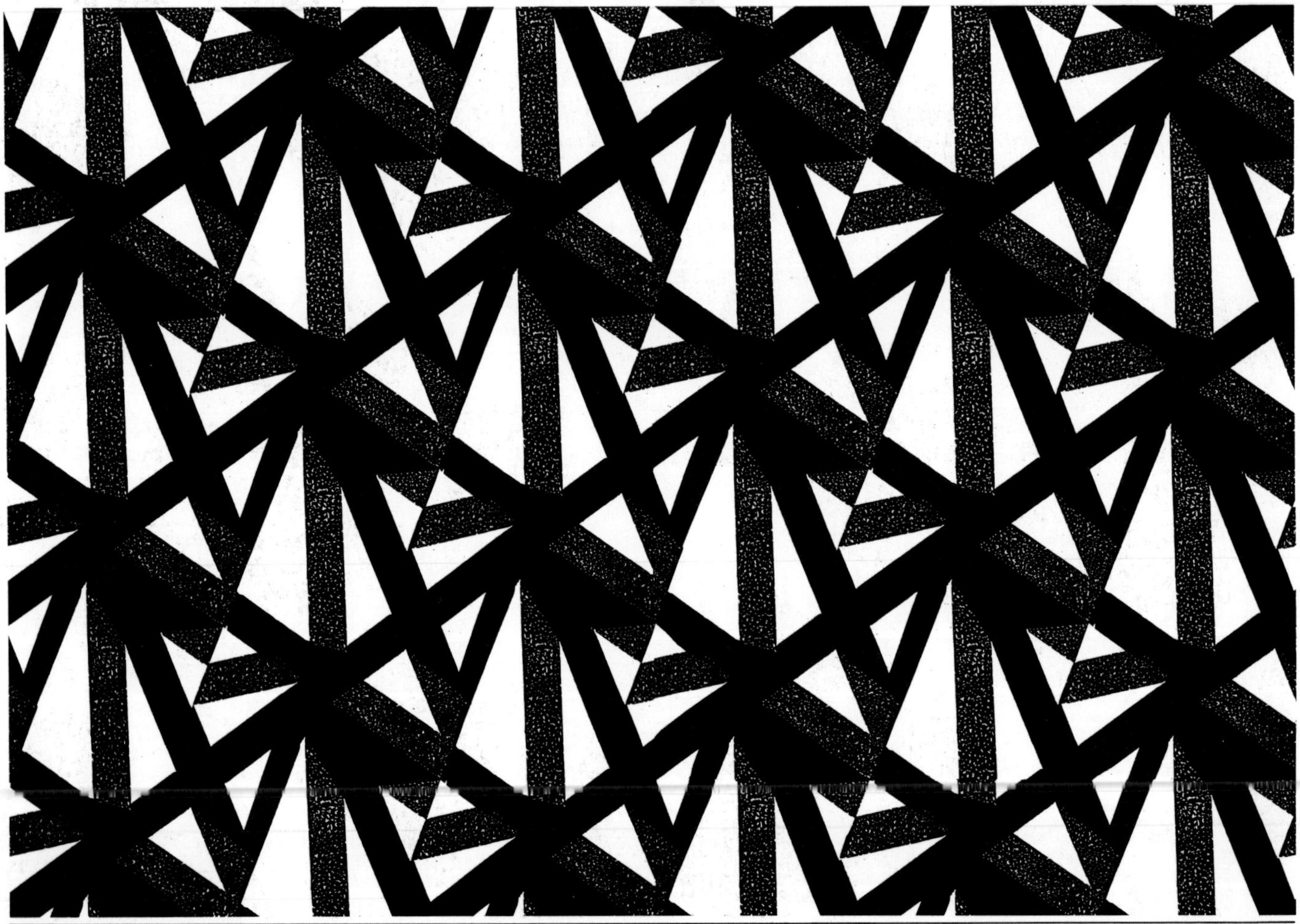

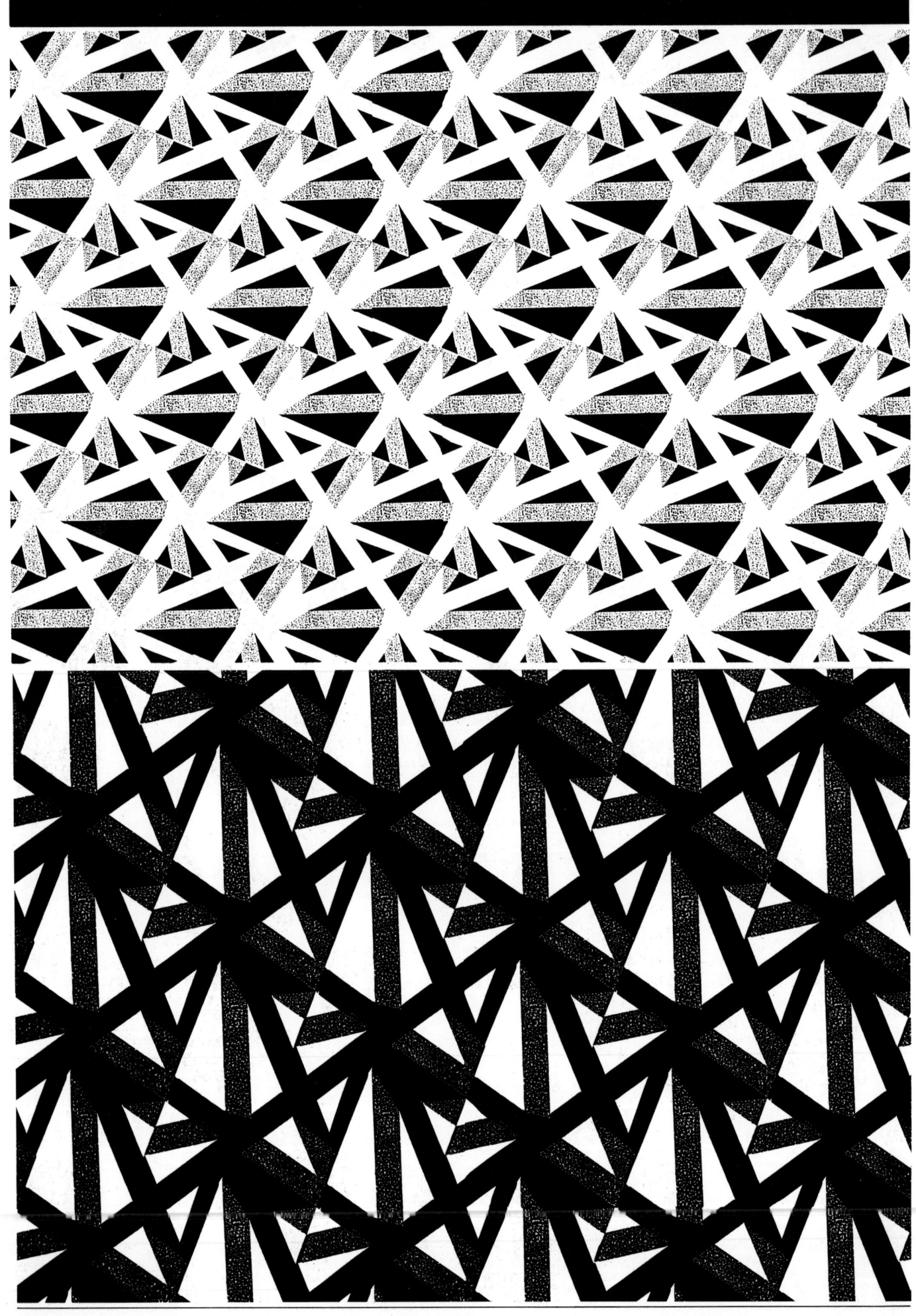

BASIC ELEMENTS BA84

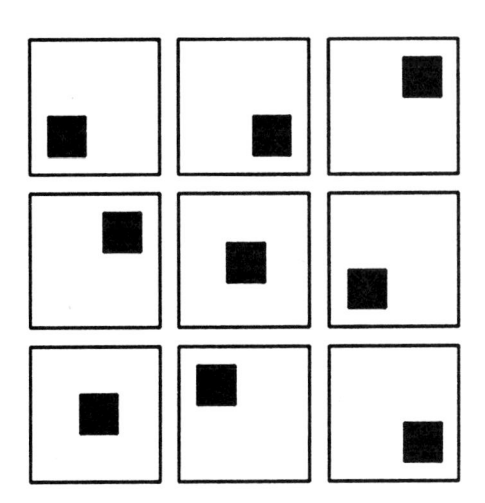

ELEMENTS
BASIC
7
BASIC

○AIM●JEUNESSE●AJ-RESEARCH-INSTITUTE●

PRODUCED BY

aim 株式会社 エーム クリエイティブ プロダクツ
〒160 東京都新宿区坂町25-1
TEL 03-353-3181(代) FAX 03-353-3299

JEUNESSE 株式会社 ジュネス プランニング コーポレーション
〒160 東京都新宿区坂町25-1
TEL 03-358-0601(代) FAX 03-358-0651

AJ RESEARCH INSTITUTE AJ 綜合研究所
〒160 東京都新宿区三栄町14番地
TEL 03-5379-3271(代) FAX 03-5379-5492

エームグループは、マーケティングに関する
全ての業務を、総合的に行なっている企画・開発・環境・創造企業です。
書籍についてのお問い合わせ、その他業務内容についてのお問い合わせ、
及び、正社員・アルバイト・外部スタッフへの応募は
上記㈱エーム クリエイティブ プロダクツまで
お願い致します。

● NEEDS HUNTING	● CONCEPT HUNTING	● PRODUCT DESIGN	● FUTURE CONCEPTION
● TREND ANALYSIS	● SEEDS HUNTING	● MD	● HARD PACKAGE PLAN
● CONCEPTUAL DESIGN	● SECONDARILY DATA	● MONITOR SYSTEM	● RENDERING
● LAND DEVELOPMENT PLAN	● CI & VI PLAN	● NAMING	● COLOR PLAN

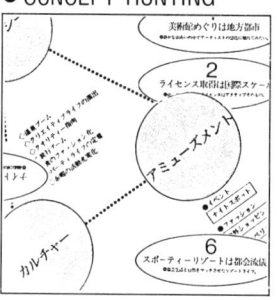

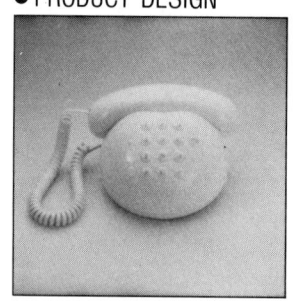

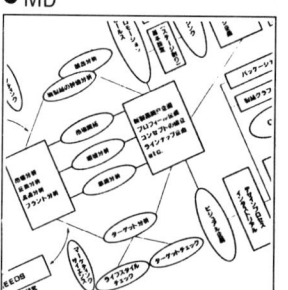

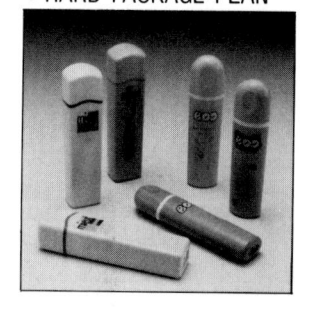

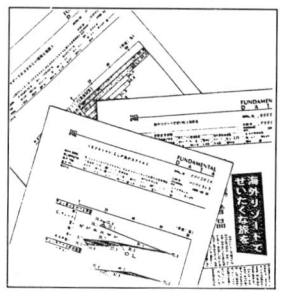

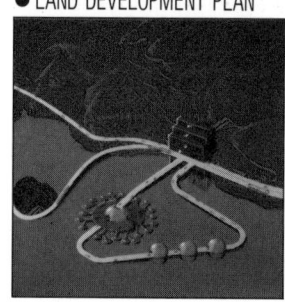

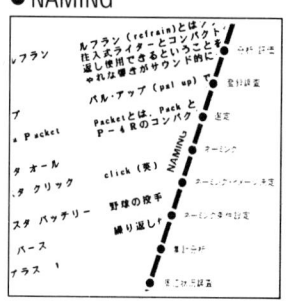

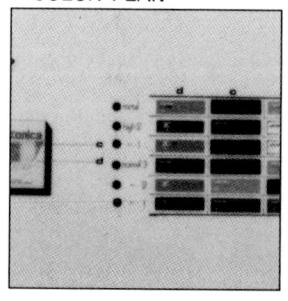

- INTERIOR DESIGN 
- TYPE FACE DESIGN 
- GRAPHIC DESIGN 
- MARK & LOGOTYPE DESIGN 
- TECHNICAL ILLUSTRATION 
- PACKAGE DESIGN 
- PATTERN DESIGN 
- ILLUSTRATION 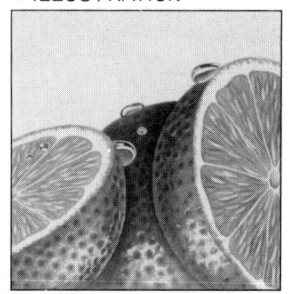
- MODEL MAKING 
- CHARACTER 
- PHOTOGRAPH 
- ISOTYPE DESIGN 
- VTR PLAN 
- POSI RENTAL 
- EDITOLIAL 
- PUBLISH

ELEMENTS
7
エレメンツ [ベーシック編]
ベーシック

初版発行
1989年10月15日
発行人
樋口健治

Creative Director

上口清幸　浦上慎一

小倉奈津江　小山美紀
Art Director
編集スタッフ
後藤節子　石田　智
西塚みゆき　福田明男
営業
小坂浩人　貞方栄子
発行
株式会社 エーム クリエイティブ プロダクツ
〒160 東京都新宿区坂町25-1
TEL.03-353-3181　FAX.03-353-3299
印刷
株式会社千代田平版社

©AIM CREATIVE PRODUCTS. Co.,Ltd.
Printed in Japan
1989
aim

ISBN4-87210-024-7

使用上の注意

このパターン集は、すべて当社のオリジナルです。
スクリーン・テキスタイル等パターンそのものの製品化、
及び販売を目的とした複製、非購入者への
コピーサービス、無断転載などは禁止されております。
製品化のご意向のある場合は、事前にご相談下さい。
オリジナルパターン制作のご依頼も承っております。
今後の企画へのご意見・ご要望及びお問い合わせは
㈱エーム クリエイティブ プロダクツまで直接ご連絡下さい。